Living with Uncertainty

Living with Uncertainty
The Messy Reality of Classroom Practice

Curt Dudley-Marling

Heinemann
Portsmouth, NH

Heinemann
A division of Reed Elsevier Inc.
361 Hanover Street
Portsmouth, NH 03801–3912
Offices and agents throughout the world

Acquiring Editor: Carolyn Coman
Cover Designer: Jenny Jensen Greenleaf
Manufacturing Coordinator: Louise Richardson

Library of Congress Cataloging-in-Publication Data
Dudley-Marling, Curt.
    Living with uncertainty : the messy reality of classroom practice
/ Curt Dudley-Marling.
        p.   cm.
    Includes bibliographical references.
    ISBN 0–435–07234–X
    1. Language experience approach in education—Ontario—Toronto—
Case studies.   2. Language arts (Elementary)—Ontario—Toronto—
Case studies.   3. Third grade (Education)—Ontario—Toronto—Case
studies.   4. Elementary school teaching—Ontario—Toronto—Case
studies.   5. Dudley-Marling, Curt.   I. Title.
LB1576.D826   1997
372.62—dc21   96–53389
                                                                                CIP

Printed in the United States of America on acid-free paper
01   00   99   98   97   DA   1   2   3   4   5   6

To Chris

Contents

Introduction
The Quest for Certainty

I was a special education teacher for seven years before I enrolled as a full-time doctoral student at the University of Wisconsin at Madison. Three years later, in 1981, I was awarded a PhD and, within a matter of days, I was offered and accepted an academic appointment at the University of Colorado at Denver. Less than four years later I moved to York University in Toronto where I continued to work with teachers who were enrolled in a graduate program or taking post-baccalaureate, in-service courses. My writing has also been directed to classroom teachers. I am best known, I think, for my efforts to translate whole language theory and practice for teachers of remedial students and students with learning disabilities.

Teaching and writing about literacy instruction assumed that I knew something about teaching reading and writing, and I'm confident that the teachers who took my classes and read my work found what I had to say helpful. I take the success of my first book, *Readers and Writers with a Difference* (Rhodes and Dudley-Marling 1988, 1996) to be a measure of my success working with teachers. However, not long after the publication of *Readers and Writers with a Difference* I began to doubt my knowledge. Most of what I was teaching and writing about I'd learned since I left the classroom. I also worried that, while I had seven years of experience teaching students in special education programs, I'd never taught in a regular classroom. More to the point, it had been over a decade since I had done any classroom teaching. The irony is that at the very time that the teachers who read my work and took my classes were granting me the status of *authority* I was growing increasingly uncertain about what I knew. If I was an authority, it seemed to me, then I should have been growing more certain in my knowledge, but I was growing less certain. More and more my assertions about teaching practice were qualified with *buts, maybes, sometimes, I'm not sures* and, most troubling, *I don't knows.*

At one level I believed these doubts merely acknowledged the complexity of working with human beings. I was rightfully suspicious of definitive, prescriptive strategies for teaching students to read and write. In the introduction to *Readers and Writers with a Difference*, for example, we warned our readers not to take our advice too solemnly. We wrote:

> The strategies we suggest . . . should be considered only as models. . . . It may be that some of them will work for you without adaptation while others may not work at all; in general, most will have to be modified in accordance with teachers' individual styles and the unique needs of each of their students. We hope teachers will use the strategies presented in this book productively and not prescriptively . . . (Rhodes and Dudley-Marling 1988, 1996, xii)

What we were saying here is that teachers, students, classrooms, and schools are very complex so we need to be cautious about the limits of our knowledge. Of course, many books and articles written for teachers are chock full of *certain* instructional strategies that promise success for all teachers, with all children, in all places.

Still, while I was making a place in my thinking for uncertainty, I was growing increasingly uncomfortable with it. The *solution* to my growing ambivalence, it seemed to me, was to return to the classroom for a year. So I talked to Stan Shapson, our dean, who talked to the director[1] of a Toronto-area school board, and before I knew it I was offered a position teaching third grade at Norwood[2] School, a relatively small, K–5 urban school in an ethnically, culturally, racially, linguistically, and socioeconomically diverse neighborhood.

There were still a couple of obstacles to teaching in Ontario: the Ontario Ministry of Education's certification branch would grant me a teaching certificate only if I first took an overview of primary education (a year-long course) and six weeks of student teaching. So in May and June I did a student teaching stint in a first-grade classroom with a masterful teacher named Peggy Bourne and in July I took the required course (four hours/day for four weeks). I'll have to admit that both of these experiences were useful but, at the time, my ego took a terrible beating. In August I also (voluntarily) took a week-long

---

1. The equivalent of a superintendent in U.S. school districts.

2. In order to protect the privacy of my students I have changed their names and the name of the school at which I taught.

workshop on manipulative math materials the school board offered its teachers, that was enormously helpful.

Despite all the preparation I'd done and the support I'd received, teaching third grade was difficult. After thirteen years at the university my skills were rusty and, in any case, as a special education teacher I'd never been responsible for such a large group of students. When I taught at Fair Acres School, a school for mentally retarded children in Hamilton, Ohio, I had 10–12 students *and* a full-time aide. When I taught students with learning disabilities in Green Bay, Wisconsin, I rarely worked with more than five or six students at one time. So the twenty-four students I faced my first day at Norwood School seemed like a lot of kids. This was also the first time I'd been responsible for students' entire curriculum—math, science, art, physical education, reading, and writing.

In addition to these challenges, I added the role of researcher to my regular classroom duties. I had some specific research questions I wanted to address (e.g., How could I encourage students to assume *ownership* of their work? How could I create a literate community?), but I also wanted to document my experience as a third-grade teacher. So each day I made field notes that included observations related to my research questions and documented each day's experience including my reflections on what was going on with me and my students. During the day I always carried a clipboard with me on which I made brief notes that I fleshed out during recesses or at home. Over the course of the school year I made approximately fifteen hundred single-spaced pages of field notes. I also did lots of audiotaping as a means of capturing large- and small-group discussions, reading and writing conferences, oral reading, and so on. I copied all of my students' written work. I took hundreds of photographs. I also saved everything I wrote, including chart stories, directions, spelling lessons, sign-up sheets, song lyrics, and anything I wrote during writing minilessons.

I spent the year after I returned to the university reading through my data and trying to generate categories or themes that would help me make sense of my experience and the questions I had asked. These themes correspond roughly to the chapters of this book which, taken together, respond to specific questions I asked (How did my students use literacy to initiate and maintain relationships? What did I do to support student ownerships? Did I treat boys and girls equitably?) and reflect on various aspects of my experience (Why did behavior problems make me feel so badly? How did I use multicultural literature? Did my knowledge of language make a difference? Did I do enough for my struggling students? Why was I so obsessed with spelling?).

I also spent considerable time reading other people's accounts of life in classrooms. I read sociological studies of schooling like Waller's *The Sociology of Teaching* (1932), Jackson's *Life in Classrooms* (1968), Lortie's *Schoolteacher* (1975), and Everhart's *Reading, Writing, and Resistance* (1983). I read Kidder's *Among School Children* (1989), a journalistic description of life in an urban classroom. Particularly helpful were first-hand accounts of teaching including Herndon's *How to Survive in Your Native Land,* (1970) Wigginton's *Sometimes a Shining Moment* (1985), and Palonsky's *900 Shows a Year* (1986), and many more.

I wasn't merely interested in the content of stories about schooling. I was also interested in *how* people told their stories and how they went about making sense of their experiences. In other words, I hoped that stories of schooling would suggest a theoretical framework that would help me interpret my experience as a third-grade teacher. The framework I was looking for began to emerge from my reading of a study by Deborah Britzman (1991) that detailed the experiences of three student teachers as they struggled to cope with uncertainties, ambiguities, and contradictions that surround the messy reality of classroom teaching. As Britzman puts it, "Enacted in every pedagogy are the tensions between knowing and being, thought and action, theory and practice, knowledge and experience, the technical and the existential, the objective and the subjective" (1991, 2). The dilemma for Britzman's student teachers was that the uncertain, ambiguous, and contradictory realities of the classroom contradicted their idealized models of the *good* teacher who always knows just what to do.

Idealized models of the good teacher are, of course, a setup created by teaching stories that efface the daily struggles of teachers, by the sanitized notions of teaching presented in teacher education programs, by the reductive research that drains teaching of its unpredictabilities, and by the popular, media-constructed *super teachers* (Newkirk 1992, McDonald 1992). McDonald observes:

> Teaching, closely read, is messy: full of conflict, fragmentation, and ambivalence. These conditions of uncertainty present a problem in a culture that tends to regard conflict as distasteful and that prizes unity, predictability, rational decisiveness, certainty. This is a

setup: Teaching involves a lot of "bad" stuff, yet teachers are expected to be "good." (1992, 21)

This tyranny of certainty (McDonald 1992) is a plague on the morale of teachers working to achieve the status of *good* teacher (Lortie 1975), an observation supported by my experience in third grade. As Jardine and Field put it, "our experience and knowledge cannot save us from the possibility that even the most theoretically aligned, carefully measured technique may not work with *this* child or *that* piece of writing or *this* community of readers" (1996, 256). Simply put: teaching is a messy, complex, and uncertain business.

My personal quest for certainty was informed by an enduring and largely unexamined faith in the role of experience and the possibility of certainty. I did not, as it turned out, learn much about teaching merely by experiencing it. I have had to reflect on that experience, but not just any kind of reflection has been worthwhile. What has been useful is a systematic, theoretically informed, deliberate reflection that acknowledges uncertainty, seeks improvement, but does not expect to attain the truth *once and for all.*

Each chapter of this book emerged from this kind of systematic, theoretically informed, and deliberate reflection. Taking up issues like ownership, gender equity, community, multicultural literature, discipline, and so on enabled me to develop my own understanding of these issues—to see beyond what I knew as McDonald (1992) put it—but my reflections have not made me more certain. On the contrary, reflecting on these issues has reinforced my earlier notion that the pedagogical experience is infinitely complicated. Viewed through the lens of uncertainty the issues I discuss in this book illustrate the complex, messy, and uncertain realities of the practice of teaching and examine how these uncertainties threatened my sense of the good teacher I wanted to become. In the end I did not become any more certain, but I am learning to live (somewhat) more comfortably with my uncertainties.

Acknowledging the messy realities of teaching third grade—including my doubts, disappointments, frustrations, and feelings of inadequacy—begins to respond to Newkirk's appeal for teaching stories that "capture the emotional underlife of teaching" (1992, 23). Teaching stories that efface the messy reality of teaching reinforce the tyranny of certainty that limits the pleasure and self-satisfaction teachers are able to derive from work. Teachers who go public with their struggles, however, risk ridicule from parents, politicians, and teacher educators who are convinced about the possibility of certainty. Admitting uncertainty may even jeopardize the careers of some teachers, especially young teachers. Telling the whole story requires courage.

Mine is not a story of courage, however. I tell my story from a privileged position—as a white, forty-eight year-old male, full professor, author, and journal editor—that minimizes the risks of honesty. I tell my story because I think it is interesting. It is not a call for classroom teachers to follow my lead and publicly share their doubts, frustrations, and struggles. For teachers who speak from a less privileged position the risks of public honesty may just be too great. It would be useful, however, if teachers learned to share their doubts with each other.

Finally, readers may find that I've been too hard on myself at various places in this book. It may be true that, in my effort to illustrate the struggles of teaching third grade, I have given too little attention to the joys and pleasures I experienced. Teaching third grade was hard for me, as I make clear over and over in the pages of this book. But it was also wonderful. I loved being part of a vibrant classroom community. I loved being part of the lives of my students. I took great pleasure in my students' growth and development. I will always miss them, and I will never forget them or the lesson in humility I learned from them.

This is a good place to acknowledge some of the people who supported this book and the experience on which it is based. I have to begin by thanking Stan Shapson, Dean of the Faculty of Education at York University. My secondment[3] to a Toronto-area school board could not have happened without his blessing and active support. Stan recognized the benefits my secondment would have for me, the Faculty of Education, and York's relationship with the schools.

I can't say enough about the generosity of the school board in which I worked. Financially, the board could have hired two entry-level teachers for the cost of my salary which was at the top of the teachers' pay scale. The willingness of board officials to enter into this arrangement demonstrates their faith in the relationship

---

3. A secondment is a kind of a loan. York University continued to pay my salary and I continued to earn service credit toward my next sabbatical. In every other way I was an employee of the school board which reimbursed York University for my salary and benefits.

between the school board and York University. I'm especially grateful to Sandie Brauti for offering me a position as a third-grade teacher at Norwood School. Sandie's confidence in her teachers' professionalism gave me the freedom I needed to implement the whole language curriculum I believed in, to experiment, and to fail, and to learn from my struggles. If all principals treated their teachers with such respect schools would be better places for teachers and students to work and learn in than is often the case. I also want to thank the teachers at Norwood School who accepted me as one of them and who were never too busy to answer my questions, offer advice, or just talk. I have particularly fond memories of my regular chats with Heather and Liz. I can't forget Peggy Bourne who had the confidence and grace to let me student teach in her class. Peggy found a way to acknowledge my *special* background and provide strong support and guidance that helped me enormously as I struggled to learn how to deal with the needs of so many children. I hope Peggy enjoys her retirement in British Columbia for many, many years. And, of course, I want to thank the wonderful children in my third-grade class with whom I laughed and cried and from whom I learned so much.

Don Dippo, my good friend and colleague, read and provided feedback to nearly all the chapters of this book. I was always amazed by the insightfulness of Don's feedback which contributed enormously to the theoretical strength of this book. I especially appreciate the way Don's feedback supported what I was trying to do. He helped me write *my* book, not *his*.

I also want to thank Carolyn Coman, my editor at Heinemann. Carolyn offered feedback, set deadlines (which I regularly missed), and provided whatever support I needed at every stage of this project. It is my good fortune to work with an editor who is herself an accomplished writer (a Newbery Honor Award winner).

Finally, I'm deeply grateful for the love and support of my family. Teaching third grade at Norwood School was a Dudley-Marling collaboration. When I went into Norwood School to organize my classroom, my children, Anne and Ian, and my wife, Chris, came and helped. When I went book shopping for my classroom, my family came along to help me select just the right books. Anne, who was only a year older than my third graders, freely offered her advice about the needs and interests of 8 year olds. Chris, Anne, and Ian were also frequent visitors to my class, sometimes accompanying us on field trips. Chris sometimes helped with writing conferences and she often spent a half an hour or more in the evening responding to notes from my students. It was Chris, a speech-language pathologist, who pointed out to me that I was overestimating the English proficiency of Nader, an ESL speaker in my class. Chris also read and responded to each and every chapter of this book. Most of all, I want to thank my family for their patience, tolerance, and forgiveness. For much of the school year I was so overwhelmed by the emotional and physical demands of teaching and collecting data that I wasn't always emotionally available to my family. I hope I've been able to make it up to them. I want them to know that they'll always be more important to me than my career.

1

Reading, Writing, and Friends
Challenging My Sense of Community

Recent work in sociolinguistics stresses that reading and writing are social practices that can only be used and understood within socio-cultural contexts (Bloome 1985; Gee 1990; Myers 1992). We humans are "inescapably social beings; and as social beings all learning occurs in social (and historical) environments. It follows then that social environments play critical roles in an individual's learning and development" (Moll and Diaz 1987, p. 196). Imagining the role of community in literacy development, Freeman and Sanders observed that "when teachers encourage students to explore the many different functional uses of writing in the community, they emphasize the vital role that writing plays in people's lives outside of school" (1987, 644). Similarly, research by Bloome (1985) illustrates how the nature of social interactions around reading influences how students both interact with and interpret a text.

Although I doubt that it was their intention, I took from writers like Moll and Diaz, Freeman and Sanders, and Bloome the belief that creating a dynamic community of learners was an essential *pre*-condition for encouraging my third graders to expand the range of (social) purposes for which they read and wrote. Even before the school year began I wrote in my notes:

> When I teach third grade in the fall I want to directly address the notion of building a community. I expect to make building a community a priority from the first day using activities which, for example, encourage students to work in pairs and in groups. (field notes, June 1991)

I also came to believe that a rich social context was essential if my students were going to learn how various social and cultural factors affect how people go about making meaning as readers and writers. In short, creating a community of learners became one of my highest priorities as I prepared to teach third grade (Dyson 1989, Freeman and Sanders 1987, Gillis 1992, Goodman and Wilde 1992).

I also believed that classrooms which evolved into democratic communities—where students and teachers worked together to negotiate the meaning of the curriculum—promoted diversity by permitting students to bring the voices of their communities and their cultures into the classroom. I hoped that nurturing a learning community would enable my students to negotiate space within our language arts program that made room for the range of cultural, linguistic, economic, and gender differences my students brought with them to school (Dyson 1993, Floriani 1994, Green and Dixon 1994, Lin 1994). Further, "when teachers are able to link their writing instruction to the social meaning of writing within the learner's culture and community, discontinuity between learning at home and at school is reduced" (Freeman and Sanders 1987, 644–645). The Foxfire experience (Wigginton 1985) is a particularly good example of this. It may also be that "when cultural differences are recognized, legitimatized, and bridged, students are allowed to read and write about things that are congruent with their home culture, they may read and write more and with more sophistication" (Bloome 1985, 138). Finally, I imagined that the creation of a learning community would provide more opportunities for my students to support each other as they struggled to increase the range of communicative functions for which they used reading and writing.

Early in the school year I planned a number of activities in my classroom that I imagined would help to *build community* in our classroom. My primary goal when I asked my students to "write a biography of another student in the class," for example, was to help students get to know each other better and to learn the collaborative skills I thought necessary for working within a community of learners. I also imagined that singing, field trips, and providing space within the "official" curriculum (Dyson 1993) for student talk would help to promote the development of a learning community in my third-grade classroom.

As I've read and reflected on the field notes I collected during my year as a third-grade teacher, I have come to believe that my explicit efforts to *build community* among my students were based on simplistic, romantic, arrogant, and, perhaps, dangerous assumptions about the meaning of community and the teacher's role in shaping classroom communities. The straightforward definition of "community" in *Webster's New World Dictionary*—a community is "a group of people living together and having interests, work, etc. in common" (1960, 296)—begins to reveal the naivete underlying my community building efforts in the fall of 1991. From this perspective, students are always part of a community in which they live and work together in a shared space even if they only come together to resist and subvert the goals of the teacher (Everhart 1983). As a group of people having shared backgrounds and interests, students are often linked by culture, religious heritage, language, neighborhood, friendship, and shared histories. This was certainly the case with most of the students in my class. If communities depend on shared background and experience then many of my students were linked in communities long before they met me.

However, notions of community based on shared work or shared interests ignore the fact that, at their core, communities are about relations—relations within the group, relations between individuals and the community, and relations between communities (Murphy 1995)—and that communities are always evolving and not fixed (Green and Dixon 1993). What makes communities more than just a collection of individuals, even if those individuals share a common background and interests, "is the beginning of a *shared focus,* a shared purpose which eventually leads to a *shared way of making sense* of some aspect of the world" (Murphy 1995, 5). Although I didn't think of it this way at the time this sense of community is probably closer to what I was trying to accomplish in my third-grade classroom. Still, there is something arrogant about the assumption that I could forge my students into a community through the force of my will without any acknowledgment that my students and I would have to work together continually to shape—and reshape—the meaning of our classroom community. I also failed to acknowledge the possibility (maybe even probability) that not all my students would choose to be a part of any community that emerged in our classroom. No matter how attractive the community I imagined, any student could—and some probably did—choose not to participate.

I also mentioned that there was something "dangerous" about my notions of community. What was dangerous about my sense of community, I think, is that it was based on a tacit, unexamined, and romantic assumption that communities are inherently good. However, as the news reports from Bosnia and Croatia indicate, the shared focus and meanings around which communities are organized can be based on exclusion and hate (Britzman, in press). Freud had an interesting way of putting it: "It is always possible to bind together a considerable number of people in love, so long as there are other people left over to receive the manifestation of their aggressiveness" (1975, 51). Classroom communities can be exclusive, too. My experience as a student and a parent indicates that many classroom communities exclude students who struggle in school, kids who are unathletic, children who are overweight, boys and girls whose behavior or appearance doesn't fit rigid gender stereotypes, children whose culture or values don't match the teacher's, and so on.

It's fair to conclude, then, that when whole language teachers talk or write about "building community" the issue isn't creating community as much as it is developing particular kinds of communities— respectful, mutually supportive communities that encourage students to engage in a range of social interactions from which authentic (i.e., not the teacher's) reasons for reading and writing emerge and which provide students with a frame of reference for making sense with and from texts. And, as I've suggested, teachers cannot imagine that they are all-powerful beings who make community merely because they wish it. At best teachers create the conditions for the development of particular kinds of communities. It remains for students and teachers to work together to give meaning to these communities.

Looking back I am not persuaded to believe that my explicit efforts to support the development of this sort of community were particularly successful. It may even be that the behavior problems that accompanied some teacher-directed, community-building activities exacerbated existing tensions within the group. Yet, I am satisfied that a dynamic, supportive, respectful community in which students read and wrote with and for each other did emerge. My students learned to use reading and writing for a wide range of (social) purposes within a dynamic community of learners. However, the relationship between community and literacy was not what I had predicted when I set the creation of community as one of my priorities. My students' varied uses of reading and writing were not a consequence of a richly interactive and supportive community. On the contrary, as the following quote by David Bloome (1985) predicted, reading and writing were primary means by which my students forged social relationships and created community in our classroom. As Bloome observed:

> In addition to being a communicative process, reading is also a social process . . . That is, reading involves social relationships among people: among teachers and students, among students, among parents and children, *and* among authors and readers. The social relationships include establishing social groups and ways of interacting with others; gaining or maintaining status and social position; and acquiring culturally appropriate ways of thinking, problem solving, valuing, feeling. (1985, 134)

School literacy will, of course, be affected "by the nature of the social community within and outside of classrooms, and by the ways in which schools and classrooms are organized" (Goodman and Wilde 1992, 3), but reading and writing also play a vital role in shaping that community. Bloome (1985) describes, for example, how a group of girls used the reading of a love note one of the girls had received to establish social interactions and display that they were part of the group.

In this chapter I illustrate the development of community in my third-grade classroom by examining how my students used reading and writing to do important "social work" (Dyson 1993)—in particular how they used literacy as an occasion for initiating, maintaining, and structuring social interactions and relations and, thereby, building community.

"ARE YOU MY FRIEND?"

Interpersonal writing—including notes, letters, apologies, and reminders—had an immediate communicative function. The most common types of interpersonal writing my students engaged in were writing notes and letters which I encouraged by designating one of our bulletin boards a "Message Corner." Some students even designed personalized "mail boxes" for the message corner, perhaps as a way to invite friends and classmates to write to them.

Sometimes it seemed that students wrote notes and letters when they couldn't think of anything else to write about, but more often students used the message corner to write to friends as a means of maintaining existing relations or initiating new ones. I recall the delight of Jennifer, who was new to Norwood School, when she received a note early in September from Connie who invited Jennifer to be her friend. I also used notes to enrich my own relationships with my students. For example, early in the year I wrote to Razika:

> Razika,
>
> Sometimes it seems that students who misbehave get the most attention. So I thought I should let you know how pleased I am with your fine work in our classroom. I'm especially pleased with how kind you are to everyone. You're a very nice girl and I'm glad you're in our class.
>
> Mr. Marling

Sometimes friends used notes as a means of carrying on arguments. Figure 1–1 was part of running dispute between Razika and Shyrose over Shyrose's attempts to expand her circle of friends.

On other occasions friends used written notes as a means of resolving disputes. Connie, for example, used a note to attempt to resolve a dispute with Catherine (Figure 1–2). I was also the frequent recipient of apologies, especially from Connie and Catherine who often acted out in class.

As Connie did with Jennifer, students sometimes used writing to initiate new relationships. Razika's fight with Shyrose led her to make the following overture to Jennifer, someone with whom she hadn't interacted much before.

> Dear Jennifer,
>
> Are you my friend? I am yours. Shyrose is not my friend. I don't like her anymore. Can I play with you at recess time?
>
> Love, Razika

Some students managed to extend our community beyond the classroom by using writing to establish relationships with my wife, Chris, my daughter, Anne, and my son, Ian. The following letter was part of a series of notes Catherine exchanged with Anne that was the beginning of a relationship that continues to this day. This note was sent the day before Anne was to visit our class.

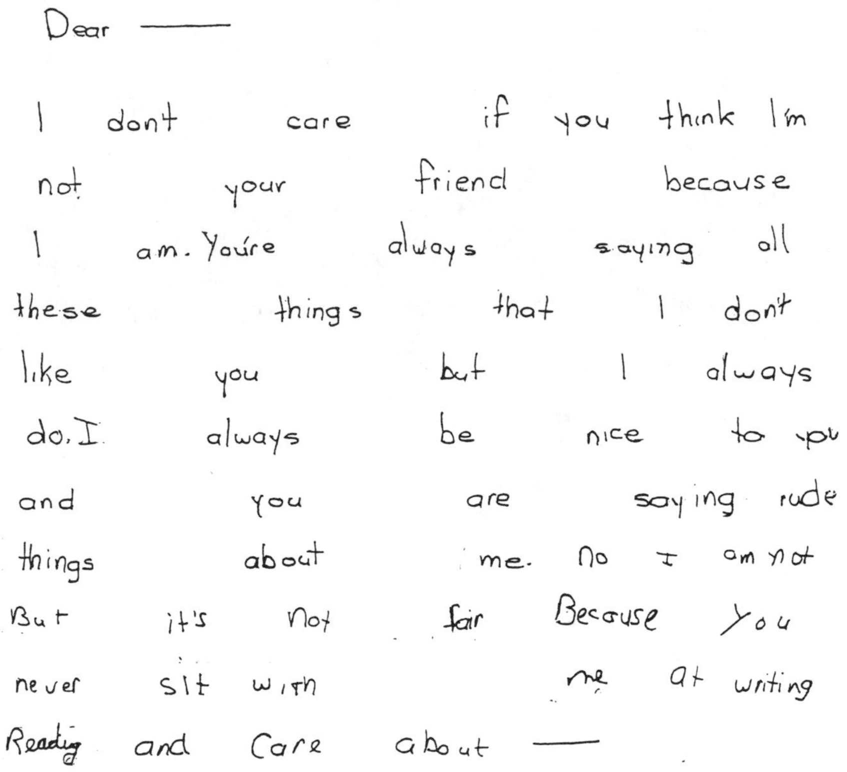

Dear ————

I don't care if you think I'm
not your friend because
I am. You're always saying all
these things that I don't
like you but I always
do. I. always be nice to you
and you are saying rude
things about me. No I am not
But it's not fair Because you
never sit with me at writing
Reading and Care about ————

FIGURE 1–1   *Carrying on an Argument*

Dear Anne,

I am sorry I didn't write you back. Well, how is life? Boring? Good?
Bad? Or mmmmmm! So-so? I just want to say that I am one of your
best friends and your dad is the best teacher I had. He said one of
these days we will come over. Oh! Don't tell anyone when you
come tomorrow because Jennifer and Barbara will say that is not
fair they won't be my friends any more. OK. Thanks for understanding.

Yours truly,
Catherine

FIGURE 1–2   *Resolving Disputes*

Many evenings my wife spent a half hour or more responding to notes from my students. A get well card several students wrote to my dad after he had surgery further tied my family to our classroom community. Notes to my family also provided me with opportunities to talk with some students about editing their writing in a way that supported *their* intentions. In late November when Roya and Lila wrote letters to Anne they were concerned that their spelling be accurate so they asked me to correct their spelling and, under these conditions, they willingly produced a second draft of their writing.

Of course, students' use of writing wasn't always inclusive or kind. I recall, for example, how pleased I'd been when John told me he'd written a note to Nader, a boy whose family had immigrated to Canada from Afghanistan and who experienced difficulty winning acceptance from the other boys. I was very disappointed, however, when I discovered that the note read, "Nader, I'm going to beat you up after school" (November 5, 1991). Similarly, Razika struck out at Wayne by writing a letter addressed to his sister detailing Wayne's "bad" behavior. On another occasion someone hurt Martin deeply by "forging" a note from Crystal that read, "Martin, I don't like you any more." And in March Denise received a note which read simply "f— off." These negative uses of writing were relatively rare, however, and, in general, letter and note writing provided students with a ready means for making space for social work (Dyson 1993) within the "official" writing curriculum. (See Lensmire [1995] for an interesting discussion of the use of writing to exclude.)

"ABOUT CRYSTAL"

On the first day of school I asked each of my students to interview another student and then use the interview to write a "biography." The writing this activity produced was neither interesting nor inspired (See Figure 1–3), but, in retrospect, this isn't surprising since this activity was mine, not theirs. I must also admit that, although we did some collective brainstorming around what kinds of questions they might ask each other, I didn't offer my students much guidance about what a biography might look like, at least not initially.

Since I had concluded that my students were not personally invested in writing these minibiographies, I was more than a little surprised when the girls[1] in my class continued to write biographies of their classmates. On November 26th, for example, my field notes indicate that over a third of my students were writing biographies. Some students produced dozens of these over the course of the year, a few students producing several biographies of the same person. At first I concluded that these "About _____" pieces were a kind of default genre produced when (some) students couldn't think of

---

1. No boy wrote an "About _____" piece beyond the initial assignment.

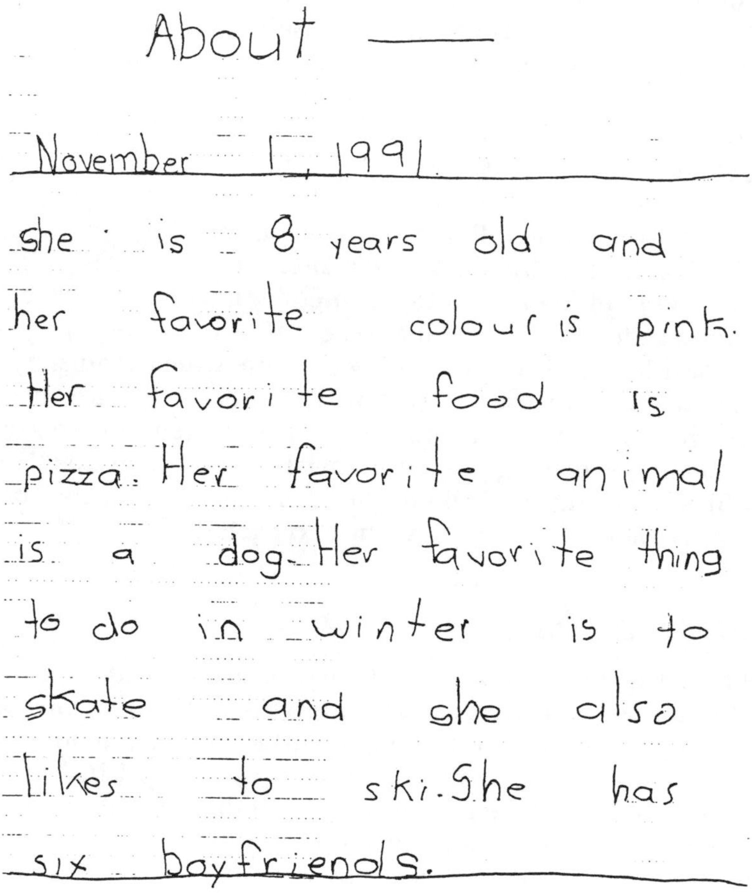

About ——

November 1, 1991

she is 8 years old and
her favorite colour is pink.
Her favorite food is
pizza. Her favorite animal
is a dog. Her favorite thing
to do in winter is to
skate and she also
likes to ski. She has
six boyfriends.

FIGURE 1–3   *"About Crystal"*

anything else to write. (Of course, this didn't explain why only girls wrote "About _____" pieces.) Therefore, I attempted to help students produce livelier, more interesting biographies by writing and sharing "About _____" pieces of my own[2]. The following story about my son, Ian, for example, was part of an effort in early

---

2. A genre study focusing on biography would have been another way to support students' writing biography but, strangely, it never even occurred to me at the time.

December to encourage students to include interesting vignettes in their biographies (as an alternative to the listing of facts that characterized most "About" pieces).

Bad for the Environment

You know Ian. He's my son. Ian's five years old and he goes to kindergarten. When Ian came downstairs yesterday morning I told him that I'd had a funny dream about monsters. He gave me a serious look and then said, "Monsters aren't funny. Monsters are scary." A moment later he added, "Monsters are bad for the environment." A funny guy, huh.

A few students, especially Razika and Shyrose, did begin to add more details to their biographies as the year progressed. I remained convinced, however, that the "About _____" pieces served no purpose other than to give (some) students something to write about when they could think of nothing else. An incident on May 26th forced me to reconsider this hypothesis, however.

Connie read me an "About Catherine" piece she was working on. The piece praised Catherine to the heavens ("Catherine is nice. She is beautiful and I like her very much . . .") and, since she read it loudly enough for Catherine—who was sitting nearby—to hear, it seemed to function as an apology for something Connie had done the previous day by reminding Catherine that they were still friends. When I suggested this interpretation to Catherine she said, "I know." (field notes, May 26, 1995)

It may be that the "About _____" pieces did function as a default genre, something to be written when students couldn't think of anything else to write (as a number of "About me" pieces suggest), but these pieces didn't *just* fill up writing time. It seems that "About _____" pieces also provided students with opportunities to celebrate their friendships, sometimes through public declarations (as in the case of "Authors' Chair"), thereby strengthening existing relations. Sometimes, but less often, "About _____" pieces functioned as bids to initiate new friendships. In either case, biographies were a means—but not the only means—by which students used writing to "manipulate the words on the page in order to accomplish particular kinds of social work" (Dyson 1993, p. 17).

Including friends as characters in their stories was another way my students celebrated their friendships (see Dyson, 1988). Lila, for example, wrote a series of stories in which Roya, her best friend, was the protagonist. Similarly, Catherine, Barbara, and Jennifer featured each other in a series of pieces each wrote about "The three girls." Wayne, Troy, and Jeffrey, perhaps influenced by "The three girls" series, produced a number of pieces featuring themselves as lead characters. Jeffrey's piece, "The four bikers," which he eventually made into a book, can be seen as an attempt to reinforce his emerging friendship with Wayne and Troy and to establish their image as "macho" guys:

The four bikers

One day Jeffrey, Troy, Wayne, and Ian[1] were doing stunt tricks on a big ramp. They were jumping off it and a manager from a stunt company was watching them. He was so impressed that he asked them if they wanted to do stunts for his company. They said, "Yes," so they were off to Hollywood.

When they got there, they made arrangements for bikes and hotel rooms. Then they went to the track where they would be doing their stunts. They got to see their new bikes . . . That night there were hundreds and hundreds of people, so they got their costumes on, and they were so good that even more people came to their next show. The fans loved them so much that they elected them for the "Bikers' of the Year" award. They got to do their stunts all around the world.

They went to Paris, Florida, and Canada. Their fans loved them. But one day when they were in Florida they had just finished their show and . . . they were in the city taking pictures when all of a sudden there was a gunshot. It was a bank robber. He had just shot a security guard. Everybody was screaming and some people were even praying. The bank robber went up to the counter and said, "Give me all the money in this bank, including the money in the vault." So the lady got all the money and she put it in a bag, but before the robber left Jeffrey got a clear picture of the robber's face with his camera. Their manager was with them and he was thinking of the reward because they were flat broke.

---

1. Jeffrey is also using my son as a character in his story. Ian was an occasional visitor to our classroom and Jeffrey, Wayne, and Troy became very fond of him.

When the robber left the bank Ian rushed out to the police department. He asked the policeman if they had any files on the robber and he said, "Yes." Ian said, "Can I have a copy of the files?" and the policeman said, "Yes." By that time Jeffrey, Troy, and Wayne were at the police station. Ian said, "Where's the boss?" Troy said, "He went back to the hotel." Then Jeffrey said, "Do you have the files," and Ian said, "Yes."

When they got back to the hotel the first thing they looked at was the robber's name. It was Mr. Jordan. His . . . address was 221 Cassandra Blvd. #1010, Orlando, Florida. When they got there Wayne said, "I'm scared" and Troy said, "Why? There's nothing to be scared about." Then Ian said, "Let's go." So they walked to the door and rang the doorbell, but nobody answered. They rang it again and this time somebody opened the door. It was a lady and she said, "If you're looking for my husband he went to the movie store." So they got on their bikes and went as fast as they could go.

It took 10 minutes to get to the movie store. When they got there they waited until Mr. Jordan came out. When he came out Troy hit him on the back of the neck and knocked him out. Then Wayne said, "Hey, let's see what movies he got." Then Ian said, "Eh, forget about that." So they picked him up and put him on the back of Wayne's bike. They got to the police station as fast as they could go. When Mr. Jordan woke up he was in jail.

The next day the mayor awarded the 4 bikers $1000 each and then they went home. THE END.

Although students can include friends' names in their stories to solidify relationships, they can use the same strategy to put someone down. Lensmire (1995), for example, describes how children in a third-grade writing workshop used the names of other students in their stories in hurtful ways leading the teacher to proscribe the use of classmates' names in stories. Similarly, Dyson found that collaborating peers sometimes "affirmed their own social cohesion by distancing a third peer, who became a critically portrayed character in their narrative" (1993, 63). (This recalls the Sigmund Freud quote in the introduction to this chapter.) This wasn't a common use of writing in our classroom, but it did happen. The following piece about Lila and Ali, written by Roya, manages to reinforce Roya's relationship with Lila while ridiculing Ali.

Lila and Ali

Lila is my best friend. There is a boy in my class who picks his nose and eats it. Lila hates him. He is a very ugly boy. . . .

After Lila wrote a piece about "A pig named Nicholas," which led Nicholas to attempt several retaliatory pieces, I banned the use of classmates' names in stories without their permission (and, like Lensmire [1995], I felt very uncomfortable about censoring students' writing in this way but did it anyway).

Anne Dyson found that for many of the children she studied "a major purpose of writing was to establish social cohesion—to declare themselves as competent kids who were members of important social groups (like "the guys")" (1993, 201). My third graders, like the children Dyson studied, also used reading and writing to claim membership in "important social groups." Students who wrote "About" pieces, for example, simultaneously celebrated their friendships and claimed membership in the group of students who did such writing. Students who read fan magazines and wrote to their favorite TV stars, declared themselves as members of a group sophisticated enough to share this interest. (I say sophisticated because most of the kids who read fan magazines in my class had teenage brothers or sisters.) Similarly, when groups of students came together to read poems, comics, or scary books an interest in these genres became part of what defined membership in these groups. In all these examples, reading and writing became shared interests that identified students as members of particular communities of readers and writers.

In summary, reading and writing provided a means for my third graders to celebrate friendships and establish solidarity within the *official* curriculum. It may be that part of the success of writing instruction organized around the writing workshop—with its emphasis on sharing and publishing—and of reading programs organized around the reading and sharing of books, is that students read and write in order to claim membership in a community of readers and writers. I certainly believe this was true with my students.

THE "SCARY, EVIL BOOK CLUB" AND OTHER STORIES

In addition to providing a means for interacting *through* texts, by which students were able to socialize and define their relationships, reading and writing also provided my third grade students with opportunities to interact around texts. Students in my class interacted, for example, as they moved about the room during writing time, sharing what they had written and seeking help with spelling and other editing concerns. Students also came together around texts as they read with and to each other. Sometimes students read texts collaboratively as a way of providing each other with needed support. In early September, for example, Lila and Roya read *Is Your Mama a Llama?* (Guarino 1989) together, taking turns reading every other page, talking about the book, and helping each other with the words. In late February, Charles and Denise spent some time looking through a picture book together, but were unable to read the text themselves until Catherine joined them and read the text to them. On another occasion I overheard Jeffrey, John, Peter, and Scott taking turns reading poems to each other from a collection of poetry. Shel Silverstein's poems were especially likely to bring students together—Crystal often found herself reading his poetry to groups of three or four students. On other occasions students read texts chorally as when Crystal and Barbara read several of Norman Bridwell's Clifford books together.

Collaborative writing was another way my third graders came together around a text. Lila, Catherine, and Roya, for example, spent several days writing and rehearsing a play based loosely on *The House That Jack Built*. Another play, full of jokes and humor, was written and performed by Paul, Nicholas, and Crystal. Hugh, Razika, Wayne, Shyrose, and Troy worked together to produce a class newsletter and Jennifer, Jeffrey, and Wayne collaborated on a get well card for my father who was recovering from surgery. When Charles wanted to write a letter to my son, Ian, he enlisted Paul to help him write it and several students sought out Hugh to illustrate their books. The stories and poems my students wrote were frequently the result of collaborative efforts. Hugh and Paul, for example, wrote the following poem together:

> *Witches, witches, they are scary*
> *They have spiders that are hairy*
> *If you see them in your room*
> *Be sure to take away their broom*
> *If you seen them in a store*
> *Be sure you don't make a roar*
> *Because if they see you will be sore*
> *So just make your move out the door*
> *Be sure not to see them anymore.* (January 6, 1992)

In general, collaborative reading and writing not only brought students together, it also enabled many students to read and write texts they could not control on their own. These collaborations weren't always successful, however. Hugh's need to take the lead in any collaborative undertaking, for example, made him difficult for most students to work with. (When these relationships ended, Hugh's former collaborators frequently explained that Hugh had "fired" them.)

My third graders also came together to read, discuss, and, in some cases, write about texts and text sets. One way this occurred was through the literature-sharing groups I organized in which 3 to 5 students signed up to read a common text I had selected. There were also occasions when students spontaneously organized themselves around a collection of texts such as fan magazines and comic books. The most interesting example of this phenomenon, however, was the emergence of the "Scary, Evil Book Club" in early May. I taped the following conversation which took place while six students were sitting on the carpet reading and discussing books they were reading.

JOHN: I was going to give that one to Nader to read . . . I'm glad Paul found these books down in the library for me. Paul got me this one. This one. And that one. . . . *Dr. Jeckyl and Mr. Hyde.* the *Phantom of the Opera,* and *The Vampire.* . . . [Catherine is looking through one of John's books.]

JOHN: Look on the second picture of that [to Catherine].

CRYSTAL: This book isn't that exciting.

JOHN: [still talking to Catherine] That doesn't kill him. That kind of does. Look at the pictures of him. You might want to read that over.

FATIMA: Here, Catherine, give it to me. We're reading those.

JOHN: Mr. Hyde is crazy. Look at him. Look at Mr. Hyde. That looks like this guy, dude.

CRYSTAL: Maybe it is . . .

FATIMA: A vampire.

JOHN: It could be. No, that's probably the driver of the coach. [pause] They're going to show his face here. Catherine. Catherine. They're going to show his face. Find the one where the girl takes off his mask [as Catherine pages through the book] There. It shows his real face.

CRYSTAL: "He has no wounds." [Reading from the book.]

JOHN: "And yet he walked on . . ." [Reading from the book.]

CRYSTAL: And it shows a picture of all the [inaudible].

JOHN: I know. Look. Listen to this Crystal. "And yet you walked on [.] the man. Some guy walked on the man." "Looked at me angrily." Oooh.

CRYSTAL: [to the teacher] We're all reading these books, these kind of books.

JOHN: I'm reading that after this. I like these books. I'm glad Paul got them out . . . Nader was the first one to ask for that one and that one.

CRYSTAL: A big scorpion.

JOHN: I know.

CRYSTAL: I hope he doesn't eat those things.

JOHN: Huh? Oh!

CRYSTAL: "Kiss to my forehead?" Huh.

JOHN: Where is it? "Because you have [inaudible]." Yuck.

CRYSTAL: Sickatating.

PETER: Look at this book. They're two pictures of him.

JOHN: Yeah. I know.

FATIMA: Yeah, that one's not too scary. Where's the other book? Did you only take out three?

CRYSTAL: She's got it.

CATHERINE: I want to read it . . .

JOHN: Come on. I want to see it.

CRYSTAL: Wait.

JOHN: This is good.

FATIMA: The pictures in it are not even scary.

CRYSTAL: I want to see it.

FATIMA: Wait!

JOHN: Look at Dracula. Look at the pictures in that one . . . [a moment later].

JOHN: This doesn't make sense.

CATHERINE AND CRYSTAL: What?

JOHN: Look. First Mr. Hyde, the bad guy, was kept in a mansion . . .

CATHERINE AND CRYSTAL: Yeah.

JOHN: . . . and now after this guy, the butler, gave Mr. Hyde some food he turned back. He's [unintelligible] it.

CATHERINE AND CRYSTAL: That doesn't make sense.

JOHN: I know. He doesn't remember anything.

CRYSTAL: That doesn't make sense.

PETER: Oh . . .

CRYSTAL: He probably didn't eat after he took the medicine.

JOHN: So whatever he drugs . . .

PETER: Probably.

JOHN: Isn't permanent yet.

CRYSTAL: Are you almost finished or are you going to read that whole book? [talking to Fatima]

PETER: Or the drug probably makes you normal once you eat.

JOHN: Yeah, probably. And then after you have something to drink or something like that . . .

CRYSTAL: Then you turn back like the potion you drank.

JOHN: Yeah, something like that. Like a hairy animal.

CRYSTAL: Like a hairy animal.

JOHN: Hey, why don't we make a little group that reads all this?

CRYSTAL: I can bring one of my dad's scrapbooks in. It has really, really old vampire pictures in it.

PETER: Real ones.

JOHN: You three could check out more. We could check out King Kong.

CATHERINE: [to the teacher] We're starting a little group.

JOHN: Yeah, we're starting a little group of, a little vampire group.

CATHERINE: He's evil, he's powerful, he's thirsty for blood.

JOHN: We're going to get out two more books and then we'll have a five group.

CRYSTAL: I'm going to get a piece of paper and write a little bit about it.

JOHN: I'm not. I'm reading more. Where's my bookmark?

CATHERINE: You know what? I have all these books here except for King Kong.

CRYSTAL: If we put all our ideas together we can make a chapter book. [They've decided to makes notes on the books they are reading.]

PETER: We'll have to get King Kong out. You will.

JOHN: Then we'll have five books.

JOHN: This is good. He coulda died if this potion didn't work. He coulda died.

CRYSTAL: My dad, my dad will let me bring his pictures in . . .

JOHN: We've got to name the club. The scary book club.

CATHERINE: No!

JOHN: It can't be a book title club. . . .

WAYNE: Are you all reading the same book?

JOHN: No . . . We're all reading different books. [Discussion returns to naming their book club.]

CATHERINE: The vampire club.

JOHN: I know. The scary creatures club.

CATHERINE: Yeah.

PETER: I was thinking . . .

JOHN: The scary reading club.

PETER: Yeah, the scary reading club.

JOHN: Yeah, that's good. And then put all the titles . . .

CRYSTAL: Who knows how to spell scary?
PETER: S-c-a-r-y.
JOHN: The scary reading books?
CATHERINE: No the evil. Evil.
JOHN: The scary reading books?
CATHERINE: Evil.
JOHN: The evil reading books?
CATHERINE: Yeah. It sounds better.
JOHN: The scary evil . . .
PETER: Yeah, OK.
JOHN: Yeah, the Scary, evil reading books, club.
CATHERINE: Yeah. . . .
CRYSTAL: I'll try to bring all my vampire books.
[Teacher ends the session.]

Over the next six weeks, thirteen students in my class joined the founding members of the "Scary, Evil Book Club" to read, write, and discuss "scary" stories. I was amazed by the power of scary books to bring together groups of children, boys and girls, who otherwise had little to do with each other. Nader, the Afghani refugee who had difficulty finding his way into the classroom community, was able to use the "Scary, Evil Book Club" as a means of forging relationships with several other students. A careful review of my field notes indicates, however, that reading and writing generally had the effect of bringing students together. Troy and Wayne, who actively shunned girls outside the classroom, eagerly sought out Jennifer, Catherine, and Crystal to talk about books and writing. Nicholas, who was always an outsider on the playground, often found companionship in the classroom around books. Hugh—distant, moody, and angry—formed his closest relationships at school through his many writing collaborations. Although I was frequently disheartened by hurtful and violent behavior in my class, the community of learners that organized itself around reading and writing was, in general, inclusive and supportive (although I did intervene to quell exclusive tendencies in the "Scary, Evil Book Club"). Why this should have been so I cannot say for sure. I can't help but wonder, however, if my reading and writing program, free from the pressure to "get things done" (see Chapter 2), may have helped to create an atmosphere congenial to the development of a supportive community. At a minimum, reading and writing were places where students could use the curriculum to do important social work (Dyson 1993).

"WHEN I CAME TO CANADA"

Just as my students used *official* reading and writing curricula to accomplish *unofficial* social work (Dyson 1993), they were also able to exploit opportunities presented by reading and writing to infuse the literacy curriculum with their personal, social, and cultural identities, what Dyson calls "staking a claim" (1993, 136).

Encouraged to write about their interests and experiences, most of my students were able to use writing to share and celebrate what was important to them in their lives outside of school. It was through writing that we learned about Wayne's hockey exploits, Catherine's cat, John's baby brother, Lila's babysitting escapades, Shyrose's family trip to Graceland, and Barbara's Newfoundland roots. Roya used writing to share the following story of her family's escape from Iran.

When I Came to Canada

I used to live in Iran. But it had too much war. We had to sleep by
the door because of the bombs and missiles. So my parents
wanted to come to Canada. We had trouble getting here. The day
we were coming to Canada I cried and said, "I don't want to
leave my Iran." When we were on the plane my ear hurt.

When we got to Canada I saw my aunt. She took us to my grandma's house. Everybody hugged. My cousin said to my mom, "What a
big stomach." My mom said, "Yes, I am pregnant." The baby was
my sister.

Now we are in Canada and we are happy.

Students also used reading to make connections between school and their lives outside of the classroom. Students frequently supplemented our classroom library with books brought from home and Charles was thrilled when I read stories from Virginia Hamilton's *The People Could Fly* (Hamilton 1985), a book he had at home. A poetry unit we did in January led to an offer by Hugh's mother to come into class to read a narrative Scottish poem. (I recall Hugh's enormous pride as he sat listening to his mother read to us in her strong, Scottish accent.) Reading folktales from different cultures and sharing information about various religious observances provided occasions for me to (at least) acknowledge students' cultural and religious heritages. (In Chapter 7 I take a critical look at this practice.)

Reading and writing frequently provided opportunities to admit a range of human emotions into the classroom, feelings that are often denied or even proscribed by the tendency to fragment literacy for purposes of instruction. In our class Denise often wrote about her loneliness and Barbara found that a book of poems on friendship helped her cope with what she perceived to be the loss of her best friend Jennifer. Reading from *A Bridge to Terabithia* (Patterson 1977) and *The People Could Fly* (Hamilton 1985) left many of us—including me—in tears. Similarly, reading sections from Barbara Park's *Skinnybones* (1982) made us laugh so hard we almost cried.

Reading and writing also provided occasions for students to talk about their lives outside of school. The following conversation, which emerged from my efforts to help Roya find something to write about, enabled a group of students to share amusing stories about their brothers and sisters.

MR. MARLING: What's the problem?

ROYA: I have nothing to write about.

MR. MARLING: [jokingly] The problem is when you have a dull, uninteresting life—

ROYA: Yeah, there's nothing to write about, especially when you have a brother. [But] when you have a brother there's so much you can write about. You can write about what a pain he is.

LILA: You do have a brother. Why don't you write about what a pain he is and stuff?

MR. MARLING: Actually, you might have something there. I think Lila is right. That is exactly the kind of thing you could write about. Those kinds of stories are funny sometimes.

ROYA: Trust me, they are. Once we went to the church when we were coming to Toronto from Montreal. On the way we went to the church with my aunt and everything. There was a cross and Jesus was on it and my brother goes "who is that?" My dad said, "Jesus." And my brother said, "Tell him to come down." It was just a statue of him.

MR. MARLING: [laughs] That's a great story.

ROYA: OK, fine.

LILA: My brother's boring. . . . All he does is sit around and watch TV—

ROYA: That's what I do.

LILA: —in his underwear.

ROYA: OK, maybe I don't do that.

CATHERINE: My brother, right, he, um, we were going to church, he had to take me to church, with Jackie, because my mom left us at my aunt's house and . . . we went, we went to Parkway Church with her. And he [Paul] went in and all the time he stared at the stained glass window, shaking his head . . . When it was time for me to go down I asked for the dollar he said I could bring. And he gives me his wallet with a two dollar bill in it and says, "Here, take this." And I asked him, "Are you sure?" He said, "It's a dollar, isn't it?" I put it back in his hands and asked my aunt and, um, she gives me the right amount of money. And while she's giving me the money my brother is still staring at the stained glass, because he thinks it's really neat. The next day when my mom got home all she could see around the room was stained glass windows my brother made from tissue paper. Now he draws a lot and gets the ideas from stained glass windows . . .

MR. MARLING: You both have something in common. You both have interesting stories about your brothers. You could write about them. They'd make good reading.

LILA: What about me? I have an interesting story.

ROYA: [Starts to tell Lila's story for her]

MR. MARLING: Let Lila tell—

LILA: I can't remember.

ROYA: The time when we were downstairs [inaudible]. Tell that.

LILA: No.

FATIMA: Tell us. Tell us.

LILA: Roya came over. We were eating popcorn and my brother kept taking the popcorn from us. Then when we were downstairs. We were making a plan to get him back for what he did to the popcorn because he spilled it all over the floor. When we weren't looking he turned the lights off on us and started scaring us. Then after we heard a knock on the door, and we were scared because we didn't know who it was. And my brother was scared too because it wasn't him. Then when we went to the door it was Roya's mom.

ROYA: I couldn't get her up. The lights were off. You should've been there.

LILA: My brother was holding me down.

ROYA: We were in the laundry room.

LILA: The laundry room is very scary.

MR. MARLING: Let's here from Jeffrey. [Jeffrey has just joined the group.]

JEFFREY:: It's not very funny.

CATHERINE: It doesn't matter if it's funny. [She proceeds to tell another story about her brother.]

JEFFREY: I can only think of one that might be funny to us. Everyone knows those cardboard things on the bottom of hangers, right? So my brother found one of those on a hanger and took one of those in the car and he started hitting the steering wheel with it while my mom was driving. She goes, "not now Jordan, don't *do it* while I'm driving." [giggles] (February 11, 1992)

Reading and writing also provided some students with a means for shaping their classroom identities. Paul's voracious appetite for books firmly established him among his classmates as a "reader" as Razika's love of writing constructed her as a "writer." Other students became well known for their interest in reading or writing particular genres. The "Scary, Evil Book Club", for example, established its members as lovers of horror books and Hugh became "famous" for his stories about the adventures of "Marshmellow Man."

The Lost Airplane

One day Mr. Marshmellow Man was having a walk . . . He tripped over something. It was an airplane. He picked it up . . . He took it to the Marshmellow study room. He examined it very carefully and he found finger prints on it. Then he took it to the police station. He showed them the fingerprints on the airplane and asked them if they knew who the fingerprints belonged to. They told him they belonged to a boy named Ian. Mr. Marshmellow Man wasted no time. He set off to find the boy. He looked everywhere. . . but he couldn't find him. Now he was looking for something different: a partner. He started looking in Australia. While he was here he found Mr. Koala W. Bear who was looking for a job . . . The first word from Mr. Marshmellow Man was, "Excuse me. Would you like a job?" Mr. Koala Bear said, "Sure." He asked Mr. Marshmellow Man, "What's the job?" Mr. Marshmellow Man told him it was detective work and Mr. Koala Bear said, "Great!" So they set off. "Have you heard of a boy named Ian?" Mr. Koala Bear said, "The name sounds familiar. Ah, yes. He used to be my friend." Mr. Marshmellow said, "Can you take me to him?" "Sure," Mr. Koala Bear said.

So they set off. Finally, they arrived at Ian's house. They knocked on the door and an ugly monster appeared. They ran for their lives . . . "We need to think of a plan," Mr. Marshmellow Man said. "I think the monster is holding Ian hostage." "I've got a plan," said Mr. Koala Bear. "I will knock on the door and get the monster to chase me and you can come up the stairs and go into the house."

Mr. Koala Bear got the monster to chase him. Now it was up to Mr. Marshmellow Man. He ran into the apartment . . . He couldn't find Ian so he ran to the balcony. There was Ian hanging from the 20th floor by a rope and the rope was on fire. The line was snapping . . . Mr. Marshmellow Man grabbed him up [but] just as he turned around he saw the monster running straight toward him. He jumped . . . and the monster flew right off the balcony. Mr. Marshmellow Man saw that an airplane had caught the monster. He thought that the person flying the plane was another monster. Then he got a close look and saw that it was Mr. Koala Bear. So they gave Ian his airplane and they flew him home. Mr. Marshmellow Man and Mr. Koala Bear shook hands and went to collect the reward for finding the monster.

CONCLUSION

"Within the social arrangements set by adults, a 'critical mass' of young children *will* construct their own social worlds, and they will do so with the tools of language" (Dyson 1993, 52, emphasis added). Arguably, this work always goes on in classrooms even if it is seen as marginal or even "illegal" by school staff. Research by Paul Willis (1977) and Robert Everhart (1983) demonstrates, for example, that even resistance to teachers' goals can be used by students as a means of establishing (social) solidarity, but peer social work need not be in contention with the goals of schooling (Dyson 1993). Progressive educators, for example, often set out to construct social contexts for learning, contexts that both support the teachers' view of what counts as learning and the needs of students to accomplish a range of social work. Reading and writing, because they *are* social acts (Bloome 1985, Gee 1990, Myers 1992), provide especially fertile ground for social interaction, but reading and writing are not the only places such interactions can occur. Group problem solving around a math or science question, for example, suggests a number of possibilities for the social work of students. Ultimately, the nature of social work in classrooms will be a function of classroom structures and opportunities mediated by a series of subtle and complex negotiations between students and teachers within physical and organizational spaces over which they do not have complete control. As Heras puts it:

The range of lived opportunities, possibilities, and constraints opened up in classrooms and schools depends on the configurations made possible by the institutional organization of the school and the classroom *and* by the social and academic interactions constructed within these institutional spaces. (1994, 276)

The children in my class found that they were able to exploit opportunities created by the official reading and writing curricula to initiate and maintain a range of social relations and to infuse the official curriculum with their social and cultural identities. Significantly, my students' ability to appropriate the official literacy curriculum in support of their social goals (usually) also advanced my (instructional) aims. As my students exploited reading and writing for their purposes they also created opportunities for discovering the power of literacy to get things done and for learning the various skills, processes, and strategies needed to do this work. I would also like to believe that the permeability (Dyson 1993) of the reading and writing curricula I constructed with my students helped to create a classroom community that was congenial to the range of social, cultural, racial, linguistic, gender, and class differences my third graders brought with them to school each day. Imagining inclusive communities in our classrooms is a much broader notion of community than I began with, but it may be crucial to our efforts to support a more just and democratic society outside of school which is, or at least ought to be, the ultimate goal of schooling. None of this occurred to me when I set "the creation of a community of learners" as my foremost priority in the summer of 1991.

2

The Teachers Work
for the Kids[1]

Ken Macrorie (1970) blamed the dead, vapid writing he found so common among the high school and college students he worked with on the lack of control students had over their writing. Macrorie's remedy for this situation was to increase the degree of control students had over their writing—what has come to be called ownership. He found that this control resulted in students producing livelier, more potent writing. Donald Graves brought the theme of student ownership to the attention of elementary teachers when he concluded that good writing is closely tied to students' personal investment in their writing. Graves put it this way: "When people own a place, they look after it. When it belongs to someone else, they couldn't care less" (in Calkins 1986, 23).

The importance of student ownership—students' ability to exercise some measure of control over the decisions affecting their learning—also extends to reading. Nancie Atwell, for example, concluded, "if we want our . . . students to grow to appreciate literature, another first step is allowing them to exert ownership and choose the literature they will read" (1987, 161). The concept of ownership isn't limited to control over *what* students read and write. Ken Goodman, for example, concluded that students must also have some control over the *purposes* for which they read and write. He says that "language development is empowering: the learner 'owns' the process, makes the decisions about when to use it, what for and with what results. Literacy is empowering too, if the learner is in control with what's done with it" (1986, 26).

---

1. An earlier version of this chapter appeared in Dudley-Marling, C. and Searle, D. (1995). *Who Owns Learning? Questions of Autonomy, Choice, and Control.* Portsmouth, NH: Heinemann.

Pappas, Kiefer, and Levstik remind us that the importance of ownership extends beyond language and literacy learning. "During the preschool years, children choose activities that interest them. Their purposes sustain their attention in projects and guide their motivation to understand. By having ownership in what they do, by following their own questions about topics, they are able to create new concepts and make new connections in their schemas" (1990, 44).

Two notable findings from a year-long study I was involved in of writing in four 7th- and 8th-grade classes provide some concrete support for the importance of student ownership. First, the students we studied didn't write very well and they rarely revised their work. When they did, their revisions were usually limited to minor editorial changes (Dudley-Marling and Oppenheimer 1995). We concluded that the poor quality and lack of care that characterized students' writing was related to the lack of control they had over the decisions affecting their writing. In these classes teachers controlled the topics and audiences of students' writing and the purposes for which students wrote.

My interest in student ownership was piqued and, as I prepared to teach third grade, Dennis Searle and I began putting together an edited volume in which university and school-based teachers and researchers address this topic (Dudley-Marling and Searle 1995). This interest led me to give a lot of attention to student ownership when I taught third grade.

OWNERSHIP IN A THIRD-GRADE CLASSROOM

When my son, Ian, was in preschool I asked him what his teachers did all day. "The teachers work for the kids," is what he told me. This is pretty close to my own vision of the relationship of teachers and students so when I taught third grade I was determined to work for my students, to support students by offering them some control over their work in school. Months before the school year began I wrote in my notes:

> To fill our classroom with our voices and our lives will be a major goal for me next year.

During those hot days of August when I worked to organize my classroom, finding ways to make the classroom theirs/ours was a guiding principle for me.

I've also tried to do what I can to make sure that it's their classroom. I've placed the kleenex on the bookcase with the writing materials, for example, because they are for their use. Putting
them on the teacher's desk . . . suggests that they're mine and
I'm sharing with them . . . The placement of books, writing materials, and art supplies is intended to send the same message . . . this is
their classroom. (field notes, August 27, 1991)

Once school began student ownership was frequently on my
mind. Early in the year I wrote:

What did I do today that encouraged student control of the classroom? I began asking students to share their writing with the class
instead of me sharing mine each day. I will still share writing to
illustrate certain aspects of the craft of writing but I'll pull back a
bit . . . What did I do to retain control? Well, there was no student
reading to the class yesterday. And I continued to assume lots of
responsibility for their behavior. Continued fairly rigid scheduling.
Still not getting much student input for units . . . Need to start
asking. There are some possibilities that emerged yesterday. Hugh,
for example, has an idea for his own science experiment. Peter is
working on directions for caring for the fish at his initiative . . .
(field notes, September 24, 1991)

Overall, I was able to offer my students some control over the
decisions affecting their work. For example, my students exercised
substantial control over *what* they read and wrote, *with whom* they
read and wrote, *why* they read and wrote, *where* they read and wrote,
and, by the end of they year, over *when* they read and wrote. As the
work of Donald Graves predicts, having some control over decisions
affecting their writing helped many of my students discover their
voices as writers. One day on the playground Roya, for example, told
me about her family's escape from Iran and their subsequent immi-
gration to Canada. At my encouragement she turned her reminis-
cences into the following story.

I used to live in Iran but it had too much war. We had to sleep by
the door because of the bombs and missiles. So my parents wanted
to come to Canada. We had trouble getting here. The day we
were coming here I cried and said, "I don't want to leave my Iran."
When we were on the plane I complained that my ear hurt.

When we got to Canada I saw my aunt. She took us to my grandma's house. Everybody hugged. My cousin said to my mom, "What a
big stomach." My mom said, "Yes, I am pregnant." The baby was
my sister.

Now we are in Canada and we are happy.

Caring about her story gave Roya the incentive to turn her story into
a book that she shared with the whole class.

Concerns with ownership also restrained my unfortunate tendency to want to be the center of attention in my classroom. I recall,
for example, telling my students a story about getting locked out of
my father's house during a recent visit, leading several students to
tell their own "key" stories. I was poised to tell another key story
"when it occurred to me that this was their show, the classroom
wasn't my stage, and, in fact, several more stories followed" (field
notes, September 18, 1991).

But, looking back, I didn't always succeed in my efforts to offer
students control over their learning and to support their intentions.
Taking a careful look at my efforts to support students' learning has
also taught me that ownership is a more subtle and complex concept
than I had ever imagined. In this chapter I draw on my notes from
my year as a third-grade teacher to illustrate what was on my mind
as I struggled to offer students some control over their work without
abdicating my responsibility to support their work. I will also discuss
what I have learned about the concept of ownership as I've reflected
on my experience in third grade.

Balancing Student Control and Teacher Support

I knew that offering students some control over decisions affecting
their learning didn't mean that I had to abdicate my responsibilities
to "teach." In fact, I saw "laissez-faireism" as one of the worst perver-
sions of whole language. Before the school year began I wrote in my
notes:

> Nudging: Even in some of the best whole language classrooms I see
> I'm not sure they "nudge" enough. Perhaps too much patience
> and too much dependence on [the power of a] language-rich envi-
> ronment. Something I can explore next year—the tension
> between nudging and taking control. Given my daughter Anne's

difficulties in first grade I would tend to want to try to nudge and challenge as much as I can.

I wasn't afraid to offer my expertise and experience to support my third-grade students' intentions. For example:

> During reading assessments a couple of the kids got really hung up on proper names (and just stopped reading as they tried to laboriously sound out the proper names, e.g., Valencia, Malcolm) so at the conclusion of reading I did a quick lesson on how to deal with proper names in text. I asked the group what they did when they came to a name like this which they couldn't pronounce (holding up a copy of *Malcolm's Runaway Soap* (Bogart and Hendry 1988)). Most volunteered that they sounded the name out, but one [student] did say that she just made up another name and went on reading. I picked up on this suggestion and noted that this is what I do. (field notes, September 6, 1991)

> I gave Crystal a quick spelling lesson. She spelled "never" "nivr" so I asked her what vowel she heard in never (exaggerating the "e"). She first said "a," then "e." I also told her that the "r" sound at the end of a word is usually going to be spelled "er." (field notes, October 29, 1991)

> Razika is writing a long story called "The Witch." She used dialogue in this story so I used this story as an opportunity to teach her about quotation marks. (field notes, October 28, 1991)

Similarly, when some of my students started writing letters to their favorite stars from *Beverly Hills 90210*, I did a minilesson on the format for personal letters, putting an example up on the wall. I found that I could also give strong direction. For example:

> Today I asked Razika and Shyrose and Jennifer and Barbara to move off letter writing . . . (field notes, October 2, 1991)

> Nicholas is spending too much time writing silly notes to people ("singing telegrams" he calls them) with nothing much on them. They seem to annoy the other students and they waste a lot of paper so I told him to stop writing them. (field notes, October 8, 1991)

But I worried about how hard I could push students without taking away control of their work. This tension is illustrated by my
response to Wayne who wanted to quit the literature sharing group
he'd (voluntarily) signed up for.

> Wayne had signed up to read a book for literature sharing and
> when I asked him to read it he said he changed his mind. At the
> time I told him that if he signed up to read the book he had to
> finish it. Part of me feels that he should follow through but I worry
> about his choice. Right now I feel justified on insisting that he
> finish this book since he made the choice. But what I need to do is
> announce this "rule" to the whole class. (field notes, January 8,
> 1992)

Similarly, when Catherine and Connie decided to stop reading the
book they'd chosen for literature sharing I insisted that they continue with their choice.

I'm disappointed that I made such a big deal over this. I never
made a fuss when students abandoned writing topics or books they
were reading individually. I eventually did back off though, perhaps
influenced by the fact that, about this time, my wife quit John Irving's *The Cider House Rules* (1985) about two thirds of the way
through because it was making her "too sad." (I did not insist that
she continue.) I was also influenced by the fact that I knew I couldn't
make Catherine do anything she didn't want to do.

> Talked to Catherine and Barbara about *Sarah, Plain and Tall*
> (MacLachlan 1985). Catherine had read to page thirty-one but she
> said she didn't like the story any more and wasn't going to read any
> more. With some of the students I'd insist that they continue but I
> know this would be hopeless with Catherine . . . (field notes, April
> 21, 1992)

Perhaps the best example of my struggle to achieve a balance
between teacher support and student control was my ongoing effort
to encourage students to produce multiple drafts of their writing.
There were instances of students revising their work early in the
year, but such efforts were rare. Getting students to revise their writing became a major goal for me as evidenced by the following
excerpts from my field notes.

Razika (and now Shyrose) continue to crank out stories at the rate of one/day. Need to get a group of these students together to start nudging them a little bit more. (field notes, September 25, 1991)

During writing spent a lot of time meeting with kids but still have had little success getting students into more sustained writing efforts. Getting students into multiple drafts is my major goal this month but other than modeling it I'm not sure what else to do short of requiring it which I'm not particularly comfortable doing. This may be something I can do as I respond to individual pieces of students' writing. (field notes, January 7, 1992)

I frequently modeled revision, but my students continued to make only superficial editing changes in their work. I also offered explicit advice to students to encourage them to revise their work. On September 26, for example, I wrote in my field notes:

Did lots of roving conferences in writing today. I talked to Razika about a story she was writing (part of "Four stories by Razika"). I talked to her about the possibility of adding more details. In this instance she had written that the kittens were naughty so I asked her why they were naughty and she gave some thoughts.

Razika listened politely when I suggested she add more details to her kitten story but, in the end, she ignored my advice. I finally concluded that I wasn't pushing individual children hard enough to revise their work. So I resolved to push harder.

I told Razika that I would insist that she take one piece tomorrow and work with it for a period of several days and then publish it. (field notes, January 13, 1992)

But this still wasn't enough.

Talked again to Shyrose and Razika about sticking with a piece. I just don't seem to be able to get them to do this. They insist that they will "just as soon as they finish this piece" but they never do. (field notes, January 28, 1992)

Finally . . .

> Shyrose was actually revising her piece about her brother. She erased lots of words—usually because of problems with spelling or grammar or just personal preference, e.g., mom—> mother; hole —> whole. I read some of what she'd written and she made more changes, e.g., I read, "Then had to fix it" and asked her if this was OK and she changed to "Then they . . . " Most of the changes she made without me and came as a result of her conferencing with Razika. (field notes, February 2, 1992)

Within a few weeks both Shyrose and Razika had taken pieces of writing and revised and then published them. Soon almost everyone in the class was working toward the publication of a book and revision was part of almost everyone's process. Initially, this reinforced my belief that I hadn't been pushing students hard enough.

> These books and the editing/revising that was part of them came about only after I began really pushing. Maybe a nudge isn't a command but it may not be a hint either . . . I think I was going too far in the direction of student control, at least in writing (field notes, March 13, 1992)

I'm now convinced that this analysis was flawed. Yes, I did push students harder but I pushed them to publish their writing.

> At the beginning of the (writing) session warned them that I would be expecting them to take a single piece of writing and work with it over a period of some time with the goal of publishing it. When someone asked if they'd have to I surprised myself by saying yes. (field notes, January 15, 1992)

In this context my students did a lot more revision, but publishing their writing gave students reasons to revise their work and gave me a genuine reason to talk about revision; that is, my talk about revision supported what they were trying to do. So it was pushing kids to publish that made the difference, not merely pushing them to revise. But I still ended up pushing a lot harder than I ever expected I would.

In this context I found it easier to respond directly to students' writing, e.g.,"I don't understand this. I think you need to make some changes." Giving students personal reasons for revising their work also made it easier for me to provide less direct support. When Catherine confessed that she was having trouble with a piece because she didn't know how to start we did a minilesson the next day on leads using a piece of writing I had been sharing with them about my daughter's birth.

Despite these successes I continued to worry about how hard I could push without taking control of students' work.

> I spent most of my time going over Ali's story with him. I was a bit intrusive and as happens too often I was frequently distracted by behavior problems as he read to me . . . I also started offering advice, or at least confessing confusion with the first line of the story. What I might have done was to listen to the whole story first and perhaps make a note or two and then "receive" his work before I commented on it. I gave him an unfortunate message I'm afraid. (field notes, February 25, 1992)

At other times I worried I wasn't pushing hard enough.

> When Crystal told me she had written something she wanted to publish I gave her what is now my standard advice that she should read over her piece, perhaps out loud, and read to a couple of other people and make any necessary changes . . . I said that we would then meet to talk about her piece, but I warned her that I might suggest some changes. She told me firmly that she really liked her piece and didn't want to make any changes. When we met I did have a couple of suggestions . . . but she told me again that she liked her piece as it was and didn't want to make any changes. So I agreed to publish her piece. It is her piece in the end. (field notes, March 25, 1992)

Despite this recognition—that it was her piece in the end—I still worried that I had failed to push Crystal hard enough.

Focusing on the Here and Now

I am relatively satisfied with the balance between student control and teacher support I was able to achieve in my literacy program. But, looking back it's clear that I didn't permit students the same degree of control in all areas of the curriculum. In math and science, for example, my students had much less control over the decisions affecting their learning than they did in reading and writing. The following excerpts from my lesson plans are illustrative.

> Science Center: Monday morning - Group activity on trees. With notebooks (and small group discussion) have them talk/write about similarities and differences between trees and plants. What is a plant? What are some of the common features of plants? (lesson plans, September 16, 1991)
>
> MATH
> 1. Do the daily survey
> 2. Do the daily estimation
> 3. Work together to solve the problems at your table
> 4. Use clocks to make the following times and record in your notebooks: 1:00; 3:00; 6:00; 9:00; 10:00; 12:00; 11:30; 3:30 (lesson plans, September 9, 1991)

These tasks are entirely teacher directed deriving from either curriculum guides or resource books. They had nothing to do with students' interests although I suppose that I hoped to "get them interested." Arguably, I set the task and offered support to help students to fulfill my intentions. Their intentions were not even considered.

My concerns about math and science, as reflected in my field notes, are just as telling. In general, my notes about math and science focus on the need for more explicit directions, better organization, behavior problems, and getting things done. The following examples are typical.

> Centers [math and science] went OK although I frequently had to ask them to be more quiet. At one point during the last center rotation I had them all come to the carpet so I could remind them to keep their voices down. (field notes, October 2, 1991)

> The last center rotation wasn't very successful with lots of kids wandering, some of the kids at the math center were doing "cat's in the cradle" because they "didn't want to do flash cards." Carl kept gravitating to the sand table even though he was supposed to be at the listening center and the science center people were all over the place because, I'll have to admit, they weren't sure what to do. (field notes, October 17, 1991)

The bubble activity was very successful, *at least in terms of keeping them interested and on task.* (field notes, April 21, 1992)

Noticeably missing from these entries is any sense of what, if anything, students were learning. In reading and writing, my focus was on supporting students' efforts to use reading and writing to fulfill their intentions. In math and science there was much more of a focus on fulfilling my intentions to get things done (i.e., cover the curriculum).

My search for ways to encourage students to finish their work was part of my overall concern with getting things done. On February twenty-fourth, for example, I sent home a note informing parents that they could expect their children to bring tracking sheets home each day. I introduced tracking sheets because I was concerned that students weren't finishing their work at the math and science centers. And when I introduced a comprehensive point system in January to try to cope with the behavior problems which were, I believed, threatening the success of my year (see Chapter Three), finishing their work was one of the ways students earned points. At various times I also used performance contracts and withheld recess from some students to encourage them to complete work.

This preoccupation with the here and now, with getting things done in math and science, contrasts with my response to students' reading and writing. When I worried early in September about students who weren't doing much writing, for example, I didn't respond with tracking sheets or artificial contingencies.

Writing wasn't very successful today. I shared a story about my cat that I had written the night before as an example of the kinds of thing they could write. Still, most wrote little if anything (Wayne wrote, "I do not like to write.") and many of the girls wrote notes to each other . . . Ali among others wrote nothing at all citing the familiar refrain, "I don't know what to write about." Clearly, I need to work hard to share something I've written each day for awhile and offer opportunities for them to share what they have written. They desperately need models and reasons for writing (which they are going to have to discover on their own). I'm also going to have to work individually with students to help them pick topics to write about. Maybe tomorrow we could brainstorm a list of writing topics for them to put in their notebooks. May also wish to enforce quiet time for the first ten minutes of writing period during which time I would write myself. Another possibility: See if any other teachers have good writing programs going. If so, their students could share their writing with my class (to model topics). (field notes, September 10, 1991)

Ultimately, my concern with getting things done in math and science resulted in few opportunities for students to exercise any meaningful control over the decisions affecting their learning. Early in the year I wrote in my field notes:

> It seems that what I want to do gets in the way of letting students assume more control of their learning. (field notes, September 23, 1991)

I also recognized early in the year that focusing on the "here and now" obscured long term learning goals (see Jackson 1968).

> Science continues to be a problem for me. We're doing experiments but we're not really learning much of anything. Need to supplement with group activities, integrate into the rest of the curriculum. Any way to fit with folk-tale study? One thing I might do is to encourage them to bring in things related to units, like plants. I also need some more support. Maybe I should involve students more in planning experiments . . . (field notes, October 6, 1991)

Despite this recognition my preoccupation with getting things done in math and science only intensified as the year progressed. In reading and writing, on the other hand, students seemed to exercise more control over their work as the year went on. This begs the question: Why was I so concerned with getting things done in math and science? Here I offer two explanations. But since I can only look back through the lens of time, distorted by the effects of personal history and growth, these interpretations are necessarily tentative and partial.

One reason, I think, for my keen focus on the here and now in math and science, with the concomitant of increased teacher control, is that I have had little experience, direct or indirect, with models of math or science that build on students' interests, experiences, and intentions. Of course, such models of math and science instruction are relatively rare.

Another explanation that may show the different ways I treated math and science on the one hand and reading and writing on the other is related to background knowledge. Perhaps my attention was so firmly fixed on the here and now in math and science while I viewed our reading and writing curricula through a wider lens was simply because, compared to reading and writing, I knew less about math and science. This explanation occurred to me early in the year.

There may be a natural tension between teacher and student control. It is interesting, I think, that I've given students the most control in the areas of the curriculum that I know the most about— oral and written language. Or perhaps these areas are easiest for teachers to give up some control over. (field notes, September 15, 1991)

It may be easier for teachers to offer students more control over their reading and writing. I'm not sure. But I am convinced that my focus on the here and now in math and science had at least something to do with my background knowledge. I know less about math and science and, more importantly, I have given less thought to what are the processes used by mathematicians or scientists.[2] Therefore, I did not have an intuitive sense for my long term goals in either math or science. It's not that I didn't have long term goals for math and science. I did. But in the heat of battle my long term goals often gave way to the exigencies of doing the curriculum.

This contrasts with the way I approached reading and writing. I know a lot about reading and writing and, more to the point, I know a lot about what readers and writers do in the process of reading and writing. Therefore, I never allowed the intense demands of life in the classroom to distract me from my long term goal to help students realize the potential of reading and writing to affect their lives. So when Wayne wanted to quit the literature sharing group he'd signed up for I finally remembered that readers (myself included) don't always finish books they've started. When students couldn't

---

2. I don't limit the terms mathematician or scientist to people with advanced graduate degrees. From a holistic perspective anyone who uses math or science to fulfill personal intentions is a mathematician or a scientist in the same way that anyone who uses reading or writing for some purpose is a reader or a writer. That we tend to think otherwise may partially explain the dearth of examples of math and science education which build on students' intentions.

think of anything to write about or if they abandoned a topic I didn't (usually) ask them to stay in for recess or offer them incentives to finish their work. I knew that this is what happens to writers because this has happened to me. And when students demanded more flexibility so that they could read and/or write during other times of the day I eventually capitulated because I knew that these are important needs for readers and writers. Recognizing what readers and writers do in the process of reading and writing made it easier for me to keep my long-term goals in the forefront.

Recently, I've found some support for a relationship between teachers' background knowledge and the construction of curriculum. Carlsen (cited in Brilliant-Mills, 1993), for example, found

> that teacher knowledge of science content influenced the patterns of interactions of teachers and students. When teachers in his study had a conceptual understanding of a topic, they opened up the conversation and engaged students in patterns of interaction that permitted examination of a range of issues and concepts of science. When they were less familiar with the content, they closed down the conversation and engaged students in patterns that sought one right answer, focused on the textbook, and were more narrow in range (1993, 302).

In my case, the issue was less a knowledge of content than a conscious knowledge of the processes used by mathematicians and scientists but I believe the results were the same.

Confusing Ownership with Independence

Getting kids to work independently—which I seemed to have equated with ownership—was a major concern for me. Consider the following three entries from my field notes.

> What did I do today to help kids own the class? Well, twice students read to the group and I continued to give them lots of freedom at the centers. (September 26, 1991)

> This afternoon went a little better. Both center rotations were very nice. They worked more independently than they ever have before. I think the combination of clearer directions and the fact that I decided to make sure that there is always one good reader at the science center seem to be very helpful. (October 7, 1991)

The students at the math center did fairly well working independently today. (May 27, 1992)

When the year began I hoped I'd be able to encourage independence as part of creating opportunities for students to explore their own interests. From this perspective it's possible to see a relationship between ownership and independence. But sometimes working independently came to mean working without teacher direction or support. I reasoned that if students could do their math and science work, for example, without too much direct support I would be free to use my time for assessment interviews, literature sharing groups, or writing conferences. For example, on September 26 I wrote in my notes:

> I don't think I'll be happy until the science and math centers are working well enough to allow me the time to work with students individually and in small groups on reading and writing.

Ironically, my goal to increase students' independence, which was rooted in my desire to increase their control over their work, may actually have decreased the degree of control students had over their learning.

> I'm very, very pleased with how the math center has worked this week. *The worksheets we've been using have allowed students to work more independently* . . . (field notes, March 27, 1992)

And when students had difficulty with open-ended tasks I tended to conclude that the problem was theirs: they just couldn't work independently.

> The activity of sorting geo-blocks didn't work much better this time than last time. The group only sorted them one way and spent most of their time recording this sorting by means of a picture. Open ended tasks like this seem to consistently befuddle even the most capable students in my class. (field notes, January 8, 1991)

I also saw a relationship between what I concluded was students' inability to work independently and the failure of some of the themes and projects we attempted throughout the year. This dubious reasoning led me to abandon a class study of the Winter Olympics.

My students just can't handle much freedom or open ended tasks. They do just fine cutting out articles for their scrapbooks but didn't do well at much else. I'm going to return to our usual routine as quickly as I can . . . (field notes, February 11, 1992)

In turn, I blamed my students' lack of independence on previous teachers.

I also think that many of these students came from more of a teacher controlled curricula and are having some difficulty adjusting to all the independence they have. (field notes, September 12, 1991)

Too late, perhaps, I recognized that the problem was not my students' ability to work independently. They worked independently all the time and did quite well. The problem was the quality of support they were receiving from me.

We haven't had much success with independent work and yet reading and writing are entirely independent and they go very well. Perhaps the problem isn't working independently but knowing what's expected of them. I just can't expect them to have entirely open ended projects. They need to know what they are to do and what kind of product they're going to have . . . They're not going to learn how to work independently unless I give them opportunities and teach them how . . . (field notes, May 4, 1992)

It is instructive to note that an animal study we did in the fall (this emerged from a folk tale unit) included significant teacher support and was relatively successful. For example:

Chris [my wife] suggested I think about studying some of the animals in the folk-tale units. So I'm going to begin by getting them to list the animals in the unit and maybe do a web to relate. Or maybe do a web more generally to build a conceptual framework from which science may emerge. May also want to start teaching them about webs as part of both science and language arts curricula. This is heartening but will keep being a challenge. I will need to work at it. It won't just happen by itself. (field notes, October 6, 1991)

Today need to give them a group lesson to support the more independent study in science, e.g., picking out some animals from our folk-tale study to learn more about (as a group). I'm asking them to pick an animal each or an animal as a group or several animals and develop a plan to learn more about them. We need to begin as a group by modeling a plan of study. I'd like to start that today. (field notes, October 18, 1991)

Continue with animal study but do several mini-lessons on the possible products for this theme. (field notes, October 28, 1991)

Last night I went to the library: got 8–10 picture books for my class. Also got a number of books to help support their animal studies: e.g., a book on saber-toothed tigers for Hugh; a book that has some stuff on crocodiles for Ali; and books on foxes and wolves for several students who are studying these animals. (field notes, November 2, 1991)

Over two decades ago Ken Macrorie (1970) drew our attention to the costs of tightly controlling students' writing. However, he found that non-direction didn't substantially improve the situation. Therefore, Macrorie argued for what he called "the Third Way" in which teachers increased student responsibility for their work, but continued to provide strong direction.

Working independently—with limited teacher support and direction—is a perverse notion of ownership. My students were able to read, write, and pursue their animal study fairly independently because, I believe, I provided them with sufficient support. There is a tension between teacher support and student control. Too much teacher support can result in teachers taking over responsibility for students' learning. But without teacher support and direction students will always find it difficult to exercise much control over the decisions affecting their learning.

An Evolving Sense of Ownership

Reflecting on my notes as I wrote this chapter has transformed my concept of student ownership. Like many educators, I believed that students could only learn to read and write if they engaged in "authentic" reading and writing. Reading and writing were authentic, I believed, only if engaged in for students' purposes. Anything else is, at best, a simulation and, the argument went, what was learned in a simulation may not transfer to instances of authentic reading and writing (Edelsky, Alwerger, and Flores 1991). So if a student wrote a book report because she was directed to by the teacher then this writing was, by definition, inauthentic (see Edelsky et al. 1991). Similar arguments could be made for reading. But there are problems with this argument (see Edelsky 1991). The reality of schooling is children are not there voluntarily (Herndon 1970; Jackson 1968). So it is doubtful that anything done at school can ever truly be authentic (Bloome and Bailey 1990). There are also examples of out of school writing where people write for someone else's purposes (e.g., writing a report for your principal) and no one would want to say that these people aren't really writing (Edelsky 1991).

Although school reading and writing may never be truly authentic, it's still important that students exercise some control over the decisions affecting their learning. There is good evidence that without a personal stake in their writing students will not write very well. I believe the same is true for reading. More importantly, if students do not use reading and writing in school to fulfill their intentions they may not discover the power of reading and writing to affect their lives. Without some control over the uses of literacy in school, students are much less likely "to use print for examining and critiquing taken-for-granted conditions in one's own life and within one's own society" (Edelsky 1991, 93–94). Critical literacy is an important factor in creating a more equitable society.

Sociolinguistic (Bloome 1987), critical (Shannon 1992) and deconstructive (Crowley 1989) voices have also encouraged me to reconsider my notions of what it means for students to own their reading and writing. These voices argue that reading and writing are sociolinguistic acts and that whenever we make meaning with language—as readers, writers, speakers, or listeners—we are influenced by the voices of our community and culture. These views have helped me to consider the subtle ways my voice affected the meanings my students made with written language.

For instance, I regularly tried to influence the meanings students made as readers and how they made meaning as writers, including the purposes for which they wrote. I often encouraged students to use their background knowledge, including their knowledge of language, to make sense of texts, e.g., "Why don't you just skip that word and come back to it?" "Does that make sense here?" By stressing the role of background knowledge in reading I encouraged a particular belief about reading: the meaning isn't (just) in the text.

There were other ways I influenced the meanings students made as readers. A major goal for literature sharing groups and for discussing books I read to the class was to encourage students to talk in literate ways, to get a sense of literary elements like plot, characters, mood, setting, and so on, and to read texts critically.

> At the end of reading I again asked them if they had come across any interesting characters in their reading and they did volunteer a number of characters. They mostly found them interesting because they were funny and did funny things. May need to model some of these things. Crystal did note that the character "lazy bear" was interesting because he reminded her of her sister who also never did anything. (field notes, September 26, 1991)

> When I read on pages 47–48 "Clouds of breath exploded from her mouth." I stopped. I read the line again. I noted how I liked the way this sounded and I asked the group to tell me what they thought it meant. One of them noted pretty quickly that this told us that it was cold outside. (field notes, May 14, 1992)

Similarly, the modeling of writing topics influenced what students wrote about.

> Writing time began with my sharing of a brief story on the chart about getting locked out of my father's house. Usually they listen in silence and we move on but today they started sharing stories about losing car keys or house keys. At least eight of them shared such stories and a couple told more than one "key" story. At least three or four of the students I checked with during writing time were writing key stories. (field notes, September 18, 1991)

I also influenced the processes students used as writers. For example:

> Catherine had started a poem about snowfall but hadn't got beyond the title. So I had her come to the window with me and asked her to look out the window and tell me what she saw. So then I asked her to try writing these thoughts down and that this would make the basis for a poem. (field notes, January 14, 1992)

Several students overheard this conversation and imitated this process.

When I noticed that students who were writing personal pieces were having more success discovering their voices as writers, I pushed several students to try personal narrative.

> Had a wonderful talk with Roya on the playground at morning recess. She told me she had a four year old brother and a two year old sister. I asked her if they were both born in Canada and she told me that her brother was also born in Iran. We talked a little about Iran and she told me she didn't want to go back there because "there's always war and everything." She told me that they had to sleep by the door at night in case "those things . . . bombs" came. She also told me about having "to cover up" and she hated that. She also told me her grandfather died recently (in Iran) and her father was homesick. (field notes, September 18, 1991)

At my encouragement Roya wrote about her experience emigrating from Iran and later returned to this theme for her first publication in early March.

I was one of the many voices my students heard when they tried to make sense of (and with) print. Recognizing the influence of my voice, and the other voices in students' communities and cultures, forced me to reconsider what it means for students to own their reading or writing. Students may be able to exercise control over when, how, why, where, and for whom they use literacy, but the meanings they make as readers and writers will always be socially influenced. That I was one of those social voices is not bad. In fact, we hope that students will hear their teachers' voices as they read and write. This is one way we might define what it means "to teach." Ownership does not mean silencing the teacher's voice. It's just that when the teacher's voice dominates, students learn only authorized meanings and are denied the opportunity to participate in the social construction of meaning (Myers 1992).

I have also begun to wonder what happens when the teacher's voice conflicts with the voices of a student's culture or community. In the following example my transactional view of literacy risked denying a kind of literacy in Ali's home which granted authority to particular interpretations of certain texts.

> Today when I read from *The Return of the Third Grade Ghosthunters* (Maccarone 1989) there was a picture of a gravestone . . . We had a

discussion of gravestones and our visits to graveyards. Among other things we talked about the date of birth and date of death on the gravestone and how to determine the person's age when they died . . . someone said they had seen a gravestone with a date of birth of 1750 and date of death of 1950. Then we figured this person would have been 200 years old when they died and we had a discussion of how long you could live. Most of us, including me, argued that few people lived beyond 100 and no one ever lived beyond 130. But Ali didn't agree, arguing that some people had lived to be over 500 years old. (field notes, November 6, 1991)

The following day:

When Ali came into the classroom he walked up to me and said sternly, "My dad said Noah lived to be 950 years old." (field notes, November 7, 1991)

I have also begun to wonder about the effects of efforts I made to push my students, who came from a range of cultural traditions, toward more personal writing. When I encouraged Razika, my most prolific writer, to draw on personal experience in her writing she resisted for several weeks, but she finally wrote a (vapid) piece about visiting Canada's Wonderland (an amusement park). Did my advice to write about herself conflict with her cultural values? I don't know. But I think it is important to at least acknowledge the possibility that the voices of our classroom communities have the potential to alienate students from their communities and culture (see Edelsky 1991).

CONCLUSION

Ownership isn't something teachers can *give* their students. However, even if we can't give ownership to students, we can create conditions which permit (or deny) students opportunities to assume responsibility for (some) decisions affecting their learning. There is no magic prescription or formula for this. From my perspective at the university, ownership seemed to be a fairly straightforward notion. I learned differently from my third-grade students. In practice, ownership is a very tricky concept.

Other teachers may discover, as I did, that encouraging student ownership requires striking a careful balance between student control and teacher support and direction. Too much teacher support risks taking control of the learning away from students. Too little teacher direction denies students access to the voices that support their intellectual growth and development limiting their ability to take responsibility for their learning. But how much is too much support? Or too little? What constitutes too much or too little support can only be determined by reflecting on our daily encounters with students.

I also found that my ability to offer students control over their learning was affected by my background knowledge and experience. I found it easiest to support students' intentions in those areas of the curriculum I knew the most about; namely, reading and writing. Offering students control over their reading and writing was also easier, I think, because I have had many opportunities to see or read about models of reading and writing instruction which built on students' interests and background knowledge. Lacking similar background knowledge and experience in math and science, I tended to focus on doing the curriculum, on getting things done. A focus on the here and now, which obscures long term instructional goals, will never be congenial to encouraging student ownership.

I think this observation has implications for teacher training. Future teachers will find it difficult to create classrooms where teachers and students share responsibility for learning without sufficient knowledge of what they are expected to teach (e.g., reading, writing, math, science) or without opportunities to observe appropriate models. Similar arguments can be made for in-service teacher education.

Students themselves may sometimes thwart our efforts to encourage students to assume control of decisions affecting their learning. Some of my students, for example, asked me to tell them what to write. My colleague Dennis Searle tells me that, in his experience, secondary students sometimes respond to teachers giving them control over topic selection by introducing taboo topics in their writing. Dennis believes that these students use taboo topics to force their teachers to return to teacher selected topics. These students resist taking responsibility for their learning, preferring the certainty and predictability of teacher control. Some students may resist their "unsanctioned" language and literacy becoming "sanctioned" (Myers 1992) because children's own language can become a "means for escaping the biases of language and culture, creating a shared and equal private world for their friendship" (Gilmore 1983, 36). Paradoxically, permitting students to bring their lives into the classroom can be potentially alienating (Edelsky 1991).

But negotiating a curriculum built on students' background knowledge and experience is worth the risks. Permitting students control over their learning is pedagogically sound and morally right. In contexts where students are permitted control over decisions affecting their learning there is good reason to believe that students will do better work. Perhaps more importantly, when students assume more responsibility for their learning it is also more likely they will discover the power of what we teach in school to affect their lives and the lives of others. Given power over how they use literacy in school, for example, students will be more likely to develop literacy practices which will contribute to the development of a more just and democratic society (Edelsky 1991; Myers 1992).

But teachers who create conditions which encourage student control over their work are not doing their students a favor. Ownership is not a gift—it is an entitlement (D. Dippo, personal communication, December 14, 1992). Children's language—their "ways with words" (Heath 1983)—and their ways of knowing express who they are and the communities and cultures from which they come. Restricting students' control over their learning limits their right to express their personal and cultural identities. Permitting students to bring themselves and their lives into their classrooms is, I believe, a moral imperative.

3

Whole Language Teachers Don't Have Discipline Problems, Do They?

Mr. Marling: You guys are really being childish!
Roya: Mr. Marling, we *are* children.

Chris Zajac, the fifth-grade teacher Tracy Kidder profiles in his book, *Among School Children*, commented on the discipline problems posed by a boy in her class named Clarence saying, "I wasn't trained for this. *I was trained to teach . . .*" (1987, 23, my emphasis). I didn't give much thought to student discipline either as I prepared to teach third grade during the spring and summer of 1991. Perhaps, like Chris Zajac, I didn't consider discipline teaching, only a related aggravation like yard duty or cleaning the blackboards and tables. Of course, you can teach with dirty tables and blackboards, but it will always be difficult for students to learn much if their teachers are unable to create some sense of order in the classroom. In *Schoolteacher*, Dan Lortie's (1975) classic study of teaching, he observed that teachers who fail to keep control over their students will soon find that teaching is intolerable work. I imagine this is why so many of my field note entries made reference to students' behavior once school began in September.

I think there may have been another reason why I gave so little thought to discipline as I prepared for third grade: the belief that good whole language teachers don't have discipline problems—at least not to the same extent as many teachers—because whole language teachers honor students' intentions. This contrasts with the practice in traditional classrooms where it appears that teachers expend an enormous amount of energy "getting their intentions to prevail over the intentions of students" (Boomer 1987, 11) or, as

Tracy Kidder puts it, "the problem is fundamental. Put twenty or more children of roughly the same age in a little room, confine them to desks, make them wait in lines, make them behave. It is as if a secret committee, now lost to history, had made a study of children and, having figured out what the greatest number were least disposed to do, declared that all of them should do it" (1987, 115).

The mismatch between the aims of students' and those of their teachers suggests the possibility that students act out as a form of resistance to having teachers' intentions forced on them. Curriculum in whole language classrooms, which claims to be based on a "negotiation of intentions" (Boomer 1987, 11) in which students and teachers jointly own and plan curricula, ought to encounter less student resistance and, therefore, fewer discipline problems. It's also reasonable to assume that whole language teachers minimize teacher–student conflicts by placing fewer limits on students' movements. In whole language classrooms students are often free, for example, to talk quietly and move freely about their classrooms. When I was in school, on the other hand, my teachers expended lots of time and energy getting us to keep quiet and stay at our desks.

I'm fairly confident that increasing students' participation in curricular decision–making and placing fewer restrictions on their movements can minimize discipline problems. Creating more democratic classrooms does not, however, change two dominant facts of life in schools. First of all, students are not in school by choice (Herndon 1970). Children have to be there under penalty of law and no doubt some of them resent these limits being imposed on them. Secondly, schools are very crowded places. In his book, *Life in Classrooms*, Philip Jackson observed that:

> There is a social intimacy in schools that is unmatched elsewhere in
> our society. Buses and movie theaters are more crowded than class-
> rooms, but people rarely stay in such densely populated settings
> for extended periods of time and while there, they usually are not
> expected to concentrate on work or to interact with each other.
> Even factory workers are not clustered as close together as students
> in a standard classroom . . . Only in schools do thirty or more peo-
> ple spend several hours each day literally side by side. (1968, 8)

There is research that shows that under very crowded conditions rats will become agitated and aggressive. There is no reason to expect that children will respond to overcrowding any differently.

Nor is there any reason to expect meaningful, child-centered education to alter the fact that many students carry some heavy emotional baggage with them to school each day. Poverty, racism, drugs, alcohol, sexual abuse, domestic violence, homophobia, and parental neglect complicate the lives of many of the students in our schools.

The freedom of movement students enjoy in whole language classrooms may also increase the possibility of student conflicts, especially among more aggressive students. The teacher who taught in the classroom next to mine abandoned activity-based learning for a more traditional classroom arrangement primarily to increase his control as a means of reducing student conflict. Similarly, one day in April when I was very tired and anxious about my father's upcoming surgery I put together a whole day of seat work for my students knowing I would not be able to handle behavior problems that day (I never did this again).

My expectation, probably unconscious, that a whole language curriculum would magically make discipline problems disappear was clearly unrealistic. In any case, my year in third grade was marked by frequent and occasionally serious behavior problems. Martin's (violent) tantrums, Denise's infantile whining, Ali's constant complaining, Catherine's and Charles's aggressiveness, Wayne's wandering about the classroom, and Jeffrey's and Paul's non-stop talking meant that large and small group activities were always a struggle. My students' behavior at lunch, in the halls, on the playground, and in the washrooms often brought them into conflict with the principal and other teachers. Violence was a more serious problem. Anyone who crossed Catherine was sure to get pushed or kicked. Hugh typically ended disputes with a knee in the groin. On one occasion Denise, who was often verbally and physically abusive, scratched Scott in the face with a pencil, just missing his eye. Peter lost a tooth in a playground dispute with Charles. In a particularly disturbing act of violence, Ali stabbed Catherine in the thigh with a pencil with such force that the tip of the pencil penetrated her blue jeans, broke off deep beneath her skin, and had to be removed surgically.

As the following excerpts from my field notes suggest, there were times I was nearly overwhelmed by behavior problems.

> After reading . . . things really deteriorated. Benizar came in crying . . . because she was upset by her new haircut. Jennifer
> cried because, she said, the boys were kicking her. Scott had one of his little tantrums and he was near tears. He was defiant and nasty

the rest of the morning. Wayne imitated him and was mouthy all morning . . . He said I yelled at him . . . Todd cried while his mother was here, but he settled down after she left. Many of them never did any writing this morning and in general many were nearly unmanageable. Reading time didn't go much better. Ali, upset because he couldn't find his book, was trouble the whole time and Wayne and Scott continued their defiance. Ali and Nader had a fight, Scott pushed Shyrose (it seems she was in his way), Wayne kicked Catherine and on and on. Denise, always hard, was the most difficult she's been to date. This morning I felt incompetent and nearly helpless. (field notes, October 7, 1991)

Catherine, Denise, Crystal, and Fatima . . . put on their costumes and practiced their play in the hall. While they were out there some of the boys going to the bathroom and the library made fun of them which created several conflicts between the boys and Catherine and Denise. While I was dealing with one of these Nader broke Denise's wand (he claimed Fatima pushed him). Catherine and Nader were then involved in a pushing match and Denise kicked him in the groin and scratched him. Finally she stormed out of the class and refused to come back in. So I sent her to the office and, in defiance of me, Connie and Catherine went with her to complain to the principal. It was a pretty awful ending to the day. (field notes, January 9, 1992)

I'm not going to use this chapter to document the behavior problems in my classroom. Yes, I had my share of behavior problems, but so do lots of other teachers including other whole language teachers. Well-known whole language teacher Cora Five (1995), for example, described a fifth-grade student who crawled around her classroom like a baby. And the stories of violence in my classroom, although disturbing, pale against the brutal reality of life in many other classrooms across the United States and Canada. Nothing I saw compared to an incident described by Mickey Harris (1993), a high school teacher from Philadelphia, who had a gang of eight girls burst into her classroom and drag a female student into the hall. Harris's efforts to intervene resulted in her being "knocked unconscious . . . with a black eye, cut lip, and a missing bicuspid" (1993, 134).

What's interesting isn't that I had discipline problems, but how I experienced them; that is, how I responded to discipline problems and how they affected the teaching identity I had constructed for myself. In this chapter I'll consider how the behavior problems in my third grade affected my identity both as a *good* teacher and a holistic educator. I'll begin by examining how discipline problems and my response to student behavior affected my sense of myself as a teacher.

"I WONDER IF REAL TEACHERS HAVE THESE PROBLEMS"

> My students' behavior was awful this afternoon. Catherine was totally out of control. She was loud and disruptive, she danced about the room, and she was defiant. Even when I put her in the hall she kept sticking her head back into the room and making loud noises. At one point she was running up and down the hall disturbing other classes. I kept her in for recess which she was supposed to spend by the office, but she kept running back and forth from the office to the classroom, attracting the attention of other teachers. Finally, I called the office and told them I was sending Catherine to the office and I hoped they would keep her there the rest of the day. I had trouble even getting her there . . . (field notes, January 21, 1992)

Incidents like this often left me feeling helpless and inadequate, wondering if I was the problem, if *real* teachers had these sorts of difficulties with their students. A rough day in late September left me wondering if I'd made the right decision returning to the classroom for the year.

> When I drove home tonight it was the first time I wasn't sure I wanted to do this anymore. I was feeling frustrated and incompetent. This despite the fact that there were lots of [good] things that happened today. (field notes, September 26, 1991)

Occasionally, I shared my doubts with Margaret, a sympathetic first-grade teacher, who often reassured me that all teachers have days when they feel helpless and out of control. There will be days like this and "you shouldn't be so hard on yourself," she'd say. I'd take some comfort in Margaret's reassurances and I often reminded myself that these were just eight year olds and I shouldn't take their behavior personally. I tried hard to keep student discipline in perspective and I often used my field notes as a means of propping up my damaged ego.

> This morning I felt helpless and incompetent . . . [but] teachers
> have days like this I shouldn't be so hard on myself . . . And
> not everyone was difficult today. It was just Charles, Ali, Wayne,
> Martin, Hugh, and Troy and even they had good moments today. I
> need to build on these good moments for their sake and mine. The
> afternoon went well, gym may have been the best yet, and lots of
> the kids had very good days. (field notes, October 7, 1991)

Even though I tried hard to keep students' behavior in perspective my field notes indicate that I continued to take students' misbehavior as a reflection of my skill as a teacher. On November 12, for example, I wrote:

> I may console myself with the fact that some of these kids—Martin,
> Denise, Charles, and Ali—have always been difficult children, but
> I'll have to be open to the possibility that I'm not great at keeping
> students under control.

On another occasion I wrote in my notes:

> I had a terrible time settling them down at the very end of the day
> and we didn't leave until after 3:35. I'm not sure what the problem
> was . . . but I felt terrible on the way home feeling that I couldn't
> control them and I was incompetent. Perhaps I am. I don't know.
> (field notes, December 3, 1991)

It seems remarkable to me now, but while I was teaching I even felt personally responsible for my students' behavior when they were under someone else's supervision. I felt guilty, for example, when my students misbehaved in the lunchroom, during French or music, or for a substitute teacher when I was sick. Conflicts my students had with the lunch supervisor led me to eat my lunch with them as if I alone was responsible for the way they behaved. Or maybe I just worried that it reflected poorly on my ability as a teacher when my students acted out publicly. Certainly I felt threatened when my students were disciplined by other teachers or the principal. I'm still convinced that Linda, another third-grade teacher, had concluded that many of the discipline problems I had with my students stemmed from my "not being strict enough." I remember feeling rebuked when Linda told me that Ali, who had spent the day with her while the rest of my class went ice-skating (I didn't allow him to go on this trip because of problems on an earlier field trip to the zoo including running away and harassing the animals), had been "as good as gold." (I took some perverse pleasure the following day when Linda told me that the mother of one of her students had complained that Ali had "grabbed her son's penis.")

Clearly there were times when I took my students' behavior personally and my struggles with discipline sometimes left me feeling inadequate as a teacher. Roya's complaints during February and March that I "wasn't funny anymore" gives some indication of the effect of behavior problems on my morale (although I'm sure fatigue was also a factor). Still, I may be painting too bleak a picture here. If someone read just this chapter they might easily conclude that I had a pretty miserable year as a third-grade teacher. This isn't true, of course. I was pleased with many aspects of my program and I still am. But student behavior was an important, occasionally overriding criterion by which I judged myself and my teaching and sometimes I'd even let misbehavior distort my perception of an otherwise successful day as in the following example.

> It's funny that I didn't feel very good about today. It started wonderfully and ended fairly well. But I was jumpy today and I allowed myself to be engaged by both Denise and Charles. And all of them were off task a lot today and a bit noisy. But so many neat things happened. Jennifer may be on to something in writing. Crystal did some real writing today. I got to work with Lila on some strategic stuff on her reading. Shyrose actually read to the class. All of them are doing great with the Olympics unit. Denise's piece of writing was really nice. We ended the day on a song and read quite a bit throughout the day. And I did some good work with the math centers. It's too bad (for me) that I was more affected by their behavior than what we actually got done. (field notes, February 4, 1992)

The question here is this: what led me to construct a teaching identity for myself that placed such importance on my ability to control my students? Certainly, I was legitimately concerned that behavior problems from students like Denise, Ali, Charles, Martin, and

Catherine would interfere with my teaching goals and the educational opportunities of my other students, that "kids like Razika had to put up with this nonsense" (field notes, November 19, 1991). I recall being stung by the criticism from Razika's mother that Razika was bored at school. (When I asked Razika about this she indicated that she was bored when she had to wait when large group activities were disrupted by other students' acting out.) Concern that my teaching year would be "lost" to behavior problems led me to implement the point system I discuss later in this chapter. And I was rightfully concerned about the threats to student safety posed by Ali and Charles which sometimes led to sleepless nights.

> Last night I laid in bed and worried about Ali's violence. We've had four acts of violence in the last couple of months and I'm beginning to worry about the safety of the other students, especially Catherine, who has been hurt twice. (field notes, April 13, 1992)

Worries about student safety led me to take the drastic step of limiting Ali's movements to always be in my sight. But none of this explains why I took behavior problems so personally. I think part of the explanation lies in popular constructions of the *good* teacher that, no doubt, had some affect on the teaching identity I constructed for myself.

In the *Sociology of Teaching*, Willard Waller's seminal study of the teaching profession, he makes the following observation about classroom discipline.

> For the beginning teacher, the class is confusion and very likely a 'big, booming, buzzing confusion.' For the experienced teacher, it is an orderly, patterned whole. Within this configuration of the class as a whole are many minor centers of tension, and the whole field may come to be organized around any one of these. The teacher who has good command over his (sic) class preserves the balance by merely shifting the center of his (sic) attention to points of incipient confusion. (Waller 1932, 162)

Among teachers, and the public at large, it seems to be taken for granted that the ability to control their classes is a defining characteristic of good teachers. Lortie observed that one of the attributes that the teachers he interviewed ascribed to their "outstanding mentors" was effectiveness in "winning student compliance and discipline"

(1975, 118). Findings such as these led Lortie to observe that teachers assessed their peers largely in terms of how well they handled relations with students, especially their capacity to establish and maintain control. Presumably, good teachers create the conditions for learning ("all eyes on the teacher") by maintaining appropriate discipline. These are the teachers who "know all the tricks," the ones who have "eyes in the back of their heads." Tracy Kidder (1987) observed that fifth-grade teacher Chris Zajac "could tell, without seeing, not only that a child was running on the stairs but also that the footfalls belonged to Clarence, and she could turn her attention to curing one child's confusion and still know that Clarence was whispering threats to Arabella. She was always scanning the room with her eyes without moving her head, seeing without being seen . . ." (1987, 115–116).

Like Willard Waller, most teachers assume that they and their colleagues will learn to maintain order in their classrooms "with experience" and, if needed, with the support of principals, consultants, teaching colleagues, university courses, and workshops. But if *good* teachers are those who learn to maintain order in their classrooms (and this begs the question about teachers who *control* their students but who are unable, for example, to teach reading or writing effectively), then teachers who do not exercise the appropriate level of control over their students—and what counts as appropriate will vary from school to school—are either inexperienced or poor teachers.

Lortie concedes that teachers may be judged on their ability to control their students because this is the aspect of their work most visible to other teachers. Few teachers have the opportunity to observe their colleagues teach a math or a reading lesson, for example, but all are likely to notice a loud, boisterous class or a class containing students who regularly run in the halls. This doesn't change the fact, however, that it is almost certain that the primary criterion by which teachers will be judged by administrators, colleagues, and, perhaps, themselves is based on their ability to maintain order in their classrooms, jeopardizing the careers of teachers who cannot maintain at least a semblance of control.

Since good teachers can (and do) have discipline problems, however, the construction of the *good* teacher may be more complicated than the picture I've painted so far. It's not that good teachers don't have discipline problems, but that they *appear* to be in control. These are teachers who are strict and do whatever is necessary to control students under *normal* circumstances. The degree to which good teachers have behavior problems then is a function of the students themselves. Violent and disruptive students like Clarence did not threaten Chris Zajac's status as a tough disciplinarian and a good teacher. And when good teachers, those perceived to be able to maintain order in their classrooms, complain about students' behavior in the teacher staffroom ("I can't do a thing with Jonathan") they tend to implicate the students and not their ability as teachers. At least this is how it seemed to work at Norwood School where I taught third grade. In the staffroom at Norwood, teachers never suggested that they couldn't control their classes (any more than they would offer that they didn't know how to teach reading or writing), but they did complain about difficulties controlling individual students. In this way they were able to portray (some) discipline problems as residing within students and, therefore, not a function either of teachers' competence or the structures of schooling (e.g., large classes, compulsory attendance, excessive rote learning, etc.).

This kind of confidence, that teachers are in control and that the discipline problems posed by individual students are independent of their skills as a teacher, is apparent in Tracy Kidder's portrayal of Chris Zajac. Zajac has more than her share of discipline problems. Clarence is at least as difficult as any student I had in my class and Zajac often gave serious thought to how she would respond to discipline problems in her classroom. And, like me, she worried about the effect behavior problems had on the other students in her class. But Kidder conveys no sense that students like Clarence ever threatened Zajac's self-confidence or in any way made her wonder about her ability as a teacher. Zajac tells her student teacher, for example, that she must never feel that the behavior of students like Clarence is *her* fault. I'm not suggesting that Chris Zajac or any other teacher should feel responsible for all student behavior. My own experience indicates that taking student behavior too personally is unhealthy. What strikes me here is that, unlike me, Chris Zajac—as she is constructed by Tracy Kidder—never seemed to wonder about the possibility that she may have been responsible for students like Clarence or at least she never admitted these sorts of doubts to Kidder.

Tracy Kidder's portrait of Chris Zajac is not unusual. The teachers portrayed in the educational literature rarely express doubts or disappointments, frustration or anger. Tom Newkirk makes a similar observation of the teachers he reads about.

> What I find most difficult to believe, the teacher never shows signs of despondency, frustration, anger, impatience, or disappointment.

If there is anger or frustration, it is directed at external forces—administrators, testing services, the government . . . but never at themselves or their students. The teachers I read about don't doubt their competence, or at least they don't admit to their doubts."
(1992, 24)

In general, there is no sense that teachers we read about are ever uncertain about themselves as teachers even if they are sometimes uncertain about their students ("I can't figure out what's wrong with Jason").

Even as the behavior problems in my classroom contradicted my notions of the *good* teacher who is always in control, my doubts about my ability to control my students further set me apart from my construction of the ideal teacher who never doubts his ability.

Good teachers, as they are constructed in both popular and professional literature, are in control, confident in their abilities, and fair. Chris Zajac may have been tough, but in Tracy Kidder's estimation she nevertheless earned the respect of her students and colleagues (and Kidder) by treating students equitably, with kindness and consideration. This is consistent with other popular portrayals of the good teacher. Lortie (1975) notes that the teachers he interviewed worried about being too harsh with their students or in other ways expressing their anger for fear this would damage their relationships with students. These teachers placed "interpersonal qualities like patience, consideration, and warmth at the heart of their 'subjective warrant' for teaching" (Lortie 1975, 158). Lortie adds "we can appreciate, therefore, why the angry outburst is so threatening to a teacher. It attacks his (sic) personal sense of competence . . . The mistake which most rapidly unravels the teacher's self-assurance as a competent teacher is the release of unbridled anger" (158).

Lortie's informants revealed, however, that they did not always manage to handle themselves in a manner which they considered "right." For example, 55 percent of the teachers Lortie interviewed talked about times they had lost their temper with students leading to feelings of "embarrassment, self-accusation, acute discomfort, remorse, and other self-punishing emotions" (Lortie 1975, 158). This is how it was for me. I was very hard on myself when I responded to my third graders' behavior in ways that I thought were unprofessional, that is, unworthy of a *good* teacher. I was especially disappointed in myself when I felt that I had been unkind to my students as the following incident indicates. We had just made popcorn and were getting ready to watch a movie and things were getting a bit out of hand.

> I ended up getting mad and when Peter kicked Catherine I told him that if he didn't stop I'd let Catherine "kick the hell out of him." I'm plenty embarrassed and I really shook him up. Yet before he went out for recess he threatened Catherine. The lack of kindness toward each other is unbelievable—hitting, yelling, threatening, etc. I need to work extra hard never to scold unkindly which I do too often. I must be very firm with this group but none of them deserves for me to be anything but kind and it's a very bad model in any case . . . Right now I'm very disappointed in myself. (field notes, October 11, 1991)

My field notes indicate that I often rebuked myself for "being too harsh," "being punitive," "allowing myself to be engaged." And I regularly used my notes to remind myself to "keep cool," "be kind," and "be patient" and, "not to take it personally." My notes also suggest that I was especially likely to lose my temper when I saw students' misbehavior as a threat to my competence as a teacher.

> Gym was a disaster today. I couldn't get into the cupboard where the equipment was stored so we had to try the same parachute activities we did last time. Since many of them had taken their shoes off I suggested we try the "popcorn" activity with the parachute using their shoes instead of balls. I already was having difficulty and soon things got totally out of hand with students running around the gym and throwing their shoes at the basketball hoop. I blew my top when Hugh's shoe landed on my head . . . I feel badly that I lost my temper, perhaps the first time this has happened this year. I also feel incompetent when I lose control like I did. This is probably why I lost my temper—I took their behavior personally. (field notes, September 23, 1991)

I also chided myself when I found that I had grown to dislike Ali, one of my most difficult students. Apparently, I felt that such feelings were unworthy of good teachers and that such feelings might lead me to treat Ali unfairly.

I'm really disappointed in my attitude toward Ali. I no longer see him as just a discipline problem but as someone . . . who interferes with what I'm trying to do here. This can't possibly be helpful. (field notes, April 22, 1992)

It seems fairly natural sitting here at my computer several years removed from my third-grade classroom that teachers will get angry and frustrated from time to time. I would, of course, distinguish between teachers who get angry and angry teachers. I believe that I fell into the former category. As a parent I accept that my children's teachers will sometimes lose their tempers although I have little use for teachers who are regularly unkind and inconsiderate to their students.

It also seems reasonable to assume that teachers will not have equal affection for all their students or even that they will like all of them. Not all children are equally likeable, although I can imagine the pain felt by children whose teachers never like them. I also imagine that teachers' fondness for their students may sometimes be linked to factors like race, class, culture, gender, ability, or sexual orientation. This, of course, is unacceptable. Teachers may not like all their students, but all students are entitled to be treated with respect and consideration.

This brings me back to the question of my teaching identity. If it is reasonable and natural for teachers to occasionally lose control of their classes, to doubt their ability as teachers, to sometimes display anger and frustration, and to dislike some students, how is it that I constructed a teaching identify for myself that made so little room for these things? At times I did have difficulty maintaining order in my third-grade classroom. I made lots of mistakes and what I learned that year would serve me well if I should ever return to the classroom. But it still seems that I was much too hard on myself when things went wrong. I too easily took my own anger, frustration, doubts and students' (mis)behavior as evidence that I was the problem. I often found that I did not measure up to my own construction of the good teacher and I berated myself for my failings. Why? For starters I suspect that I was influenced by popular constructions of the ideal teacher who is always in control, who never loses her temper, and who never doubts his teaching ability. I often felt like Linda Christensen who wrote: "Over the winter break I read a book on teaching that left me feeling desolate because the writer's vision of a joyful, productive classroom did not match the chaos I faced daily" (1994, 1).

I imagine I was also influenced by the teachers whose classes I have visited, teachers who, at least in my presence, were always kind, confident, and in control. (I recall how my own class was the model of perfection the day two teachers, both of whom were former students of mine, visited.) And certainly I was influenced by accounts of whole language practice which rarely acknowledge even the possibility of behavior problems or that present whole language as an antidote to behavior problems. My faith in my maturity, experience, and expertise may have also contributed to unrealistic expectations (if whole language teachers don't have behavior problems, certainly an experienced, forty-three-year-old, over-educated whole language teacher shouldn't expect any.)

In general, I fell victim to the "tyranny of certainty" that pervades the teaching profession (McDonald 1992), and Western society more generally (Dewey 1960, Saul 1992), a certainty that is reinforced by the silences in teaching stories (Newkirk 1992) uncontaminated by the messy reality of life in classrooms. McDonald observes that:

> Teaching, closely read, is messy: full of conflict, fragmentation, and ambivalence. These conditions of uncertainty present a problem in a culture that tends to regard conflict as distasteful and that prizes unity, predictability, rational decisiveness, certainty. This is a setup: Teaching involves a lot of 'bad' stuff, yet teachers are expected to be "good." (1992, 21)

The construction of the ideal teacher as a "super teacher . . . without cracks" (Newkirk 1992, 23), confident and in control, may demonstrate possibilities, but such an ideal makes no room for certain uncertainties of life in a classroom with twenty or more diverse and complicated people, creating a sense of inadequacy in all of us who fall short of the ideal (Newkirk 1992). The messy reality of teaching insures that we will all fall short of the ideal—robbing many teachers of professional satisfaction (Lortie 1975) and driving some teachers out of the profession altogether. Newkirk puts it this way:

> Problems occur . . . when we don't feel these "normal feelings," particularly when what we feel is less than noble—anger, envy, frustration, inadequacy, disappointment, or lack of affection. Often in cases like these we remain silent, and conclude there is something wrong with us. To admit these feelings, to tell a different narrative,

is to risk being thought weird, perverted, not a good teacher, not a good parent, not a good person. (Newkirk 1992, 21)

To not admit these feelings, however, insures that we will always feel less than worthy. Worse, to shut these feelings out of our teaching creates classrooms devoid of human emotion, forbidding places for little (and big) humans to live. The antidote to what McDonald (1992) calls the "tyranny of certainty" is to complicate our teaching identities by changing the nature of our stories to include our failures and well as our successes, making room for the ambiguities, contradictions, and uncertainties that are naturally part of life in a classroom. There are risks to admitting that we are not certain and there is always the danger of using uncertainty as an excuse for incompetence. But, as Newkirk points out, the long-term benefits to teachers and to the profession more than offset the short-term risks. Certainly a more realistic teaching identity would have made my year as a third-grade teacher more satisfying. More importantly, teachers who acknowledge the uncertainty which attends any practical activity like teaching (Dewey 1960) can use uncertainty as an occasion for growth and, ultimately, professional growth and development. McDonald, summarizing the work of John Dewey, puts it this way:

> Uncertainty saves a place for novelty and genuine growth and change. When we accept uncertainty . . . we transform our relationship to practical problems. They become the means by which we may see beyond what we think we know. (1992, 7)

Clearly the behavior problems in my third-grade classroom, doubts about my teaching ability, and inconsistencies in my own behavior created a reality that fell far short of my vision of the ideal teacher, an ideal, as I have argued, that may have little basis in reality. In the next section I discuss how my ultimate response to discipline problems, the implementation of a token economy, contradicted and, therefore, threatened my identity as a holistic educator.

What Kind of Whole Language Teacher Would Implement a Token Economy?

The behavior problems in my third-grade classroom clearly threatened my identity as a good teacher, but I don't want to create the impression that I positioned myself as a passive victim of student behavior. I did more than merely attempt to keep discipline problems in perspective. For better or worse, I employed a range of active strategies to create what I imagined would be a classroom environment that was safe and congenial to learning.

I regularly reflected on my interactions with students in an effort to identify how I might have been contributing to behavior problems. I thought a lot about the attention I gave individual children wondering, for example, if I was too hard on Charles and Nader, if I gave Denise too much attention for negative behavior, or whether I was too willing to ignore Catherine's acting out. Sometimes I reminded myself to be stricter, but this always involved putting on a false front, something I'm not very good at. Other times I tried to use strategies that encouraged students to examine the consequences of their behavior (e.g., "How do you think it makes me feel when you interrupt me while I'm reading to the class?"), but this never felt natural either.

I also considered how my lessons and classroom structures might have affected student behavior. For example, when students at the science center were distracted by students working at the computers, I moved the computers. When some of my students had difficulty settling down for reading or writing I decreed that the first ten minutes of reading and writing periods be silent. When I guessed that one of the reasons students were having difficulty getting down to work at the science and math centers was because they weren't sure what to do, I tried to provide clearer directions. Rambunctious behavior at the end of the day led me to move reading to that time period, at least for awhile.

I often sought the help and advice of parents, the principal, other teachers, consultants, and students themselves. For example, I phoned Ali's and Wayne's parents once a week to keep them informed and to enlist their support. To solve the serious behavior problems I was having in gym I sought the guidance of one of the school board's physical education consultants to plan more interesting lessons. And through class meetings my students were able to suggest a variety of solutions to disruptive behavior including shortening the length of some activities, clearer directions, and keeping my sense of humor. Lila explained some difficult behavior toward the end of October by observing that, "Kids are being bad because they're excited about Halloween."

I was all too willing, however, to resort to punishments. At the suggestion of a second-grade teacher, for example, I sometimes deducted time lost due to disruptive behavior from our recesses (punishing my students and me). Occasionally, I kept some students in for the whole of their recesses, usually as punishment for not doing work or for aggressive behavior. I was never very consistent about these punishments probably because they cost me some quiet time. And I wasn't above sitting students in the hall or sending them to the office. Sometimes students did need a quiet place to compose themselves but more often, I think, I was just getting rid of the problem.

I also imagined that field trips, singing, and the occasional movie or ice cream party would improve classroom behavior by reducing classroom tension. I tried to keep classroom rules to a minimum—I recall being very irritated when a classroom assistant chided me for failing to enforce two rules: no gum and no hats. But more than anything else, I tried to remain calm, convinced as I was that there was a strong causal relationship between my behavior and theirs. I wasn't so naive as to think that remaining calm would eliminate behavior problems, but I was convinced that the tension that arose when I got angry only made things worse.

In general, I was able to maintain a safe and orderly classroom, although I cannot say if my successes in this regard were because of or despite my active interventions. Then in January things began to deteriorate so rapidly that I feared that a big part of my year in third grade would be lost to behavior problems. Finally, perhaps out of desperation, I implemented a point system, really a token economy, to restore order. On January 21 I wrote in my notes:

> I need to go to a point system that rewards students for good behavior. I would like to start tomorrow but I need to think it out carefully so that I'm able to follow through consistently. I want to withdraw all of our privileges (e.g., using the computer, free choice, library) and make all these (and more) contingent on good behavior and the points. I've been reluctant to try a point system because I'm worried about the time this management system would take. But the behavior problems we are having are taking far more time. This afternoon, for example, I had little involvement in either the last center rotation or reading because I was pre-occupied with behavior. I need to get this under control or my personal goals for the rest of the year could be lost. (field notes, January 21, 1992)

Over the next several days I introduced my third graders to a point system by which they could earn points for behaviors such as being "considerate" during circle times and center rotations, participating in gym, and keeping track of their pencils.

PRIVILEGES YOU CAN EARN	COST	CONDITION
Free choice	1000 points	twice/week
Play games on the MacIntosh	50 points	during free choice
Go to library	50 points	20 minutes/3 times per week
Stay in and help during recess	50 points	teacher is available
Use pillows	20 points	
A week off from your job	50 points	let me know on Friday
A whole day off from class-work	2000 points	2 people at a time
Your own set of markers for a day	50 points	4 people/day
Write in the hall	50 points	2 people at a time

Students lost points for violence or leaving the classroom without permission. Points were redeemable for such "privileges" as: a free choice activity, playing games on the computer, or having the whole day off from classwork.

POINT SCHEDULE

IF YOU:	THEN YOU EARN:
Are considerate during morning circle times	10 points
Are considerate during center times	10 points
Are considerate during afternoon circle times	10 points
Are considerate during writing time	10 points
Work hard during writing time	5 points
Are considerate during reading time	10 points
Come promptly to circle times all day	10 points
Are considertate during gym	10 points
Participate during gym	10 points
Do your job and help tidy up at day's end	5 points
Do not lose your pencil	5 points
If you fight	YOU LOSE 100 points
If you leave classroom without permission	YOU LOSE 20 points

I also awarded points to the whole class each day which were redeemed for movies, popsicles, field trips, and (once) an ice cream party.

Managing the point system was time consuming but, except for some fine tuning, I stayed with it through the rest of the year. The point system wasn't a panacea, however. There were still difficult days and occasional violence. Some students, Catherine, Denise, and Charles in particular, weren't the least bit interested in or affected by the point system. Still, students' behavior did improve considerably although I'm inclined to believe the success of the point system lay in its effect on my behavior. A few days after implementing the point system I observed:

> The best part of today was that I didn't raise my voice, I didn't threaten anyone, and I didn't really punish anyone beyond asking a few of them to sit out briefly during gym. This system may make it much easier to follow my personal rules. (field notes, January 27, 1992)

What interests me about the point system isn't why it worked or how it worked, but how it happened that a holistic educator (me) who had consciously rejected behaviorism as a pedagogical framework came to embrace a quintessentially behavioral solution to discipline problems.

From my perspective, behaviorism is the antithesis of holistic education. Behaviorism is informed by the assumption that all human behavior—including higher level skills like reading, writing, and problem solving—is reducible to a finite collection of discrete skills and subskills. Conversely, from a holistic point of view, human behavior can only be described in terms of complex, interacting systems each affecting and affected by other systems (see Heshusius [1982] and Poplin [1988], for a thorough discussion of the paradigmatic differences between holism and behaviorism). Since the whole is greater than or different from the sum of its parts, holistic educators do not believe that human behavior can be understood by reference to discrete skills.

Arguably, the assertion that human behavior cannot be reduced to its parts applies only to higher cognitive skills like reading, writing, or problem solving and behavioral principles like reinforcement and punishment adequately describe human social behaviors. There have been times when I thought this was the case. It seems to be an unassailable conclusion, for example, that the manipulation of certain contingencies can affect the frequency of human behavior. But it isn't clear that altering the frequency of behaviors is the same as teaching, if teaching is to be understood as a supportive relationship in which teachers support learning by honoring students' intentions. For example, my token economy may have inhibited Paul's chattiness during whole group activities, but I am not confident that he really learned anything about getting along in groups, unless you're willing to accept the behavioral view that equates learning with performance. I can say with confidence only that I controlled or managed his behavior through the use of behavior-management techniques that subtly, but clearly, exploited the power differential between us. I, as an adult and a teacher, had power and he, for the most part, did not. From Paul's perspective earning rewards and avoiding punishments depended on compliance and I am fearful that the one lesson that Paul and my other students learned from our token economy is that what really matters in human relationships is power.

It may be, as some readers are no doubt thinking, that life often works that way. Perhaps. I also suppose that the use of raw power can be justified when student safety is at issue. And it is, of course, silly to pretend that teachers don't have power. What troubles me, however, is the way I used that power. The use of an explicit system of rewards and punishments to control students' behavior echoes the theme in Golding's *Lord of the Flies* (1974) that children, if not continually subjected to the controls of a civilizing society, will quickly and certainly revert to their savage selves. Is that how I thought of my students? In my field notes I frequently reminded myself to be considerate and respectful of my students, but there isn't anything considerate or respectful in the conscious, deliberate way I manipulated my students through a token economy. This isn't the way I treat my family or friends nor is it the way I wish to be treated. So how did I come to treat my students this way? How did I come to be a part-time behaviorist?

The only way I can account for this jarring contradiction in my teaching identity is to recall how desperate I was at the time. I felt that I'd invested considerable time, energy, and prestige in returning to the classroom and I had high hopes for this experience. I imagined that I would have an opportunity to try for myself all the whole language practices I'd been sharing with teachers and students over the years. I also hoped to collect lots of useful and interesting data. When classroom behavior deteriorated in January, I nearly despaired that my personal goals would have to be sacrificed, that my year would be "lost." I was open to drastic measures and, since my background in special education included training in token economies and other behavior modification techniques, a token economy seemed a natural solution to our behavior problems. In a sense, I implemented a token economy because I knew how to.

I must admit that when I was teaching third grade I was willing to ignore the theoretical contradictions of a whole language teacher implementing a token economy although I was aware of them. I did not, however, give much thought to the ethical problems of token economies although I knew that my university colleagues were more than a little surprised to hear about my point system. At the time I was just too caught up in fixing a problem. Writing this chapter is the first time I've taken the time to deliberately and systematically reflect on the ethics of my token economy and, I must admit, the experience has left me disappointed and embarrassed.

I should not, however, be surprised to discover contradictions in my teaching practice. Contrary to some popular myths people, including teachers, are not always consistent. I know from my own experience that "nice guys" can, for example, drink and drive or indulge in a little embezzlement. And whole language teachers can sometimes act like behaviorists. My experience suggests that the key to resolving these contradictions is active reflection that supports the current movement toward teachers as reflective practitioners. It is not enough, however, to merely observe these contradictions. We must also seek to resolve them. In my case the observation that the token economy I implemented fundamentally contradicted the theoretical and ethical beliefs I hold dear is useful only if it changes how I interact with students in the future.

CONCLUSION

This chapter is based on more than two hundred pages of field notes that address various aspects of discipline in my third-grade classroom. The sheer volume of notes I had on classroom behavior led me to expect that this would be an easy chapter to write. As it has turned out this has been the most difficult chapter I have written for this book. It has taken nearly two months to write and I have agonized over each section. This has puzzled and frustrated me but the difficulties I had writing this chapter are now clear to me. Reviewing the problems I had with students' behavior has once again threatened my identity as a *good* teacher. Writing about these problems for all the world to see is especially threatening. My reflections on class-room discipline are helping me create a teaching identity that lives more comfortably with the uncertainties and ambiguities of student behavior, but this reflection has also revealed a particularly disturb-ing theoretical and ethical contradiction—a token economy in a whole language classroom. Whole language classrooms have enor-mous potential to create space for the range of student voices that are present in our classrooms, taking up Carole Edelsky's (1994) challenge to educate for democracy. The control and surveillance implicit in a token economy is, however, an anathema to Edelsky's goal of creating a more just and democratic society.

I worry that this chapter may be seen as an elaborate exercise in self-deception. Valorizing uncertainty can easily become the refuge of incompetence. Still, I am confident that the kind of deliberate, systematic reflection I have done in this chapter is a partial antidote to this danger.

Finally, I worry that this chapter paints too bleak a picture of life in my third-grade classroom. As much as the preponderance of suc-cess stories in the educational literature efface the daily struggles of teachers, an explicit focus on the uncertainties, ambiguities, and contradictions of life in classrooms masks the pleasure of working each day with twenty-four interesting, loving children. Life wasn't always easy in my third-grade classroom, but a week after the school year ended I wished I could go back and I could wish it because I knew I wouldn't.

4

Students for Whom School
Is a Struggle

Before I taught third grade all of my teaching experience was in special education, first as a teacher of students labeled moderately retarded and then as a teacher of students with learning disabilities. In my life as a teacher trainer and university-based researcher my work has continued to focus on students in special education and other students for whom school is a struggle. In *Readers and Writers with a Difference* (Rhodes and Dudley-Marling 1996), for example, Lynn Rhodes and I attempted to translate whole language theory and practice for teachers working with struggling readers and writers. Similarly, my book *When School is a Struggle* (Dudley-Marling 1990), inspired by my daughter's struggles in school, speaks to both parents and teachers of students in special education programs. Given my background and experience it isn't surprising that I was anxious to address the needs of the struggling readers and writers in my third-grade classroom.

Since whole language has been such a hard sell with remedial and special education teachers, who tend to favor reductive approaches, I begin by (briefly) reviewing the case for the appropriateness of whole language instruction for students in special education and remedial programs.

My reading of the special education and language arts literatures reveals three versions of instruction for special and remedial students, each informed by a different set of assumptions. The first version is that special learners require qualitatively different sorts of instruction (see, for example, Hallahan and Kauffman 1976, Lerner 1993). Proponents of this point of view typically point to evidence of neurological dysfunction (e.g., minimal brain dysfunction) to support arguments for unique instruction, but the case for unique instruction is usually put more simply: since students in special and remedial education programs did not profit from the normal curriculum, something fundamentally different is needed. That fundamentally different something has often focused on the training of perceptual, sensory, and psychomotor abilities thought to underlie the development of reading and writing. Although these particular approaches to instruction have been largely discredited (Coles 1987, Kavale and Forness 1985, Ysseldyke and Algozzine 1982) special education was founded on, and is sustained by, the assumption that these students require something qualitatively different from their normally-achieving peers.

Eclecticism, a common alternative to the model of unique instruction, holds that "*multiple* perspectives and approaches will be necessary to accommodate the needs of children who possess differences in abilities and learning histories" (Kameenui 1993). The eclectic teacher selects the best teaching and learning activities from various approaches to literacy as a means of meeting the diverse needs of learners. This approach seems eminently sensible until you realize that underlying different approaches to literacy instruction are fundamentally dissimilar notions of what it means to read or to write. I'll say more about this later.

A third version of instruction for struggling students assumes that there are models of literacy learning that best describe the reading and writing development of all children. From the perspective of whole language theory and practice, for example, there are universal language-learning principles from which instructional practices derive (e.g., Edelsky, Altwerger and Flores 1991, Weaver 1991).

Whole language theorists and practitioners dispute unique instruction for struggling students because they assume that these language-learning principles apply to all learners regardless of ability. Whole language practitioners also reject eclectic models of literacy instruction because the eclecticism in these approaches is informed by fundamentally different and often contradictory assumptions about how people learn to read and write and what it means to read and write. Underlying skills-first approaches to literacy instruction (e.g., DIS-TAR), for example, is the implicit assumption that meaning resides in the text and that the reader's task is to unlock the meaning by "breaking the code." This conflicts with transactional, whole language views of literacy instruction that hold that readers construct meaning from texts by simultaneously drawing on their knowledge of the (phonetic) code, their knowledge of language, and their knowledge of the world.

Therefore, skills-first and meaning-centered approaches to literacy instruction represent more than different sets of instructional activities—they indicate different meanings of what it means to read, what people do in the process of reading, people's relationships to texts and, in the case where certain readings of texts are privileged, to each other. Eclecticism involves teachers in theoretical, pedagogical, and political contradictions.

From a whole language perspective, however, the assumption of universal language learning principles does not mean that all learners should be treated the same. Whole language practices recognize differences in students' ability, life and learning experiences, and cultural and social histories as the foundation upon which teachers can build—not as the basis for qualitatively different sorts of instruction. But even though whole language advocates do not believe that struggling readers and writers need qualitatively different sorts of instruction, they recognize that struggling readers and writers often require frequent, explicit, individual support and direction from their teachers.

This chapter offers me an opportunity to reflect on my own efforts to support my students' reading and writing development, especially the struggling readers and writers in my class. Lila, Charles, and Martin—three students in my class who found reading and writing particularly difficult—are the principal players in my story so I'll begin by briefly describing their reading and writing development.

LILA

When I listened to Lila on the first day of school she read slowly and haltingly, pointing to each word with her finger as she read. When she encountered an unknown word her preferred strategy was to sound it out—no matter how long it took. Because Lila's phonics skills were weak, this was rarely a successful strategy. The following excerpts from her reading of *Clifford the Big Red Dog* (Bridwell 1985), are illustrative.

Text	*Lila*
My dog is a big red dog.	My dog is a big r- red
I have the biggest,	I have the biggest,
reddest dog on our	reddest dog on our str- (10 sec)
street.	street.

We play games.	We play ga, We play gums, We play agums, We play gums, gu--mz, We play gu--mz, games (over 30 sec.)
I throw a stick,	I thr-, I thr- (over and over for over 1 min. before I gave her the word.)
and he brings it back	and he br-, br-, br--ing--z, (after
to me.	30 sec. I gave her the word)

In general, Lila rarely used contextual information to make sense of text and her miscues often resulted in a significant change of meaning. There were rare exceptions, however. For example, on October 1:

> Lila asked if she could read *The House that Jack Built* with the class because she'd read it with her mother. First, I asked her to read it to me and she did well. One interesting miscue was the "cock awoke" for the "cock crowed" which resulted in little change in meaning. (field notes, October 1, 1991)

Lila wrote willingly, but slowly, laboriously sounding out most words as she wrote. In early September she wrote a piece about her grandmother's cat.

> My gamoow has a cat the cat has a bookun boon me and my bagg brradr want to the dactrr he had to stae in the hospital for to days (My grandma has a cat. The cat has a broken bone. Me and my big brother went to the doctor. He had to stay in the hospital for two days.)

School was hard for Lila, but she never lost her easy going manner and she worked hard to improve her reading and writing. Unlike Charles and Martin, Lila had never been formally identified as having special learning needs. I imagine she'd never been referred for special education because she was so well behaved and hard working. Charles was another matter.

CHARLES

Charles loved to sit on the carpet and look at books. However, he rarely selected books he could read independently and there were few texts he could read independently. One day late in September, for example, he spent an entire reading period sitting in the reading corner looking through a book in which he could recognize only a few words. When he read text orally he struggled mightily. In general, Charles's oral reading was slow and dysfluent and when he came to an unknown word he either dismissed it with "whatever" and read on (Charles often dismissed unknown words with "whatever") or he relied on his very weak phonics skills to try to sound out the word (e.g., "be-its" for "brings"). Occasionally, Charles would use contextual information to make sense of words in text, but only if he was receiving individual support from me. Charles's miscues often resulted in meaningless text as in the following excerpt from his oral reading of *Clifford the Big Red Dog* (Bridwell 1985), a book with which he was already familiar.

Text	*Charles*
This is my dog—Clifford.	This is my dog—Clifford
We play games.	We play great (pause) whatever.
I throw a stick, and he	I with, (pause) catch, (pause) I co-inss-i a stick, and he
brings it back to me.	be-its, bong, brah, big it to me brung it to me (sighs) whatever.
We play hide-and-seek.	He, he plays, We play hiding and go, hiding and seek.
I'm a good hide-and-seek	I'm a, I'm, I am coming, or
player.	something, she, (long pause) he and sick, seek, pra, praynar.

Charles was a reluctant writer and when he did write, he pestered other students for the spellings of words. Still, when I supported him by exaggerating isolated sounds of words (e.g., "p-p-p—arrrr—k") he was able to produce phonetically acceptable spellings (e.g., "prk"). A story about a trip to the circus, produced with considerable teacher and peer support (Crystal is responsible for many of the spellings here), may have been Charles's longest piece of writing all year.

I whent to the curcrse with my famale and my cuson and we hab fyn togeter andb we saw peole jamping on the hrempin.
(I went to the circus with my family and my cousin and we had fun together and we saw people jumping on the trampoline.)

Charles often surprised me by what he didn't know. From September to November I discovered, for example, that Charles couldn't spell his last name, didn't know his address or telephone number, and couldn't count to twenty.

Charles was formally identified as learning disabled and spent two hours each day in a special education resource room. He was clearly embarrassed and frustrated by his difficulties. When he read Margaret Wise Brown's *Big Red Barn* (1956) orally, for example, "his head was bent down and he frowned the whole time" (field notes, Jan. 6, 1992). I also suspected that embarrassment accounted for his tendency to select books that were much too difficult for him. Charles's frustration may also have contributed to his frequently disruptive—and sometimes violent—behavior.

MARTIN

When Martin arrived in our class in October it was hard for him to sit with a book (or do anything else) for more than a few minutes. He read word by word with little sense for the whole of a text. His miscues tended to look like the expected response (e.g., "horse" for "house"), but often resulted in text that made little sense. When I did a miscue analysis with Martin in mid-October he chose to read *The Very Hungry Caterpillar* (Carle 1987), a book with which he was already familiar. A few (representative) excerpts from his reading are presented here.

Text	Martin
He started to look for some	He saw to look for some
food.	food.
On Monday . . .	One minute . . .
. . . but he was . . .	. . . patted he was . . .
On Thursday . . .	On a tree . . .

Martin liked to write, but early in the year his handwriting and spelling were so poor that neither he nor I could read his writing. The piece of writing presented here was written sometime in January, after Martin had been placed on Ritalin, and represents considerable progress.

The Sampsns

Bart is on hiis way to school wan he got to school was ovir he had to go all the way haem Bart's DaD sad way our you haem new BeCais school was out oh at 6:00 it was saprtaem.

The Simpsons

(Bart is on his way to school. When he got to school [it] was over.
He had to go all the way home. Bart's dad said, "Why are you
home?" "Because school was out." "Oh." At 6:00 it was suppertime.)

Like Charles, Martin was identified as learning disabled and spent
two hours each day in a special education resource room. Martin's
violent outbursts often required that he be removed from the classroom for varying periods of time.

Charles, Lila, and Martin struggled with learning to read and
write, but they were not the only students in my class for whom
learning to read and write was difficult. Nicholas, for example, was a
willing writer but struggled as a reader. John read fairly well but
found writing difficult. Nader and Fatima spoke Farsi at home and
faced the formidable challenge of learning to speak, read, and write
English. Denise enjoyed reading and writing, but her skills lagged
well behind most other students (and were complicated by serious
emotional and behavioral problems).

I've acknowledged how important it was for me to do well with
struggling readers and writers and, when I was teaching third grade,
I worried that I wasn't doing enough to meet the needs of struggling
students, particularly Charles, whom I seemed to believe I should
have been able to handle better because of my long experience as a
special educator. For example, on October 16 I wrote in my notes:

> Continue to have very difficult time with Charles . . . At this point
> he's learning almost nothing in our class. *I'm a special educator.* This
> shouldn't be happening (field notes, October 16, 1991).

And:

> Had another problem with Charles today. He returned a few min-
> utes before the next center rotation and played in the sand table (I
> asked him not to). I reminded him that he needed to work at the
> centers in order to earn points to use the computer. He wouldn't
> leave the sand table which the math groups were going to
> use . . . and when I put my hand on his shoulder and moved
> him . . . he huffed off to the reading corner and starting kicking the
> pillows (he started laughing when he did this). At this point I'd

had enough and I sent him to the principal's office . . . Overall, this is pretty frustrating. Charles hasn't done any work at all this week . . . I'm especially frustrated *since I'm a special educator* and should be able to deal with kids like Charles . . . I just don't know. (field notes, October 18, 1991)

My sense of inadequacy wasn't limited to Charles. I generally worried that I wasn't doing enough for my struggling readers and writers. For example:

One other frustration: the work I am doing with the students who are struggling. Need to do much more work for them recognizing that it is going to require more preparation. (October 6, 1991)

I continue to be excited about what we're doing in reading, but I want to do better for the students who are struggling. (October 18, 1991)

There is a sense among teachers that the expertise acquired through experience, reading, conferences, workshops, and university coursework enables them to deal more easily with difficult students. I imagine that education and experience are helpful but, in my case at least, my acquired expertise led me to develop unrealistic expectations about my ability to teach struggling students. Why wouldn't I struggle to meet the needs of Charles, Lila, and Martin? Did I really expect that, because of my background and experience, their difficulties would magically disappear? Knowing more I expected too much of myself—especially early in the year—and, unable to achieve these expectations, I felt frustrated and demoralized.

When they were all reading the chart story Charles exclaimed, "Shyrose, it's your birthday?" I asked him how he knew and he told me he read it (pointing to the chart). (field notes, October 17, 1991)

Each morning before school I wrote a chart story which I hoped would invite my less able readers to read. First thing in the morning, after they'd hung up their coats, I asked my students to sit on the carpet and read the chart story. Then I'd either read the chart story to them or invite the whole class to read it chorally. Again, this was largely for the benefit of struggling readers. Comments like Charles's about Shyrose's birthday indicate that the chart stories did invite reading. A few days later Charles glanced first at the chart story and then at me and asked, "You ran thirty miles last night?" (I had written "Last night I ran three miles . . .") On another occasion I overheard Nader carefully sound out "Mayy-pull Lleeefs" as he read the chart story.

My more able readers were also attracted to the chart stories. Most students read the chart stories as they entered the classroom, sometimes gathering to read the chart story even before they hung up their coats as in the case of the chart story that referred to the "Norwood learning center and hair salon" (the girls in my class were forever grooming one another's hair).

> Good morning, boys and girls. Welcome to the Norwood learning center and hair salon. Today is Wednesday, October 2, 1991.
> Last night the Blue Jays won and the Red Sox lost. The Blue Jays have clinched a tie for the pennant. Yesterday's highlights: Nicolas read his circus story to the class; Roya read her story about Iran to us; and, Razika and Benizar read the *Velveteen Rabbit* to us. And Martin joined our class. For me yesterday was a terrible, horrible, no good, very bad day. I'll bet today is a lot better day.

> Must work to see that there are lots of invitations (reasons) for reading and writing in my third-grade class (field notes, August 10, 1991).

People learn to read by reading. This was the fundamental assumption that guided my reading program. The common practice of limiting struggling students' reading (and writing) opportunities until they are ready (e.g., Allington 1983) will, I believe, exacerbate students' difficulties by denying them access to the data they need to develop as readers (how, for example, do readers use their knowledge of phonics while simultaneously drawing on their background knowledge to make sense of texts?) The emphasis on reading and writing skills insures, perhaps, that struggling readers and writers get better at the skills (see Myers 1992, for a discussion of the generalizabiltly of school literacy), but without addressing what I think should be the basic goal of literacy instruction: learning to read (and write) for a variety of purposes in a range of (social) settings.

I tried to take advantage of every opportunity to invite reading and demonstrate its uses. A discussion prompted by a picture of a gravestone in Grace Maccarone's *The Return of the Third Grade Ghost-hunters* (Maccarone 1989), for example, led me to bring in a collection of grave rubbings. I displayed the grave rubbings around the classroom and they captured the interest of many of my students, especially the more able readers. I finally read them to the class only after they'd had a few days to read the grave rubbings themselves.

I tried to play my guitar and sing with my class as often as possible and, largely for the benefit of struggling readers, I copied the lyrics to the songs we sang on chart paper. Sometimes I'd invite the class to read song lyrics chorally before we tried to sing it. As it turned out, song lyrics were a powerful invitation for many students, especially the girls. A few days after I introduced the song "The Cat Came Back," for example, I saw Jennifer, Catherine, and Barbara—all good readers—alternately reading and singing the lyrics which I had taped on the blackboard. Unfortunately, because I was so concerned about behavior problems (especially disruptive behavior by Charles, Martin, and Ali), we did much less singing than I had hoped.

At least once my concerns about student behavior almost led me to forget the power of songs to invite reading.

> I copied out the lyrics to the Beatles' "Birthday" this morning. After copying the lyrics I started to put the sheet away reasoning that the lyrics might get them excited (i.e., wild). But then I realized how stupid that was since the point of environmental print is to invite the students to read, something not likely to happen when it's in the cupboard. (field notes, October 8, 1991)

In retrospect, the posting of written directions, announcements, samples of students' written work, comics and articles from the newspaper, posters, sign-up sheets, chart stories, and song lyrics frequently engaged my students' interest. To insure that environmental print wouldn't lose its power to invite reading I also worked hard to keep the environmental print in my classroom fresh (see Loughlin and Martin 1987). But perhaps the most obvious way I invited my students to read was by the presence of books—lots of books.

We had over 700 books in our classroom many of which I had purchased at book sales and garage sales. I regularly supplemented these with library books, books from my own children's library, and books published by my students. I worked to ensure that we had plenty of interesting, but not-too-difficult books for struggling readers and more challenging books for more able readers. Before I went to a book sale in early October I put up a sign-up sheet and asked the students to use "post-its" to let me know the kinds of books they'd like me to buy[1]. Still, by the end of the school year, I was having a difficult time finding enough challenging books for more able readers like Razika, Shyrose, Peter, and Hugh. I do not have a strong background in children's literature and this made it more difficult for me to locate appropriate books for my more able readers. I'm not sure why I didn't take better advantage of our school librarian, who was very knowledgeable. I recall feeling so overwhelmed that it was difficult to even think about doing one more thing. But it may also be that asking for help may have threatened my status as someone who was supposed to know something about literacy.

It helped that students often brought their own reading materials to school. A group of boys spent weeks reading and discussing comic books they had brought from home. Charles eventually joined this group. Earlier in the year a group of students that included Nicholas brought fan magazines to school. They spent several weeks reading about and discussing their favorite characters from the TV show *Beverly Hills 90210* eventually sending them fan letters. When a group of students came together to read and share "scary" books (see Chapter 1) Crystal brought a couple of her dad's books on vampires to class.

Sometimes my students discovered unexpected reading materials in our classroom. Jennifer, Catherine, and Barbara, for example, often read song lyrics from my song books, sometimes chorally. When they discovered the Beatles' "Sexy Sadie," which they thought was a "dirty song," it became a must read for everyone in our class.

Perhaps the easiest, most enjoyable and powerful way I demonstrated the power of reading and invited my students to read was by reading to them. I read to my class three to four times each day and I took advantage of any opportunity to read more often. When we had to wait outside the gym to perform for a concert, for example, I read *Cloudy with a Chance of Meatballs* (Barrett 1982). If we just had a couple of minutes to fill I often read a poem or two. Sometimes, when students were getting a little wild, I'd call them to the carpet and read them a story to settle them down. Charles often acted out in class, but a story from *The People Could Fly* (Hamilton 1985), a

---

1. I am indebted to Jane Murphy, a first-grade teacher in the York Region Public Schools, for this idea.

collection of American Black folktales his mother read to him at home, would always settle him down.

But not all the books I read to my class worked equally well. In general, my students preferred picture books that could be read in a single sitting to longer "chapter" books. I think this was especially true for Charles and Martin who, because they spent two hours a day in a special education resource room, often missed readings from longer books. It may also have been that I didn't always select appropriate chapter books to read orally. Many of the boys got very restless, for example, when I attempted to read *Ramona Forever* (Cleary 1984) (I abandoned this book after a few days) and both girls and boys claimed to be bored when I attempted to read *Sarah Plain and Tall* (MacLachlan 1985) (almost as soon as I started reading this book some students started asking when they could write). Connie Proctor, a fifth-grade teacher and a friend of my wife's from Perry, Michigan, warned me that *Sarah Plain and Tall* was more suitable for fifth graders. Apparently, she was right. She offered the same advice about *Bridge to Terabithia* (Paterson 1977) which I also read to my class with similar results although I did read it to completion. There were, however, other chapter books that worked quite well with my class. My students loved James Howe's Bunnicula books and Gertrude Chandler Warner's Boxcar Children books were a big hit with almost everyone. Barbara Park's hilarious novel *Skinnybones* (1982) turned out to be my students' favorite book.

Encouraging students to pass notes turned out to be another way I invited my students to read (and write). Many students used our "message center" (see Chapter 1) to share notes with each other although this was not as popular with the boys. I also wrote notes to students, sometimes singling out struggling readers. When I heard Charles referred to my Volkswagon van as a "turtle van" I wrote him the following note:

Dear Charles,

I thought it was funny yesterday when you called my van a "turtle van."

Mr. Marling

This may, however, be the only note I wrote to Charles and I may have missed a nice opportunity to engage him in meaningful reading. Similarly, in early October Charles, a very reluctant writer, asked me to help him write a note to my son Ian. It was the end of the writing period and I promised I'd help him the next day. Unfortunately, I didn't follow up on this opportunity. Looking back it's clear that writing notes to and with my students was, potentially, a powerful invitation to read (and write) and to establish relationships. That I didn't do enough of this may be related to how often I felt overwhelmed by competing demands and behavior problems.

Even in some of the best whole language classrooms I see I'm not so sure they "nudge" enough. Perhaps too much patience and too much dependence on language rich environments. Something I can explore next year—the tension between nudging and taking control. Given my daughter Anne's difficult experience in first grade I want to nudge and challenge as much as I can. (field notes, August 10, 1991)

Immersing students in a print-rich environment is necessary, but I don't think it's a sufficient condition for students' reading development. Many students, especially those for whom school is a struggle, also require explicit, individual support and direction from their teachers. Lisa Delpit (1988), in her critique of writing process classrooms, argued that explicit literacy instruction is critically important for students who do not come from white, middle-class backgrounds, students who are less familiar with the middle-class discourse practices favored in schools (see Gee 1990). A failure to provide explicit support and direction to students is the result of a laissez-faireism which is, I believe, a perversion of whole language.

One way I tried to provide explicit support and direction for my third graders was by helping them learn to select appropriate books to read. Here I was reacting to my concern that many of my struggling readers, especially Charles, often selected books which I judged to be much too hard for them. This led me, for example, to dedicate a bookshelf to not-too-difficult books so students could easily find these books. I encouraged—but did not insist—that Charles, Lila, and Martin, among others, choose books from this shelf, but they continued to select books I thought too difficult. At the time I guessed that students chose books that were too difficult to protect their self-image, but I learned that struggling with difficult texts can be worthwhile. Lila, for example, managed to cope with texts like *Amelia Bedelia's Family Album* (Parish 1991), which she couldn't read independently, with the support of her friend Roya. Nader, an ESL student, spent six weeks struggling with Barbara Park's *Skinnybones* (1982), a book we'd read in class, and, to my surprise, by the time he was done he was a much better reader.

The most common and, perhaps, the most powerful strategy I used to support struggling readers was assisted reading, a strategy that may be especially useful for students like Charles, Martin, and Lila who read word by word, in a choppy, stumbling manner (Rhodes and Dudley-Marling 1996). Usually I began by sitting next to the student and reading a book to them, sometimes pointing to each word as I read. Then the student and I would read the book together, but I would lower my voice when the student's reading was strong and raise it when the student needed support. For example:

> Read *The Big Enormous Turnip* (Shannon 1988) with Nader. At some points I paused and he finished the lines (the more predictable/repetitive ones). At other points he read along with me . . . After I left him he re-read the story on his own. (field notes, September 26, 1991)

I also used assisted reading in an attempt to encourage students like Lila and Charles to make better use of contextual information to make sense of words in text.

> Did assisted reading with Lila again using *Finders Keepers* (Will Nicholas 1989). Today I continued to read with her, even providing support for the parts I knew she could read. I was trying to use assisted reading to encourage her to read more quickly. She still tends to plod along making it difficult for her to take advantage of contextual clues in the process of reading. (May 20, 1992)

Later in the year I read texts chorally with Charles, Martin, and Lila to make more efficient use of my time. This didn't always work out, however. Martin, for example, often got frustrated with Lila who read too slowly for him. Other variations of assisted reading I used included reading along with audiotaped stories and paired reading. Early in the year I required my students to read with their partners on Fridays. I tried to pair struggling readers with students who I found were able to provide helpful, unobtrusive support for their partners. Typically these were students who, like Catherine, Tiffany, and Razika, had younger brothers and sisters. We also did some whole class mini-lessons on how to support reading partners. When paired reading was no longer required, many students—including Charles, Martin, Lila, Nader, and Fatima—continued to read with partners. Charles often preferred reading with Ali to reading with me.

I also tried to increase struggling students' reading fluency (and sight vocabularies) by encouraging the repeated reading of texts. When I did assisted reading, for example, we repeatedly read the same text until students could read it independently. I also found that opportunities to encourage the repeated reading of texts often arose naturally. When students started asking to read to the class (by late October students took over most of the oral reading to the class) I put up a sign-up sheet, but insisted that students practice their books before reading them to the class. A school-wide reading program which partnered my students with a first-grade class also encouraged students to practice books they were going to read with their younger "reading buddies." Lila, Martin, and Charles, perhaps anxious to avoid embarrassment, worked especially hard to practice their books. Regrettably, reading buddies was usually scheduled when Charles and Martin were in the resource room denying them a useful opportunity. Still, I could easily have asked to have Charles and Martin excused from the resource room for reading buddies. The resource room teacher was very flexible. Why didn't I? I can't be sure, but I'm afraid I was all too happy to have a respite from Charles and Martin and their disruptive, sometimes violent, behavior.

During reading I read with Lila and Charles again using assisted/ choral reading with *Where the Wild Things Are* (Sendak 1963) . . . When one of them read, ". . . roared their terrible eyes . . ." I went back and asked "Do they ROAR their terrible eyes?" and they corrected their miscue. (field notes, April 6, 1992)

I regularly used explicit strategies to help students learn to make sense of texts. When I read with struggling readers like Lila, Martin, or Charles, I often drew their attention to miscues and suggested specific strategies for making sense of words in text. For example:

Martin read the first few pages from *Frog and Toad are Friends* (Lobel 1970). Some miscues: He read "Frog ran up the path to Toad's house." He stopped on "path" until I encouraged him to skip this word and go on. He did and was able to come back and get the word. When he came to "knocked" ("He knocked on the front door.") he paused and I again encouraged him to skip the word and come back. He read ahead and then came back and correctly read "knocked." When he read the line "Blah" (I gave him this word). (field notes, March 24, 1992)

I also took advantage of opportunities to model strategies for making sense of words in text when I read to my class. If I came to a proper name I couldn't pronounce, as often happened when I named authors and illustrators, I made a point of telling the class that I wasn't sure how to say the name. I told them I would have to make up a name (until I learned the proper pronunciation). Since many of my struggling readers seemed to believe that the good readers in our class never made miscues, I sometimes pointed out miscues that I made when reading aloud. And, if my miscues didn't change the meaning of the text, I'd tell them that miscues which didn't result in meaning change were acceptable (and natural). I'm not sure they were convinced, however.

I also prepared cloze tasks to encourage struggling readers to use contextual information to make sense of words in text. For example, in early April I prepared a cloze task for Martin, Charles, and Lila based on the book, *I Know an Old Lady* (Chambliss 1987) which they were reading with my assistance.

I know an old _____ who swallowed a _____ .

I don't know why she _____ a fly.

_____ old lady.

I guess she'll _____

Cloze tasks didn't work equally well for all students, however. Martin and Denise usually tried to locate the book on which the cloze was based and use the book to find the missing words. Copying from the book did encourage reading, but missed the point of the exercise. This was easily solved by briefly removing the books from circulation. But for Charles cloze was always a problem. Despite my instructions ("Put in any word that makes sense"), he tried to faithfully reproduce the text as it was in the book. I eventually overcame this difficulty by making up my own cloze passages although Charles still needed some convincing that he could put any word in the blank.

Charles was confused at first, saying that he didn't know this (he meant he didn't know the story from which the cloze came). I assured him that I had made up the story and he commented, "I can put anything in?" I told him he could as long as it made sense. (field notes, March 24, 1992)

I found cloze to be helpful for encouraging students like Charles, Lila, and Martin to use context to make sense of words in text, but I recognized that cloze was not a substitute for students reading actual texts.

> I had intended to start Lila, Martin, and Charles on a new cloze task but Lila was so productively engaged in reading *Piglet Is Entirely Surrounded by Water* (Shepard 1991) that I didn't think it was a good idea to interrupt her. (field notes, February 18, 1992)

> When Charles came to the sentence, " . . . under the hen was quite an egg" he asked for help with "under" and I suggested he go on. When he came back he still had difficulty so I covered up "der" in under leaving "un" for him to sound out to which he responded by guessing "unicycle." (field notes, January 6, 1992)

There is a popular perception that whole language teachers don't teach phonics, but good whole language teachers do teach phonics directly and so did I. The above lesson with Charles didn't work out like I hoped, but I routinely did phonics minilessons with my students. I also used whole group lessons and predictable books to help my students discover some of the regularities in English orthography.

I think my students learned the most about phonics, however, through our individual and whole class spelling lessons (these lessons are described in more detail in Chapter 8). The following interaction was typical of the kind of support I'd offer students.

> While I was with Crystal, Benizar asked me how to spell "operation." I suggested she listen for the sounds and she said, "o-p-r" (then I told her that "e-r" was usually spelled "er" not "r" and then I said, "shun" and Crystal volunteered "s-h-u-n." Then I started to say that "shun" is usually spelled "t-i-o-n" but before I could, Razika said it. Then I talked about "t-i-o-n" and noted that other words like "vacation" and "celebration" (this one came from Crystal) were also spelled "t-i-o-n." (field notes, October 11, 1991)

This is my dog Clifford. He is the only pet I ever had . . . except one time last year a kitten came to our house . . . Mom said we could keep him until we found his owners . . . I think Clifford was a little jealous. That night Clifford slept as close to me as he could get . . . He was a playful little kitten. He chased butterflies. Clifford chased butterflies too. He saw a very big one. He caught it. Dad paid the boy for his kite. Kittens love to play with spools. Clifford had never played with a spool. He found one in the street . . . I took the kitten for a ride in my doll carriage. I never did that for Clifford. Clifford wanted a ride too. While I was explaining why I couldn't push him . . . the kitten jumped out of the carriage and started across the street . . . The kitten didn't even say, "Thank you." He just sharpened his claws. Clifford tried to sharpen his claws . . . While Clifford was busy putting the light pole back, a big dog came into our yard and growled at the kitten. He didn't notice Clifford. The big dog decided to go back into his house to play. While I was hugging the kitten, a little boy rode up. He said, "Oh, you found my cat. Thank you! . . . " That sure was a cute kitten. I hated to see him go. (Charles, June 17, 1992, reading Bridwell 1985)

Looking back I find that I was able to provide frequent, intensive, individual support and direction to my struggling readers and writers, but how did they do? As the above excerpt from Charles's miscue analysis indicates, Charles made significant progress as a reader. By the end of the year he was able to read a range of texts independently, using an array of strategies (e.g., skipping unknown words, rereading) and cueing systems (graphophonics, syntax, and semantics) for making sense of words in text. Charles made much less, if any, progress as a writer, however. At the end of the year Charles was still a very reluctant writer overly concerned with spelling, but I had few opportunities to support Charles's writing development since he wasn't with us during writing time.

Lila also made nice progress as a reader. At the end of the school year she was still reading slowly and she tended to rely heavily on graphophonic cues to make sense of words in text. But she was also able to use contextual information to make sense of texts, sometimes skipping unknown words or substituting words which didn't change the meaning of the text. When she read *Jillian Jiggs* (Gilman 1985) to me in March she skipped the word "thought" and, after reading the rest of the sentence, came back and read "made up" for "thought up." Lila also attempted to read more challenging texts. In early January she proudly announced to me "I'm reading a chapter book . . . *Karen's Ghost* (Martin 1990). Perhaps most important, Lila learned to enjoy reading—sometimes I had difficulty getting her to stop reading and move on to something else. Sometime in May she paid me the ultimate compliment: "All because of you I learned to like reading."

Lila also made substantial progress as a writer and in April she published her first book, a story about a little boy who tricked his babysitter. Spelling was still difficult for her, but, by the end of the year, her spellings were phonetically appropriate and were beginning to take on features of standard English orthography (e.g., "fiting" for "fighting"; "frand" for "friend"; "grlle" for "girl"; "asct" for "asked"; "navr" for "never") (I discuss Lila's spelling development in more detail in Chapter 8).

Martin also made good progress as a reader. Like Lila and Charles, he learned to use a variety of strategies and cueing systems for making sense of texts. In late March, for example, when he came to the word "voice" in an Arnold Lobel Frog and Toad story he skipped it and then came back and substituted "monster" and read on. When he came across the word "voice" a second time he read it correctly and then went back and pointed out that the word he read as "monster" was also "voice." Martin, like Charles, didn't participate in our writing program and made relatively little progress as a writer.

Evaluating the progress Lila, Martin, and Charles made as readers and writers has been an interesting exercise. In Dan Lortie's (1975) sociological study of teachers in five different communities, he reported that the uncertainty and ambiguity of student evaluation made many of the teachers he interviewed very uneasy. Teachers worried, for example, about their ability to gauge student progress accurately. They fretted over students who did not appear to learn much in their classrooms. And, even if students made satisfactory progress, teachers wondered about the effect their teaching had on students (perhaps students would have learned to read, for example, even without their efforts).

It has surprised me the degree to which reflecting on the progress of Lila, Charles, Martin and other struggling students in my classroom has evoked an uneasiness that echoes the concerns raised by Lortie's teachers. I wonder about my influence on Charles, Lila, and Martin. Could the resource teacher be responsible for Charles's reading development? How much of Martin's progress was due to his medication? I also find myself guilt-stricken about students like Crystal who didn't make much progress as a reader or a writer and who, by the end of the year, seemed to be doing worse in math. And, despite the accomplishments my struggling readers and writers made, I find myself wishing that I had done more for them.

I'm disappointed, for example, that I couldn't have found some way to support Charles's and Martin's writing development. I tried scheduling reading at the end of the day so they would be in our class for reading and writing, but reading didn't work well late in the day so, for the sake of the rest of the class, I returned to our earlier schedule (reading first thing in the morning, writing after lunch). Still, I might have supported Charles's and Martin's writing by working more closely with the resource room teacher. I asked her early in the year if she was willing to collaborate on Charles's reading and writing program and she was. But I never made a serious attempt to work with her. Why? It's hard to be sure. I know I worried about stepping out of my teacher role and into my professorial role and, because I was a guest in the school, I worried about the possibility of conflicts arising from theoretical differences. But I think time was an even more important factor here. As I've already said, I just felt so overwhelmed by the burdens of teaching (and researching) that I couldn't bear to take on one more thing. Still, since my university work frequently emphasizes the importance of collaborations between special education and regular classroom teachers, I'm disappointed that this is something I was unable to do myself. Perhaps if I spent another year in the classroom this is something I would have taken on. I can only hope I would have.

5

"We Only Learned What the Boys Did"
Doing (and Undoing) Gender in a Third-Grade Classroom

Don Dippo, a friend and colleague at York University, has read and responded to drafts of most of the chapters of this book. As Don has read my accounts of life in third grade he's pointed out to me how often I have marked gender when I wrote about my students. A rereading of my field notes from this perspective supports Don's observation. I often made gender relevant when I described students' behavior even when it wasn't. In early September, for example, when I took my class outside to make and record observations about plants as part of a science unit I wrote, "The *girls* all got right to it, but many of the *boys* were reluctant to write." When we went outside to play dodgeball on the second day of school I observed that "the *boys* dominated and the *girls* stood around." And, when I showed a movie to my class in December, I wrote that "even though the *boys* complained that they wouldn't like the movie ... they all watched intently."

It's interesting how natural it was for me to foreground gender when discussing my students. Of all the social or physical categories I might have used to characterize my students gender is the one I chose most often. (In my field notes I referred to "boys" a total of 130 times and "girls" 153 times.) I did not categorize my students by age, height, eye or hair color. I never wrote, for example, that the seven-year-olds got right to work, but the eight-year-olds dallied or that the blue-eyed children liked an activity and that the brown-eyed students didn't. Nor did it even occur to me to attempt to explain students' behavior on the basis of categories like race, language, ethnicity, religion, or class although I did construct the category of "struggling readers" (see McDermott 1993, for a discussion of how schools construct school failure) to describe several of my students who had difficulty reading and writing texts independently. In general, when I tried to make sense of my third graders' behavior gender mattered and the problem for Don Dippo was that I *made* gender matter. Certainly I could reasonably describe each of my students as either a boy or a girl (and refer to their actions as the behavior of *a* boy or *a* girl), but it wasn't just gender that made my students unique and interesting people.

In retrospect, it is clear that I had a tendency to give gender a salience—and explanatory power—it did not warrant. It may have been, for example, that some of the boys balked when I asked them to record their observations when we went outside to study plants. But it wasn't all and only the boys who were reluctant to record what they had observed. Some boys wrote willingly and some of the girls did not. More boys than girls may have resisted this activity, but gender alone cannot explain these behavioral differences since neither the boys nor the girls exhibited unique behavioral patterns (e.g., all the girls wrote and none of the boys did).

It seems that my observations of the boys and girls in my class may have been shaped by the lens of expectation. For instance, I was most likely to make gender salient in situations in which other researchers have reported "statistical differences" between boys and girls in play, in conversation, in social skills, and so on (Swann 1992, Tannen 1990, Thorne 1993). The problem with invoking *the boys* or *the girls* to account for differences in students' behavior, however, is that it risked creating expectations that were self-fulfilling. It may seem that there are real (i.e., biological) differences between boys and girls, but the reality is that differences among groups of girls and groups of boys are often greater than the differences between boys and girls (Thorne 1993). My tendency to talk about *the boys* and *the girls* obscured differences among the boys and the girls in my classroom and may have affected my own behavior toward them.

In this chapter I reflect on how my students and I did gender—including my search for gender differences; my concerns about the differential treatment of boys and girls in my classroom; my observations about gender relations; and, my (modest) efforts to challenge—that is, undo—conventional assumptions about how we did gender in my third-grade classroom.

LOOKING AT GENDER THROUGH A PINK
AND BLUE LENS

> Much of what has been observed about girls and boys, especially in
> the relationships they create apart from the surveillance of adults,
> can be fitted into the model of 'different worlds or cultures.' But as
> I've tried to line up that model with . . . empirical observations and
> with the research literature, I have found so many exceptions and
> qualifications, so many incidents that spill beyond and fuzzy up the
> edges, and so many conceptual ambiguities, that I have come to
> question the model's basic assumptions. (Thorne 1993, 90)

When I viewed my students through the expectant lens of "the
pink and blues" (Thorne 1993, 159) it seemed that my observations
generally supported many of the stereotypic assumptions about the
behaviors of boys and girls; that is, the boys, compared to the girls
in my classroom, seemed to be more competitive, more dominant,
more active, more aggressive, and so on. A careful and thoughtful
analysis of the data (my field notes), however, reveals the same fuzzy
ambiguities that troubled Barrie Thorne. In this section I use several
accepted gender differences to demonstrate how my observations
first supported, then finally contradicted, both popular gender stereotypes and the conclusions of much statistically-based research on
gender differences.

Boys Seek Hierarchical Relations;
Girls Seek Intimacy

Stereotypically, boys are always jostling to establish their positions in
various social hierarchies. Girls, on the other hand, are believed to be
more interested in establishing connectedness (Goodwin 1991, Lever
1978, Schofield 1982, Tannen 1990). Presumably, this explains the
tendency of boys toward competition and girls toward collaboration.
Certainly, this is the way it often seemed to me as I observed my third
graders interact. I was intrigued by the ways the girls in my class
provided emotional and physical support for each other. When I read
books to my class many of the girls often groomed one another's hair
or laid their heads on the shoulders of other girls. I recall being
amazed at how easily Jennifer wrapped her arms around Connie and
held her hands when Connie leaned against her during a presentation in the library. Connie and Jennifer weren't friends and they

rarely had much to do with each other, but when Connie signaled her need for comforting Jennifer willingly provided it. Similarly, whenever Catherine was upset about some real or imagined disaster at home, or Fatima was embarrassed by a new haircut, or Barbara was in tears after another fight with her best friend Jennifer, there was always a girl in our class ready and willing to offer some comfort. In general, I admired the kind of emotional support the girls provided for each other, support that seemed to be missing from my male experience. On April 21, for example, I wrote in my notes:

> The girls often offer each other nurturing by physical touching, by playing with each other's hair, and holding each other. Watching them makes me realize what the boys are missing. Is this part of what makes *us* [males] more aggressive? I wonder. (field notes, April 21, 1992)

If I imagined that the girls worked to provide each other with an emotionally safe and supportive space in our classroom, I was just as certain that the hierarchical tendencies I observed in the boys helped to create what was, for them, an emotionally hostile place. After all, it seemed that it was the boys who were always putting each other down with insults. It was the boys who pushed, shoved, kicked, punched, and threatened. It was the boys who harassed Nicholas for his immature habits. It was the cruel taunts and exclusion by (some) boys that sent Nader home crying each day after school early in the year. And it was Alex and Jason, two fifth-grade bullies, who dominated the other boys on the playground.

My sense that the boys in my class created a hostile environment for one another while the girls created an emotionally supportive environment for themselves was reinforced by my observation that the girls seemed more likely than the boys to work collaboratively. Girls like Jennifer, Catherine, Lila, Roya, and Crystal, for example, regularly came together to read chorally, chant rhymes, or sing songs. Conversely, it seemed like it was always the boys, particularly Wayne, Troy, Ali, and Nicholas—who balked at paired reading and wouldn't work together at the science center. This recalls, of course, the prototypical hero of American fiction—strong, independent, and male, presumably deriving his strength from this independence.

My initial observations of my third graders seemed to support popular stereotypes and a considerable body of research which holds that females tend to seek symmetry in their relations while males seek asymmetry in theirs (e.g., Tannen 1990). The problem with this all too tidy generalization about the boys and girls in my classroom is that it wasn't true, at least not to the extent I had imagined. Although the girls were demonstrably more affectionate with one another at least one boy, Hugh, occasionally groomed the hair of other boys and, on at least one occasion, the hair of a girl. That he didn't continue to groom the hair of classmates may have more to do with how my third graders constructed gender (girls groom, boys don't) than any intrinsic differences between boys and girls. Nor is it the case that all girls engaged in grooming and stroking each other. I never observed such behavior from Denise or Razika, for example. And the conclusion that the girls provided an emotionally supportive environment for themselves ignored the many ways the girls in my class hurt and excluded one another. The "tense triangles" (Thorne 1993) involving Catherine-Jennifer-Denise, Jennifer-Barbara-Catherine, and Catherine-Razika-Shyrose, for example, did not provide a very friendly environment for Barbara, Denise, or Razika. (I'm also learning at the dinner table from my teenage daughter, Anne, just how hurtful young girls can be.) Girls, like boys, could be mean, even cruel. The girls were just less likely to hit, punch, or kick and, even then, girls did sometimes hit, punch, and kick. (More about this later.)

Looking at my students through *pink and blue* lenses led me to focus my attention on stereotypic, negative behaviors in my male students and positive behaviors in my female students. Based on this stereotypic view of male dominance I concluded the boys in my class had created an emotionally unfriendly space for themselves even though this isn't how I recall my own boyhood. I seemed to have forgotten the emotional support and sustenance I derived from my own boyhood friendships, and I seemed not to notice the various ways the boys in my class signalled their support and affection for each other. Yes, Wayne and Troy were often exclusive and domineering, but they fiercely defended each other in disputes with other children and they frequently made a public display of joint interests—all in the name of friendship. It was also Wayne, Troy, and Jeffrey who so warmly (and affectionately) accepted my then five-year-old son, Ian, when he visited our class. And what was true of Wayne and Jeffrey was also true of Peter and John and Ali and Charles. Blinded by stereotypes, I seemed not to notice.

A more circumspect analysis of my field notes also contradicts stereotypic images of the "social" girl and the "independent" boy. It may have been that the two most dominant boys in the classroom, Troy and Wayne, often shunned collaborations with other students (they sometimes did work together) and Paul usually preferred to read by himself. But many boys regularly collaborated. John and Peter routinely wrote together and Ali often read with Charles. Hugh frequently read and wrote with other boys. On the other hand, some girls, notably Denise and Connie, hardly ever collaborated with other students. In some situations the boys appeared to be more collaborative than the girls. For example, when my third graders worked with their first-grade reading partners early in April I asked them to first read a book with their partner and then draw a picture to go with their stories. Given these instructions most of my girls divided a piece of paper in half so they and their reading partners could draw separate pictures. All of the boys, on the other hand, worked with their reading partners to draw a single picture. Again, when girls were social and supportive, I noticed. When the boys were social and supportive, I didn't. Overall, my seeming preference for simple, stereotypic notions of independent boys and social girls was contradicted by the subtle, complicated ways the boys and girls in my classroom actually interacted with one another.

Boys Dominate Talk

There is a considerable body of research that, contrary to popular opinion, males—not females—are apt to dominate conversational interactions (supported by my daughter's complaints about her brother and her father). Specifically, males, relative to females, are likely to take more turns and longer turns in a range of conversational settings (Graddol and Swann 1989, Tannen 1990). The observation that unequal access to the conversational floor disadvantages girls in school has led many feminist educators to seek strategies to remedy this imbalance (Swann 1992, Weiler 1988) including the establishment of all-female schools featuring feminist pedagogy.

Influenced by this research on differences in the conversational styles of males and females, I began the year expecting that my third-grade boys would dominate the conversational floor in both small- and large-group, mixed-gender settings. Such evidence didn't take long to emerge. On the very first day of class I wrote in my field notes:

We broke into small groups to talk about their summers . . . Interestingly, the boys did seem to me to dominate the discussions.

When we got back together on the carpet I asked the large group what they had learned about each other. Roya quickly volunteered, "We only learned about what the boys did." (September 3, 1991)

Similarly, an analysis of the written transcript of the discussion that led to the formation of the "Scary, Evil Book Club" (this conversation is excerpted on pages 16–19) reveals that the overall number of turns taken by the two boys who participated in this discussion, John and Peter, exceeded the total number of turns taken by the three female participants, Catherine, Fatima, and Crystal. By himself, John took the same number of turns as the three girls combined and both the total and the average length of his turns exceeded the girls. The boys also dominated the discussion by taking slightly longer turns as measured by the number of lines spoken on the transcript.

Boys	Number of turns	Length	Avg. length/turn
John	61	86	1.41
Peter	10	11	1.10
Total:	71	97	1.37
Girls			
Catherine	18	25	1.9
Crystal	33	44	1.33
Fatima	10	12	1.20
Total:	61	81	1.33

This quick and dirty analysis apparently supports the general finding that, in mixed-gender groupings, males dominate the conversational floor. A more careful analysis of these data, however, indicates that this conclusion needs to be qualified. It may be that in the "Scary, Evil Book Club" discussion John dominated the conversation and that combining John and Peter's contribution to the discussion seems to demonstrate the conversational imbalance between the boys and the girls. Yet it is John who dominates, not Peter who stands with Fatima as the two participants who took the fewest number of turns. In fact, Crystal took over three times as many turns as Peter and in other contexts John, who dominates here, rarely spoke at all. (Arguably, John spoke so readily here because the books they were discussing were his books.) There were also other conversations throughout the year in which girls dominated although these seemed to be less common. So it is more than a little misleading to suggest that all boys will dominate all conversations all of the time

even if, on the average, boys are more likely to dominate these interactions than girls. This isn't to deny that many males use conversational strategies that have the effect of oppressing females or that
these tendencies, where they exist, shouldn't be challenged (see
Cameron 1992, Weiler 1988). It's just that asserting that all males or
all females behave in certain ways effaces the complexity of the
behaviors of individual males and females. Each of us—male and
female—is a complicated, contradictory, context-embedded person
and dichotomous ways of talking about ourselves will never capture
this complexity. Stereotyping will never lead to either better communication or greater understanding between males and females and,
more seriously, monolithic claims about the language of males and
females have and will almost certainly continue to be used against
women and girls by portraying their language as deviant compared
to males (Cameron 1992).

It might be argued that the tendency of males to seek domination
in social relations (by dominating conversations, for example) is a
function of their more aggressive nature or, alternatively, an aggressiveness nurtured by male culture, which brings us to another stereotypic difference between males and females.

Boys Are More Active and Aggressive than Girls

I'm fairly certain that most Americans and Canadians readily accept
the assertion that boys are both more active and more aggressive
than girls (Hartup 1983, Maccoby and Jacklin 1974, Paley 1984).
(This accounts, I think, for the sympathy often given to mothers of
boys.) My early assessment of my experience as a third-grade teacher
reinforced my own belief in this stereotype. After we played dodgeball on the second day of school I wrote in my notes that "the boys
dominated and the girls stood around" (September 4, 1991). This
was how I usually saw it. It seemed that it was always a boy who
spoiled a game of kickball or baseball or a song or a story with overly
aggressive play or noisy disruptions. Conversely, it was always the
girls who refused to participate in gym and the girls who stood
around on the playground.

None of these generalizations were entirely true, however. On the
whole my third-grade boys may have been more physically aggressive, but few of the boys outdid Catherine or Denise for either physical or verbal belligerence. Denise once poked Peter in the face with

a pencil narrowly missing his eye and no one rivaled her use of sexually-explicit curses. While Catherine's assaults were not as violent as those of Ali or Charles, no one in my class resorted to physical aggression as quickly and as often as she did. And anyone crossing Fatima was likely to get an elbow in the ribs. (Fatima was so quiet that I rarely even noticed her physical aggressiveness.) Both boys and girls in my class often resorted to violence to solve their disputes. It was just that the boys were somewhat more likely, compared to the girls, to resort to violence and that, because of their greater strength and size, the consequences of their violence were usually more serious. (The girls, unlike the boys, rarely drew blood.) Again, (some) boys may be more aggressive than (many) girls, but it isn't all and only boys who are physically and verbally aggressive. Unfortunately, the belief that aggression is natural in boys fosters a willingness to overlook some acts of violence among males (including violence against women) on the grounds that "boys will be boys."

It also seemed to me that the girls in my classroom were less active than the boys, but girls like Fatima and Catherine enjoyed physical play as much as any boy. And no one disliked sustained physical exercise more than John. And, yes, it was only girls who refused to take part in gym, but not all (or even most) of the girls refused participation. Possibly the girls and the boys in my classroom were equally likely to avoid participating in gym, but they tended toward different strategies for non-participation—some of the girls resisted by sitting out; some boys (and girls) resisted by acting out (which resulted in them being told to sit out).

My sense that the boys in my third-grade class were more likely than the girls to tend toward aggressive behavior and active resistance, reinforced by how I interpreted my experience as a third-grade teacher, led me to worry more about the boys' responses to large- and small-group activities. I now fear that we may have done less singing than I had hoped, for example, because I feared disruptions by the boys. (Although singing was often difficult with my class I cannot say that it was only boys who disrupted singing. Here I may have been acting on my own experience with music in school. I hated music in school, most of the other boys in my class hated music, and we frequently acted out during music, so perhaps I expected a similar response from the boys in my third grade class.) In an attempt to avoid disruptive behavior by the boys I may also have been more inclined to read books to my class that I believed would interest them. This, of course, betrays an assumption that boys and girls are not interested in the same books. Certainly, no boy in my class ever read a Babysitter book and Troy and Nicholas rejected any book that featured female characters. But several boys enjoyed the Ramona Quimby series and, as the broad participation in the "Scary, Evil Book Club" indicates, horror books were not strictly a male genre.

What's important here, however, is that my expectations—and my reading of my own experience—may have influenced some of the choices I made as a teacher including which books to read to my class and a reluctance to do much singing. Believing that boys were a problem, I may have catered more to their needs and desires, at least to the degree that their needs were different from the needs of the girls, and, more seriously, ignored the needs and desires of (some) girls—and, of course, the boys who shared their interests. This raises an uncomfortable question for me: to the degree that I did cater to the stereotypic needs and desires of my male students, did I encourage those characteristics in all or some of my males students? Paradoxically, my negative stereotype of boys (aggressive, disruptive, etc.) may have led me to (sometimes) privilege their point of view (as far as it was their point of view) and, by so doing, encourage the behaviors I found so distasteful.

On the other hand, my relations with the boys in my class, influenced, perhaps, by differential expectations, were often strained and generally less satisfying. Aware of my discomfort with my perceptions of the behavior of the boys in my class I gave much thought to the question: is my treatment of the boys and girls in my third grade class equitable?

"I Don't Joke with the Boys"

Yesterday morning before school I looked through the double doors and saw Shyrose hanging up her coat outside the daycare center. I caught her eye and made a funny face. She responded by sticking out her tongue. Later in the day I gave Roya a little hug after she'd said something particularly funny. Catherine asked me to give a card she'd made to Anne which read: "Dear Anne I have heard a lot about you. I like your name and our (sic) Dad. He is a good teacher. From Catherine." Naturally I was thrilled . . . But what about the boys. I don't have these kinds of interactions with them. I don't seem to ever joke with them, they don't write to me, and, although I do touch them to express my support, I'm much

more likely to be locked in battle with them . . . But of course the
girls seek me out. They write me notes and they hang around
me on the playground and in the classroom. . . . worry about the
gendering of primary education, but I now wonder how I myself am
contributing to it. I'm not sure I'm treating the boys and the girls
the same and, therefore, I may be contributing to the divisions
between boys and girls which I claim to abhor. And I may be inad-
vertently letting the girls into a private little club where they
share jokes and affection with the teacher, a club from which many
of the boys may be excluded. (field notes, November 2, 1991)

As this excerpt from my field notes indicates, I often worried
about the quality of my interactions with the boys in my class which
didn't seem as positive, or as satisfying, as my interactions with my
female students. Even now, it seems that I rarely had the kind of
warm, personal moments with any of the boys that I had with Catherine, Roya, Razika, and Shyrose, for example. I joked with the girls.
I learned about their families. I got to know them. With the boys I
always felt like a police officer—a role I really hated. I engaged the
girls and controlled the boys—at least that's how I often felt.

Early in the school year I was also concerned that I was harsher,
less patient, and more punitive with the boys. In late October I wrote
in my field notes:

When Ali had a tantrum this morning I made the mistake of getting engaged [i.e., angry]. It was unkind of me to let him know that
he had to stay after school for tripping someone on the playground right after the lunch recess. I could have waited. This is
how I treat Catherine and Roya. I worry that I am unkind when I
discipline Ali, Charles, and some of the other boys. On the
other hand, I'm almost apologetic when I discipline some of the
girls. (field notes, October 24, 1991)

Another entry in my field notes several months later indicates that
the equitable treatment of boys and girls was a concern for me
throughout the school year.

I'm sure I mishandled the incident with Charles today. I didn't talk
to him about what he did and I'm sure he doesn't understand why
he got sent to the office [for violently pushing Catherine against

the wall] and Catherine didn't. She pushed him, too. The difference, to me anyway, was the level of violence—he could have hurt her. Still, I'm afraid that I just contributed to his alienation by the way I handled this incident. I should know better. Catherine has pushed kids hard (once she pushed Peter at least as hard) and I haven't sent her to the office. I must treat everyone with as much respect and consideration as I give to Catherine and the other girls. And although I always strive to do this I don't always manage to follow through, especially with Charles and Ali. I'll just have to keep trying. (field notes, February 11, 1992)

[The following day I did apologize to Charles and I explained to him why I thought I took the action that I did.]

Treating students fairly is an important concern for most teachers (see Lortie 1975) and so it was for me. I was concerned then, as I am now, that I did not always treat my students equitably. In particular, I worried that I was kinder to the girls than I was to the boys. I was stung by the criticism from one of the boys in my class that "you like the girls better" because I feared it may have been true. As much as this disappoints me I take some comfort in the fact that I did work hard to change my behavior as the following quote from my field notes suggests.

. . . if I can reflect on this [how I treat boys and girls] then I can make some changes. For example, I'm much too hard on Nicholas and Nader and even Wayne and Troy. I can try harder to be more gentle. I can seek out the boys and share the kinds of jokes and conversations I have with the girls. I can try to join in their games on the playground from time to time, perhaps throwing the baseball or football with them. In general, this is a serious concern so I need to ask myself almost daily the question: "Did I treat the boys and the girls equitably today?" (November 2, 1991)

Throughout my year as a third-grade teacher, I often asked myself this question sometimes highlighting it in my lesson plans (e.g., "Today's goal: Work harder to be kind to the boys"), and I frequently reminded myself of the "Catherine rule" (treat everyone with the same respect and kindness with which I treat Catherine, Roya, Razika and the other girls) when I interacted with boys (especially Nader, Ali, Wayne, and Nicholas). I reasoned that all of my students—boys and girls—would benefit from the kindness, affection, and understanding that marked my relationships with Razika, Shyrose, Catherine, and Roya.

Looking back I also suspect that I never managed to resolve the tension between equitable treatment and equal treatment. I was right to be troubled by issues of fairness, but fair treatment (equity) doesn't necessary mean identical treatment. I'm sure I should have been kinder to (some of) the boys, but the ways I expressed kindness to boys and girls needn't have been identical. But, writing this chapter four years after third grade, I'm not so sure I was so hard on the boys. The problem may not have been the boys at all, but certain aggressive, seemingly insensitive, behaviors that were more common in (some) boys. I wasn't so much hard on the boys as I was hard on boys (and girls) who exhibited certain behaviors. So I sometimes got very angry with Ali, Charles, Wayne, and Martin for pushing, shoving, hitting, and being verbally abusive. I also got angry with Denise and Connie for similar behaviors. I tended not to get mad at Shyrose, Razika, Roya, Lila, Jennifer *or* John, Scott, and Paul. So it is at least arguable that I did not always treat students the same because they didn't behave in the same ways, but that these differences, while unequal, were equitable.

Although I learned to live more comfortably with the boys in my classroom, I'm not sure I completely overcame my worry that I preferred the company of the girls in my classroom. It seems more likely, however, that it wasn't a question of preferring girls to boys as much as preferring behaviors that were more common in the girls and disliking certain behaviors that were more common among boys. To the degree that boys were more aggressive, for example, I preferred girls *and* boys who were kinder and gentler souls. So I preferred Shyrose's warmth and humor to Ali's anger and hostility, but I also favored John's kindness and empathy to Denise's hateful spite. So my sense that I preferred the company of girls to that of boys may have been a result of mixing up issues of behavior and gender. I preferred certain behaviors which I was all too willing to equate with gender. Still, I suspect that I did find aggressive, competitive, and disruptive behaviors in boys menacing. For me these behaviors foreshadowed the macho, insensitive, crude, sexist actions and attitudes of (some) men (admittedly another stereotype and a self-serving one at that) that have led me, as an adult, to prefer the company of women (*and* other men who have rejected dominant conceptions of masculinity). There was also a sense in which, as the father of a daughter, I saw the boys' actions as a potential threat (to her).

Whatever the source(s) and the degree of my discomfort with the boys in my class, the rejection of aggressive, insensitive behavior is not the problem. Some might even consider this praiseworthy. However, did I reject the behaviors or the boys and, to the degree that I rejected the boys, did I contribute to the behaviors I abhorred by fostering a sense of alienation in my male students? And, to the degree that I may have favored the girls in my class in the short term, did I do them harm in the long term by reinforcing gendered views of the world in which people's worth is tied to their gender? These are complicated questions worthy of serious reflection and, although I'm not sure I can ever be sure of the answers to the questions, I am certain the issues raised here are more questions about humanity and morality than of gender. This does not mean, however, that teachers should ignore gender any more than they should ignore the race and class of their students (in the name of equal treatment). Students live gendered (and classed and raced) lives and to ignore gender is to efface the lived experiences of our students. Similarly, to ignore gender is to pretend that sexism does not limit the opportunities of our female students. The challenge is to acknowledge the influence of gender on the way males and females live their lives, but to confront sexist stereotypes that limit the life chances of girls and women.

Girls' Space and Boys' Space: The Social Geography of Gender

One of the most familiar patterns of the social geography of the schools I visit is the overwhelming tendency of students to divide themselves along gender lines (recalling the enforced gender segregation of my own schooling at a Catholic elementary school in northern Ohio) and so it was for my third graders. On the playground, for example, the girls in my class tended to congregate on the blacktopped area near the rear entrance to the school. Some of the girls played ball games, but most preferred to stand and talk (at least that's how it seemed). The boys, however, played games like football, soccer, tag, and baseball in the field well away from the school building. The boys came onto the blacktop (the girls' space) only to play handball against the side of the school, to disrupt the girls' games, and, sometimes, to do both at the same time. The girls complained whenever the boys invaded their space and they rarely ventured into the boys' space although there was one fifth-grade girl who regularly played baseball with the boys. (These patterns, in which girls stick close to the school and boys claim the spaces further away from the school building, have also been reported by other researchers [see Thorne 1993].) There was also a space on the playground of Norwood School, at the boundary between the blacktop and the field, where (some) of the boys in my class occasionally chased the girls who drifted into this space. Girls who strayed across this neutral zone into the middle of the boys' games (e.g., soccer, football, tag, etc.) risked being knocked down and/or verbally harassed (e.g., "Get OUT of here."). In this way, gender segregation on the Norwood playground wasn't simply a matter of preference (i.e., the girls naturally chose to stick close to the school in the same way young girls are thought to play close to their homes). The boys' physically policed the gender boundaries on the playground preserving for themselves significantly more space relative to the girls. This, of course, raises the possibility that the girls in my class were less active on the playground because of the quantity and quality (the hard blacktop may have discouraged certain games and activities which risk falling down) of the space they chose to inhabit rather than any innate tendencies to be less active than the boys. (This reminds me of the argument that the socially constructed practice of girls carrying around dolls limits their development by "disabling" one of their arms.)

Similar patterns of gender segregation were evident inside our classroom. Whenever we gathered in a circle on the carpet, for example, the girls sat in the area closest to me and the boys gathered in the semi-circle furthest from me (Sometimes I'd disrupt this pattern by moving across the circle to sit with the boys.) When we lined up for gym the boys gathered (sometimes they pushed) in the front of the line, the girls in the back. Reading partners and collaborative writing also tended toward single-gender groupings (There were many exceptions to this pattern, however, which I'll say more about later.) The comic book reading group, which emerged alongside the "Scary, Evil Book Club," was exclusively male. Boys also gravitated toward books featuring male characters (e.g., Robin Hood, Hardy Boys, etc.) while the girls seemed to prefer books and stories featuring females (e.g., Ramona Quimby, Amelia Bedelia, Babysitter books, etc.).

The pattern of boys' and girls' activities dividing in the familiar geography of gender (Thorne 1993) is so commonplace that it is often taken as natural. However, there was nothing natural about the boys in my class reading comic books or the girls hanging around the blacktop. I've already described the less than natural process by which the boys enforced gender boundaries on the playground. The gendering of comic book reading was no more natural. First of all, not all and only boys read comic books. In fact, comic book reading *became* a boys' (i.e., gendered) activity in my classroom despite the fact that it was two girls, Catherine and Jennifer, who first brought comic books into our classroom. It was only over a period of several months that the students in my class constructed comic book reading as a boys' activity. And, since I have good reason to believe that several girls in my class continued to enjoy reading comics at home, comic book reading became a *boys' activity* only in that public space known as third grade.

Two other literacy practices that became gendered over the course of the school year were reading and writing poetry and the reading of joke books. Early in the year many of the boys in my class loved listening to and reading poetry, especially Shel Silverstein, and joke books were a genre that attracted both boys and girls. However, these preferences began to shift in gender specific ways over a period of several months. The gendering of poetry and joke books was nearly complete by January when it was my class's turn to take responsibility for reading school-wide announcements over the intercom. The usual practice was for students from each class (usually two at a time) to read a few announcements and then read a "saying of the day" from a book provided by the principal. My class, however, decided (I don't know how this happened) to offer an alternative to the saying of the day by reading either a poem or a joke. Remarkably, all the boys in my class read jokes over the intercom and all of the girls read poems (I allowed students to sign up to do morning announcements which produced only same-gender pairs.) My students' participation in the morning announcements became a particularly visible part of the process by which certain literacy practices—in this case poetry and joke books—became gendered. Arguably, the public nature of the morning announcements may have influenced students' choice of readings although, even if this were true, it still indicates my students had a sense that boys should prefer joke books and girls should prefer poetry. And, although I can't be completely sure of this, my recollection is that this pattern—boys read joke books, girls read (and wrote) poems—was fairly rigid during the second half of the school year.

The practice of writing notes was another literacy practice that developed into a gendered activity over the course of the school year. At the beginning of the school year, boys were just as likely as girls to write and send notes to their friends. Several of the boys facilitated this practice by constructing mailboxes which they hung up in the message corner (see Chapter 1). However, by the middle of the year only girls were sending notes to each other. Somehow, over the course of the year, note writing was gendered by virtue of being associated with girls (who did it) and boys (who did not). Similar processes seemed to be at work in defining certain pieces of literature as "girl books" (e.g., Ramona Quimby) and other works as "boy books" (e.g., Robin Hood, Tarzan). Again, there is no natural explanation for these preferences since, for example, early in the year several boys acknowledged having read and enjoyed Ramona books.

Subtly, but surely, the students in my class, as in the broader culture in and out of school, learned to associate certain activities and characteristics with boys and girls as part of the practices and processes "through which children and adults create and recreate gender in their daily interactions" (Thorne 1993, 4). This, in turn, enabled students to define themselves in terms of these activities (e.g., boys play active sports in the field, don't write notes, prefer comic books to Babysitter books and jokes to poetry). Boys were boys because they didn't do girl things and not because of any biological differences (my boys always based their claims of superiority on the basis of preferred activities or characteristics (e.g., size, strength, courage) and never anatomical differences). Similarly, girls were girls because they didn't do boy things. Constructing gender largely on the basis of activities provided a tidy means for policing the boundaries of gender. For a boy to do girl things, for example, risked being "like a girl" with the concomitant loss of status that goes with being a female in late twentieth century North American society. Boys' activities, therefore, weren't as natural as much as they were safe, part of not being a girl. Girls, on the other hand, could more safely risk being like a boy since boy things have a higher social status (which is why being called a "sissie" or a "girl" is, for a boy, pejorative in the same way that associating females with male characteristics is not).

The social construction of gender, as my field notes demonstrate, is not natural. Nor is it benign. Constructing particular activities or spaces as male or female, for example, foreshadows the historical practice of limiting the social and vocational choices of adult females

by defining certain occupations and spaces as male (women's movements are restricted by the threat of sexual assault much as the
threat of being knocked down or threatened limited my third-grade
girls' movements on the playground). Perhaps this is why I found
the increasing tensions between boys and girls in my classroom so
disturbing.

One manifestation of this tension was the tendency of some of the
boys in my class to shun the girls and, to a lesser degree, for girls to
shun boys. For instance, my efforts to organize reading buddies in
our class on the basis of reading was undermined by the outright
refusal of some boys to work with (any) girl. Denise was the only girl
who refused to read with a boy (although she wouldn't work with
many of the girls either). The antagonism between (some) boys and
girls led me to allow students to select their own reading partners,
eventually making reading partners optional (but encouraged).
Although there were situations in which many of my students would
engage in mixed-gender interactions, Nicholas, Peter, and Nader
never had much to do with the girls. The girls would avoid particular boys (usually Ali), but only Denise avoided all boys all of the
time. Nicholas, perhaps my most overtly sexist student, literally had
a tantrum when a girl suggested that he might even know a girl
named Fern in his life out of school.

An ugly incident, described in the following excerpts from my
field notes, demonstrated the need of (some?) boys to avoid even
the appearance that they might be associating with girls.

> Just before our Writers' Workshop Roya gave an invitation to her
> birthday party to Troy and Wayne. Before they began writing they
> ripped up the invitation into a thousand piece and handed it back
> to her. This struck me as one of the unkindest things I've seen this
> year. I let them know how unkind this was and how disappointed
> I was that they could be so mean to each other. They justified their
> behavior by saying that they were getting even because she's always
> bugging them although I don't think this is actually true. (field
> notes, December 2, 1991)

Wayne and Troy's actions struck me as cruel and hurtful. However,
Nicholas's angry response to the suggestion that he might even know
a girl named Fern suggests another possible interpretation. It may be
that Troy and Wayne were threatened by Roya's public invitation to

her party which, if they had accepted it, would have risked ridicule and jeopardized their identity as boys. After all, as I've already suggested, the essential characteristic of boys is that they are not girls. Showing an interest in girls and girl things may have risked this identity (see Thorne 1993).

Another way the boys and girls in my class demonstrated their gender biases was through their response to literary characters. For example:

> After we read the chart story I finished reading *The Washout* (Carrick 1978). [I had started this the previous day.] Then we had a brief discussion about Chris, the main character in this book. We talked particularly about what kind of boy Chris was and whether or not they'd like him. Unfortunately, this divided along gender lines. The boys [at least those who spoke up] liked Christopher and the girls didn't "because he was a boy." (field notes, January 7, 1992)

Similarly, when I asked Wayne to talk about the characters in the Boxcar Children book he was reading he indicated that, while he like Henry and Benny, he didn't like Violet and Jessie because the things they said "were stupid." Roya's response to the giant in a version of *Jack and the Beanstalk* is a particularly amusing example of the way gender influenced my students' responses to literary characters.

> After morning announcements I read another version of *Jack and the Beanstalk*. During the subsequent discussion the children debated whether this was a "good guy" or a "bad guy" story. Naturally, this discussion focussed on whether Jack and the giant were "good" or "bad." There were differing opinions about whether Jack was good or bad, but everyone agreed that the giant was bad. However, at the end of the discussion Roya volunteered her opinion that the giant was "a good guy." When I asked her why she thought so she replied, "because he eats boys." (field notes, October 11, 1991)

To many people these stories of gender segregation may seem harmless enough since they recall our own experiences as children. It might even be argued that some degree of gender separation is a necessary part of the natural process by which children learn the gendered identities that figure so prominently in social relations in

North American society. However, this process has done women and girls no good. Boys who learn to define masculinity in opposition to femininity will almost certainty come to see girls as the antithesis of the qualities they value in themselves. If girls are the opposite of boys (as in the opposite sex), then boys are strong and girls are weak, boys are brave and girls are timid, and so on, thus justifying the whole range of sexist practices by which males dominate females. I need to own up to my own participation in this process. To the degree that I showed any preference for the girls in my class I no doubt helped to "produce a sense of gender as dichotomy and opposition" (Thorne 1993, 5).

The common practice of using war metaphors ("battle of the sexes," "sexual conquest," "fending off sexual advances," etc.) to describe male-female relations suggests another way of interpreting the separation of boys and girls in my classroom. If we understand gender relations as a war (see Lakoff and Johnson [1980] for a discussion of how metaphors form a basis for world views) then it makes sense that many boys and girls would want to avoid fraternizing with the enemy. Gender relations as war also suggests one interpretation of an unfortunate episode that occurred in October.

> We agreed to play kickball outside for gym. At their urging (they voted) we divided into girls and boys and the girls got to go first. Unfortunately, several of the girls refused to participate so I suggested that I help the girls a bit. This was a huge mistake. After I made a couple of outs for the girls four of the boys stomped off because they felt this wasn't fair. Wayne was in tears saying I was "against the boys" . . . There was also a lot of violence. Catherine and Ali got into a fight. Later Charles shoved Catherine. Peter threw a ball at her when she was on the ground. We had a class meeting to air it all out and it was difficult but we agreed in the end that I wouldn't participate next time. I drew the condition that we would never divide up by boys and girls again. Wayne was still so upset during this discussion, almost forty-five minutes after the fact, that he started crying again. (field notes, October 16, 1991)

Clearly it was foolish of me to sanction a game of girls against the boys (a mistake I never made again). But I also believe that taking the side of the girls led Wayne and those who took his lead to conclude that I had betrayed the boys (a traitor to my gender). I believe this sense of being a traitor to my gender poisoned my relations with some of the boys in my class throughout the school year.

There is, of course, a much more sinister side to the battle of the sexes. If males and females are engaged in a war we might also expect physical casualties (a study of domestic violence sponsored by the Canadian government concluded that there is currently a war against women going on). It was this sense of gender relations that I found particularly disturbing in my third-grade class. Throughout the school year girls complained about being pushed, shoved, and kicked by the boys in and out of the classroom. In a particularly violent incident Ali stabbed Catherine with a pencil with such force that the tip of the pencil had to be surgically removed. As the altercation around the play practice demonstrates, the girls could fight back and in some cases they initiated violence. More often, however, the boys were first to resort to physical force and, because they were usually stronger than the girls, it was usually the girls who were hurt.

There were also several incidents in our class that foreshadowed the sexual harassment that plagues girls in the upper elementary grades and high school (Larkin 1994). On a single day in November Martin was accused of looking up Melissa's dress (although he denied it I later overheard him boasting to other boys that he had done it) and looking under the stalls in the girls' bathroom (he was caught by another teacher). During one week in March I had to talk to Jeffrey, Hugh, and Nicholas about pinching girls' bums.

Both boys and girls contributed to an oppositional sense of gender by actively shunning one another. The boys, however, were more likely than girls to resort to intimidation and violence in the "battle of the sexes." The girls, for their part, were more likely to use taunting as a means of creating a gendered sense of US versus THEM. For example:

> Today when we sang the "Cat Came Back" the girls adapted the lyrics to taunt the boys. Instead of "the cat came back . . ." they inserted the names of boys, e.g., "Wayne came back . . ." and, at the end of the chorus they improvised "He just couldn't stay away (pause) **FROM VERONICA**." (June 16, 1992)

Ironically, in this example the girls managed to put the boys down by associating them with girls which had the effect of diminishing their own status.

Undoing Gender

Taunting, fighting, shunning, and avoidance did not, however, characterize all the interactions between the boys and girls in my classroom. Readers will recall that one of most interesting aspects of the "Scary, Evil Book Club" (discussed in Chapter 1) was that both boys and girls came together to read, discuss, and write about scary books. There were many other examples during the year of mixed-gender groups coming together to share a book or a poem or collaborate on reading or writing a text. Early in the year, for example, it was common for two or three boys to sit at Crystal's feet as she read Shel Silverstein poems to them. Later in the year I observed Jeffrey and Crystal taking turns reading to each other. Shyrose sometimes sought out Charles as a reading partner. Many literature sharing groups (that were determined by sign-up sheets) included both boys and girls. The group of students who wrote a get-well card for my father included boys and girls. Both boys and girls were in the group of students that read fan magazines and wrote fan letters to the stars of *Beverly Hills, 90210* early in the year. Troy, who claimed that he and his mother burned Ramona Quimby books to underscore his assertion that he would never be interested in a book featuring a female character, was among several boys who willingly (and warmly) read with first-grade reading buddies who were girls. Over the course of the school year, almost all the boys in my class interacted with girls around reading and writing (Nicholas and Ali were, I think, the only exceptions). Reading and writing also provided many occasions for girls to interact with boys (here Denise may have been the only exception).

Barrie Thorne (1993) found in her research that the most comfortable cross-gender groups emerged around small group activity like creating a play or some crafts project. In my class reading and writing provided a relaxed space for boys and girls to work together in support of a common goal. These events stood in sharp contrast to the mutual antagonism that dominated cross-gender interactions in many other contexts in my third grade class. Overall, gender relations in my class were strongly affected by the social setting. Public spaces (e.g., the playground) and large group activities seemed to heighten tensions between boys and girls while more relaxed, small group activities often provided a space where boys and girls could comfortably work together. This supports Thorne's observation that:

> When kids maneuver to form same-gender groups on the playground or organize a kickball game as 'boys-against-the-girls,' they

produce a sense of gender as dichotomy and opposition. And when girls and boys work cooperatively on a classroom project, they actively undermine a sense of gender as opposition. This emphasis on action and activity, and on everyday social practices that are sometimes contradictory, provides an antidote to the view of children as passively socialized. Gender is not something one passively 'is' or 'has'; . . . . we 'do gender.' (1993, 5)

In my third grade classroom we *did* and *undid* gender in contradictory ways. If I'd had a clearer idea of what was going on at the time I might have been able to take better advantage of activities that had the effect of dissolving the boundaries of gender and, at the same time, avoided activities that emphasized the oppositional identities of boys and girls (Thorne 1993). There were moments, however, when I did attempt to confront sexism directly in my classroom.

Feminist Tales

Recognizing the harm sexism does to girls and women, I often took advantage of opportunities to confront sexist behavior and beliefs. When I read to my class, especially during our folktale study early in the year, I often drew my students' attention to sexist stereotypes. After I read versions of *Cinderella* and *Sleeping Beauty*, for example, I tried to get my class to consider the ways females were portrayed in these stories. In the following discussion (if it can be called that) I tried to get my students to take up the ways males and females tend to relate to each other in folktales and fairy tales and the effect this might have on our perceptions of females and males more generally. The following is an excerpt of a discussion also taken up in Chapter 6.

MR. MARLING: In what ways are these two stories alike?
ROYA: Both are about girls.
RAZIKA: There are fairies in both.
MR. MARLING: How do they describe the prince in both stories?
CATHERINE: They have curly hair. It looks white, like a wig . . .
MR. MARLING: In both stories who rescues whom?
ROYA: The boy rescues the girl, but the girls don't like it because it's a boy.
MR. MARLING: How does that make the girls feel to always be rescued?

CATHERINE: Horrible. They feel horrible because they have to get married, they have to have children, and they don't live happily ever after.[1]

ROYA: It makes them feel silly.

MR. MARLING: Why is that?

ROYA: They always have to get rescued by boys.

WAYNE: [But] boys are more daring. The boys take greater chances. [presumably explaining why the boys always did the rescuing]

MR. MARLING: Wayne has a point. In the books they do portray the boys as being more daring and brave and they portray the girls as being weak. [At this point the discussion disintegrated[2] and we moved on to the next activity.]

I followed up this discussion over the next several days by reading and discussing with my students several folk tales with strong, independent female protagonists. These included Robert Munsch's *Paper Bag Princess* (1980) which features a strong, independent-minded princess who rescues—and then rejects—a chauvinistic, weak-willed prince. Parts of the discussion of the *Paper Bag Princess* are excerpted below.

MR. MARLING: How is this story like other folktales? How is it different? [Troy and some of the other boys were particularly hostile to this story and the discussion was momentarily sidetracked by a discussion of whether or not kids liked folktales.]

MR. MARLING: What made the *Paper Bag Princess* different from other folktales?

FATIMA: There were dragons.

JOHN: There were castles.

SHYROSE: There were princes and princesses.

MR. MARLING: Which stories were most like the *Paper Bag Princess* that we read? [no response]

---

1. It is worth pointing out that Catherine's attitudes toward prince charming were probably affected by the abuse her mother suffered at the hands of her father who no longer lived with them when I met Catherine.

2. Listening to this tape was not a pleasant experience for me. Many of the students were very poorly behaved during the discussion, which clearly went on much too long. It seems that I was bound and determined to address my agenda here with the result that my students were nearly out of control. I would have done better to have moved on and returned to this discussion on another day.

MR. MARLING: We read a bunch of stories we called rescue stories where somebody rescued somebody? Is this a rescue story? [There was some disagreement, but most everyone agreed that this was a rescue story.]

MR. MARLING: Who rescued whom in *Sleeping Beauty* and *Snow White?*

FATIMA: In *Sleeping Beauty* and *Snow White* the prince rescued the princess.

MR. MARLING: Who rescued whom in the *Paper Bag Princess?*

ROYA: The princess saved herself.

DENISE: The princess saved the prince.

FATIMA: No, the princess saved the boy. [She seemed not to have noticed that the "boy" was a prince.]

SEVERAL VOICES: The princess saved the prince. Prince Ronald.

MR. MARLING: I wonder how the girls feel about that.

[When Roya offered that this showed girls were pretty and boys were ugly there was a brief exchange of insults between several boys and girls.]

MR. MARLING: If I was always rescued by a boy, do you know how I'd feel?

CATHERINE: I wouldn't like being saved by a boy.

[My repeated efforts to get different girls to offer an opinion did not meet with much success.]

ROYA: They should find out if girls want to be saved by boys . . .

PETER: Roya, if you had your legs cut off would you want a boy to save you?

ROYA: Well, yeah . . .

MR. MARLING: One of the things I notice in books that I think is kind of bad . . . It isn't who is saving whom, it's that in most books the boys save the girls and this is one of the few books I've ever seen where the girl saves the boy. What do you think about that?

CATHERINE: I think this is better than any of the other books . . .

[When some of the boys volunteered that if they were in danger they wouldn't mind being saved by a girl I made the point that I agreed with this sentiment. And when Wayne suggested that boys were more daring because they had bigger brains I first offered that many of the smartest people I know are women. I then asked Andrea, who was the tallest person in our class to stand next to Wayne, who was at least five inches shorter. I then told them that bigger people had bigger brains, but this didn't necessarily mean that Andrea was smarter than Wayne.]

My heavy handed approach to these discussions denied my students an opportunity to come to grips with sexist stereotypes on their own terms and, for that reason alone, these discussions were probably ineffective. But I kept trying. Books like Robert Munsch's *Giant, or, Waiting for the Thursday Boat,* (1989) for example, provided additional opportunities to discuss non-traditional portrayals of girls and women. Giant is a story about a struggle between St. Patrick and a giant who both end up in heaven and meet God who, in Munsch's tale, is a little girl.

> After we finished *Giant* I asked the class who they thought the little girl was. Some suggested that maybe she was an angel. Someone else suggested that she was St. Patrick's daughter. Someone even suggested that she was the giant's little girl. When the discussion had run its course I suggested that I thought the little girl might be God. No one agreed, but one student was willing to concede that maybe she was God's daughter. They all agreed, however, that God was "a boy." Someone said that God was a boy because "he" made boys first. . . . (field notes, October 23, 1991)

I was no more successful using this discussion to engage my students in an in-depth look at the portrayal of males and females in folktales although the discussion of *Giant* gave some indication of the tenacity to which both boys and girls held onto gender stereotypes (i.e., God couldn't possibly be a girl). Worse, these discussions may have only had the effect of pitting the boys against the girls that I fear only fuelled the gender antagonisms that already existed in my classroom. In any case, I'm disappointed I didn't handle these discussion with more skill although I would have done better if I had used literature to engage my students in a long-term study of gender stereotypes (Russell 1995).

One other way I attempted to challenge sexist practices in the classroom was by trying to insure that girls and boys had equal access to all activities, spaces, and materials in our classroom. I refused, for example, to let the boys control the computers or certain board games (e.g., basketball) during free times like indoor recesses. And when a school board consultant set out to teach my students how to use electronic mail I demanded that equal numbers of boys and girls received this training even though it sometimes meant insisting that some of the girls (who were reluctant) took advantage of this opportunity. Still, it doesn't seem that I was particularly successful translating my own beliefs about the evils of sexism into effective anti-sexist pedagogy.

CONCLUSION

When I was teaching third grade my attention was drawn to presumed differences between the boys and girls in my classroom, differences in the ways I treated boys and girls, and differences in the ways they treated each other. At the time my casual observations reinforced a range of gender stereotypes and my suspicion that I tended to favor the girls in my class. A closer examination of the data reveal a more complicated story. I observed no behaviors that were unique to either girls or boys although, over the course of the school year, some behaviors and activities did become gendered (i.e., associated with boys or girls). I am also less certain that I favored *the girls* over *the boys* as much as I preferred behaviors more common (but not unique) among girls than boys.

Still, over the course of the year my students' identities became more and more gendered, but gender was typically defined in oppositional ways. That is, boys were boys because they weren't girls and didn't do girls' things. Girls were girls because they weren't boys and didn't do boys' things. This sense of gender as opposition permeated my students' relations with one another, at least in many settings. Certainly I worked to overcome gender-based animosity in my class and, although our classroom structure provided opportunities for relaxed, mixed-gender interactions, I failed to notice the potential of these kinds of interactions to promote alternative ways to construct more congenial gender relations. In some ways, my efforts to intervene may have actually increased the alienation of boys and girls in my class by highlighting perceived gender differences.

To the degree that the ways I thought about and treated my students and the ways my students thought about and treated each other were based on biological differences then my students and I participated in an oppositional construction of gender. It doesn't matter that these differences appeared to favor the girls. History indicates that the inequitable treatment of males and females has never favored women and girls. Creating gender dichotomies will surely ratify "the dynamics of separation, differential treatment, stereotyping, and antagonizing, and antagonism" (Thorne 1993, 163) which, at this point in our history, always works to the disadvantage of females. This does not mean, however, that teachers should pretend that gender differences do not exist. As Thorne puts it, "Teaching practices that ignore or try to play down gender differences . . . may have unintended negative consequences. Without guidance and positive intervention, boys adopt definitions that set masculinity in opposition to femininity and reproduce male dominance" (1993, 169). Instead, adults should demonstrate that there are a variety of ways of being male (and female). But drawing boys and girls together and demonstrating alternative gender identities is not enough. The "dynamics of stereotyping and power may have to be explicitly confronted" (Thorne 1993, 167). Taking up the issue of systemic sexism requires considerable skill, however. Thoughtless interventions can easily have the effect of polarizing students along gender lines, heating up the "battle of the sexes" by increasing the tensions between male and female students. Failing to do anything to confront systemic sexism, however, endorses a status quo which limits the opportunities for vocational and personal happiness for half the population for mere biological differences. Again, teaching is a complicated business and the only antidote to certain uncertainties of teaching is thoughtful, deliberate, theoretically-informed reflection.

6

Certain Knowledge in an Uncertain World
Creating a Rich Language-Learning Environment in a Third-Grade Classroom

Early in the fall of 1991 the letter carrier delivered to my house six brand new copies of *When Students Have Time to Talk* (Dudley-Marling and Searle 1991), a book I'd written with Dennis Searle. Although this wasn't my first book I was still excited and I took a copy to school that I shared with my students in the context of a writing mini-lesson on publication. I confess that I was also anxious to use this commercially-produced text to enhance my credibility with my third graders as someone who knew something about writing. Of course, I was also hoping that *When Students Have Time to Talk* would strengthen my reputation as someone who knew something about language within the academic community.

When Students Have Time to Talk drew on what Dennis and I had learned about language over the years including what we'd learned from our sociolinguistic training and the classroom research we'd done separately and together. Dennis and I hoped that *When Students Have Time to Talk* would help classroom teachers create language learning environments that expanded the range of purposes for which children used language and the settings in which they used language and create opportunities for students to use language as a means of drawing on their background knowledge and experience to support classroom learning.

I expected that my knowledge of language would be a valuable asset as I endeavored to create a supportive language learning environment in my own classroom. Certainly my background in language influenced me to place a high priority on oral language in my classroom. Several weeks before the beginning of the school year I wrote in my notes:

> Oral Language: DELIBERATELY give opportunities . . . [for students] to use language for lots of purposes (assert, question, describe, report, hypothesize, problem-solve, predict, project into others' feelings) with a range of conversational partners (teacher, classmates, other teachers, students from other classes, adult visitors). This should emerge naturally if given appropriate opportunities in science, social studies, reading, and writing. Also give opportunities for students to use language in large groups and small groups including pairs. I'd also like to encourage oral story telling throughout the year in part by encouraging parents to share stories with us. Oral language will not be a separate study but part of the entire curriculum. My most important *personal* goal here is learning to be a better listener. (field notes, August 16, 1991)

There is every reason for me to have been confident in my ability to create a rich language learning environment for my students. But did my knowledge of language make much of a difference when I was teaching third grade? Courtney Cazden, who is widely recognized as an expert in language learning and language development, asked a similar question twenty years ago in her article, "How knowledge about language helps the classroom teacher—or does it: A personal account" (Cazden 1976). Like me, Cazden returned to the classroom "to go back with children, to try to put into practice some of the ideas about child language and education that . . . [she] had been teaching and writing about, and to rethink questions for future research" (Cazden 1976, 74). In general, Cazden's experience suggests an uneven relationship between teachers' knowledge and language instruction. Knowledge of language did help Cazden deal with invented spellings and dialectical differences. However, the structures of schooling, the physical environment, and student characteristics were among the factors that limited the influence of her expertise on the language curriculum.

This chapter draws on analyses of my field notes and nearly twenty–five hours of audiotape, portions of which I transcribed, to examine the nature of the language learning environment I created for my students and to speculate on the degree to which the language learning environment I created for my students drew on my knowledge of language and language instruction.

LANGUAGE INSTRUCTION IN A THIRD-GRADE CLASSROOM

When students have time to talk "they are able to try out their language, to listen to others respond to their language, and to hear other children . . . use language, getting the information they need to continue developing as language users" (Dudley-Marling and Searle 1991, viii). As I indicated in an earlier chapter ("Reading, Writing, and Friends") my students had lots of opportunities to talk in our classroom including, for example: as they read and wrote; at the art, math, and science centers; between lessons; as they came and went from the classroom; during literature sharing; and, to a lesser degree, during large-group discussions. The only time I prohibited talk in my classroom was for the first ten minutes of writing time (and later in the year for the first ten minutes of reading) and even then I often used this time to conference with individual students. In the rest of this chapter I'm going to focus my attention on opportunities for talk in my classroom during four different classroom routines: whole-class literature discussions, literature-sharing groups, writing time, and small and whole group science lessons. I begin with an analysis of talk during whole class literature discussions.

How Is This Story Like or Different From . . . ?

In *When Students Have Time to Talk* Dennis and I wrote, "In general, whole-class discussions will never be a good way to encourage language use for many students . . . Large-group discussions tend to be dominated by more capable or outgoing students . . . [and] teachers devote a lot of time to calling students to attention or asking them to be quiet" (Dudley-Marling and Searle 1991, 25). We also warned that large-group discussions—because they tend to be dominated by teachers who ask circumscribed, factual questions to which they (usually) already know the answer—limit opportunities for verbal interactions among students.

Still, I imagined that whole-class literature discussions would be a useful way to help my third graders learn to talk about story elements like plot, setting, and character development. So each morning after our oral reading time I asked my students questions about the stories I'd read to them. During our folktale study, for example, I asked questions I hoped would draw students' attention to characteristic features of folktales or features that distinguished among different types of folktales. Consider, for example, this discussion that followed the reading of a Cinderella story in late October.

MR. MARLING: Any comments about that story? [pause] I'd be particularly interested in hearing how it was like and how it was different from other folktales we'd read. [another brief pause]

MR. MARLING: Catherine?

CATHERINE: It was different because it had two balls. [This comment leads to a lot of snickering by the boys.]

MR. MARLING: How is this story like or different from other folktales we've read?

NADER: It's been retold.

MR. MARLING: OK, it's been retold. It's a story handed down among the common people. [Here I repeated a definition of folktales Troy had found in the dictionary and shared with us.]

MR. MARLING: What else? Crystal, how is this like or different from other folktales?

MR. MARLING: [silence] Let me ask you a different question. Which story have we read that's most like *Cinderella?*

MR. MARLING: Paul?

PAUL: *Sleeping Beauty.*

MR. MARLING: Why do you think so?

PAUL: I don't know.

MR. MARLING: I agree with you, but I want to know why, why do you think so?

SHYROSE: Because Cinderella, she gets married in the end and in *Sleeping Beauty* the other person gets married.

MR. MARLING: Connie?

CONNIE: There's a prince in both of them.

MR. MARLING: Roya?

ROYA: They're both about girls . . . and the boys are all ugly.

MR. MARLING: How do they describe the prince in both stories, guys? Do they describe them as ugly? [Many of the girls say they did and the boys object.]

CATHERINE: They have long curly hair. [She's interrupted by lots of talking.]

JENNIFER: Like George Washington. [Again there are lots of interruptions.]

MR. MARLING: Catherine? [asking for Catherine to continue]
CATHERINE: They have long curly hair and it's white, it looks like gray.
SCOTT: It's a wig. [Another series of interruptions.]
MR. MARLING: I want to hear . . . Razika? [Razika has raised her hand.]
RAZIKA: There are fairies in both stories.
MR. MARLING: Other similarities between *Sleeping Beauty* and *Snow White?*
[Here I misspeak myself.]
SCOTT: Snow White?
MR. MARLING: I mean *Sleeping Beauty* and *Cinderella.* . . . How are they the
same? [Again no one takes up my question but I plod along.]

This excerpt is a good example of what language educators find
so problematic about whole-class discussions. I asked a series of stereotypic questions that I had asked many times before (How is this
like or different from . . . ?) and students responded with brief, predictable answers. There is no interaction among students and,
although it isn't clear from my transcription of this excerpt, most of
my time is spent calling students to attention or disciplining individual students. Later the same day I wrote in my field notes:

> They were OK [i.e., well behaved] for the reading of *Cinderella* . . .
> but the discussion was *awful.* Many of them were chatty and disrup-
> tive . . . [and] I ended up raising my voice and I finally resorted to
> being punitive. (field notes, October 23, 1991)

This discussion—such as it was—was fairly typical of folktale discussions we had early in the year. I recognized that these discussions
weren't very good and yet I continued to ask the same tired questions.
Eventually I suspected that the problem with these discussions was the
quality of the questions I asked so I began consulting sources like Joy
Moss's *Focus Units in Literature* (1984) in an effort to find better questions. But better questions didn't improve the quality of these discussions. I began a discussion after reading from one of Beverly Cleary's
Ramona stories, for example, by asking, "Is Ramona a folktale?" This
question had at least the potential to stimulate some interesting talk
but the discussion which followed was marked by disruptive behavior
and a series of yes/no responses. For me, at least, better questions
were not the key to improving large-group discussions.

In time I guessed that (some) students didn't like the folktales I'd
been reading (they often complained they were "boring") so I
worked harder to locate more interesting books which I hoped

would stimulate richer, livelier discussion. But that didn't seem to happen either. Before resuming the reading of *The Great Brain Reforms* (Fitzgerald 1973) I asked my students a series of questions I hoped would teach them something about the role of setting in narratives. But the discussion which ensued followed the all-too-familiar pattern of Initiation-Response-Evaluation (Cazden 1988) that gave students little room to share their personal responses to a story they really enjoyed.

MR. MARLING: Before I start reading a little bit more from *The Great Brain Reforms,* we've read quite a bit now, does anyone remember the name of the town where they lived?

PAUL: Adenville?

MR. MARLING: It's called Adenville. What do we know about Adenville?

JEFFREY: There aren't a lot of people.

MR. MARLING: There aren't a lot of people in Adenville. Why do you think that?

JEFFREY: It sounds like there are only a little bunch of people there.

MR. MARLING: What else do we know about Adenville?

HUGH: There's not much money going around?

MR. MARLING: What makes you think so?

HUGH: The houses and everything. If they had lots of money the could spark the place up.

JOHN: There's a very smart kid in the town.

MR. MARLING: Who?

JOHN: Tom.

MR. MARLING: What else do we know?

ROYA: It's a small town.

MR. MARLING: You agree with Jeffrey . . . What else do we know about this town?

HUGH: There's a lot of tricksters . . .

MR. MARLING: What else do we know about this little town?

WAYNE: There's a lot of betting.

MR. MARLING: What else do we know?

NICHOLAS: They don't have stuff that we have.

MR. MARLING: Why not?

NICHOLAS: Because they hadn't invented yet.

MR. MARLING: Yeah, it was a long time ago.

MR. MARLING: You guys all seem to agree that it was a small town. Is that important to the story?

STUDENTS: Yeah.

MR. MARLING: Why? Would the story have been the same in a big city?

HUGH: There'd be more stuff going on.

MR. MARLING: How else would the story have been different if it happened in a bigger town?

SCOTT: There'd be more people.

MR. MARLING: How would this change the story? This is the story about a boy who does what?

HUGH: Tricks people . . .

Sometimes I tried to turn these discussions in a direction that I hoped would raise students' awareness of issues like sexism or racism which led me to ask even more leading questions. The following excerpt, part of which is also presented in Chapter 5, is a continuation of the earlier *Cinderella* discussion.

MR. MARLING: Here's another question for you. In both stories [*Cinderella* and *Sleeping Beauty*] who rescues whom?

ROYA: The prince rescues the girl but the girls don't like it because the prince is a boy. [lots of laughter]

MR. MARLING: I was talking to a friend of mine the other day who asked me to talk about this . . . [lots more interruptions] I want to know how the boys and girls feel, how does that make the girls look, Roya, to always be rescued by the boys?

CATHERINE: Horrible. [more interruptions] They feel horrible because they have to get married and have children and they don't live happily every after . . . It's bor-ring.

MR. MARLING: Roya, how do you think it makes the girls look to always be rescued by the boys?

ROYA: It makes them feel silly. They always have to get rescued by the boys. [inaudible but more interruptions]

SHYROSE: They got a godmother in *Sleeping Beauty* and there is a fairy godmother in *Cinderella*.

MR. MARLING: How do you think it makes the girls feel to always be rescued? What do you think about the girls always being rescued?

WAYNE: The boys are more daring . . .

MR. MARLING: Wayne's got a point. The boys are always portrayed as more daring. . . .

When I listened to this part of the *Cinderella* discussion I sensed that my students were restless and bored. It seems that I was the only

one interested in this discussion although Shyrose seemed to be trying to make the point that the role of the fairy godmothers in the
two stories contradicted my assertion that only the boys did the
rescuing.[1] Yet I persisted with my own agenda to do a bit of anti-
sexist education. I didn't seem to notice that my class was bored and
restless, my questions weren't interesting, and students' responses
were dull and predictable. Nor did I pick up on Shyrose's observation about the role of the fairy godmothers. I was too busy teaching
to notice what my students were learning. And what's true of *Cinderella, Ramona,* and the *Great Brain Reforms* was true of dozens of other
literature sharing discussions we had over the course of the school
year. The language that emerged in these discussions was rarely
interesting and keeping order was always a chore, but I just wouldn't
give it up. Why? I'm not entirely sure. It may be that I really wasn't
paying attention. I may have been working so hard keeping order
that I wasn't listening to what was really happening. Had I followed
the advice I often give to teachers in my classes and listened to the
tapes of these discussions while I was teaching I might have recognized the futility of these discussions earlier. But I was so overwhelmed with the demands of teaching and collecting data that I
never took the time to listen to these discussions—until now. I also
think I persisted with this routine—following oral reading with a
discussion—because of a stubborn determination to get things done.
I was determined to discuss the books I read because this is what I
planned to do (and what I'd seen so many other teachers do) and,
while I wasn't bound to any written curricular guide, I was bound to
my own lesson plans—at least to some extent. Being bullied out of
my lesson plans by student disruptions made me feel inadequate so
I refused to give up. I also believed that technological fixes—better
questions, better discipline techniques, changing schedules, and so
on—would magically create better whole-class discussions. The evidence indicates, however, that large-group discussions would have
always been difficult with my class and, in any case, it is doubtful that
twenty-four children talking to their teacher one at a time could ever
be conducive to rich, interactive discussions. What's disappointing is
that I knew this long before I taught third grade.

Arguably, large-group literature discussions mainly taught my students how to participate in a kind of discussion peculiar to schooling.

---

1. I am indebted to Chris Dudley-Marling for this observation.

Students didn't learn how to talk about books as much as they learned a particular way of talking about books (short answers, speaking one at a time, etc.). It pains me to say it, but, in whole-class literature discussions learning to sit quietly and (appearing to) listen may have been more important than anything my students had to say about the books I read to them. Fortunately, these whole-class literature discussions were usually brief, rarely longer than 5–10 minutes. This was also one of the few times each day when I did whole-class activities with my third graders and the kind of language I hoped for in the whole-class literature discussions did emerge in our small, literature-sharing groups.

Tarzan, Son of Caliph?

I organized literature-sharing groups (see Peterson and Eeds 1990, Short and Pierce 1990) in the following way. First I'd announce that I was putting out several copies of a particular book title. Then I'd invite my students to sign up to read the book together (first come, first serve). Once a literature-sharing group was established I met with the group every couple of days during our regular reading time to talk with them about their book. Of course, students often talked among themselves about the books they were reading (recall the discussion of the Scary, Evil Book Club in Chapter 1). In the context of small-group discussions my students shared varying perspectives, argued over meaning, took up issues of plot, setting, and character, and drew on their background knowledge and experience to make sense of texts. In short, what didn't happen during the large-group literature discussions did occur in literature-sharing groups. The following excerpt is from a teacher-moderated discussion with a group of students reading a book about Tarzan. In the first part of the discussion I challenged several students' interpretations of a particular detail leading to a lively discussion in which students appealed to the text to support their arguments.

ALI: Tarzan killed the ape. And then there was a lion and a tiger.
HUGH: It wasn't a lion and a tiger. It was a saber-tooth tiger.
MR. MARLING: There was a saber-tooth tiger in this book?
NICHOLAS: Yeah.
MR. MARLING: Really?
ALI: There's a lion and there's a [interrupted]. I think there's proof [opening the book and paging through it]. There's a saber [pointing to a picture of a tiger on the page].

SCOTT: Saber . . .

HUGH: It'll say saber.

MR. MARLING: Do they call it a saber-tooth tiger?

HUGH: They don't call it saber-tooth.

ALI: But they call it Saber.

MR. MARLING: [speaking to Hugh] You know a lot about saber-tooth tigers. Do you think this could be a saber-tooth tiger?

HUGH: We-l-l . . .

SCOTT: It could be.

HUGH: It certainly doesn't look like one 'cause his teeth aren't real big. His teeth should be bigger.

MR. MARLING: Have saber-tooth tigers been around recently or have they been gone a long time?

HUGH: They've been gone a long time, back when the dinosaurs . . .

ALI: No, look [indicating a page in the book he starts reading] "She shot and the arrow hit Saber in the chest."

A few minutes later this group argued among themselves over details about Tarzan's parentage and, again, students appealed to the text to support their arguments.

NICHOLAS: Page 19. It tells you who that boy was on page 19.

MR. MARLING: What boy?

NICHOLAS: [reading from the text] "My mother was an ape." And this is a boy so it must have been Tarzan.

HUGH: His mother wasn't really an ape. He just thinks it because he was RAISED by an ape.

ALI: Yeah, he was raised by an ape. Apes killed his mother. [Several students indicated their agreement with a chorus of "yeahs."]

PAUL: Where was his dad?

HUGH: Someone killed 'em.

ALI: Yeah, someone killed 'em.

SCOTT: [paging through the book] This is where that man saves him.

MR. MARLING: Who?

SCOTT: Tarzan. [For several minutes more students page through the book talking about what happened at various points in the book and making reference to the pictures but continuing to discuss and argue about various incidents in the book. When one of them pages back to a picture of Tarzan as a boy, Nicholas asks:]

NICHOLAS: Is Tarzan crying?

ALI: He lost his [inaudible] because he didn't know what to do and his father died. And the ape heard the baby crying and the ape was called Caliph . . .

OTHERS: [a chorus of "No-o-o]

HUGH: Geez, man.

ALI: [pointing to a picture of an ape] This is his mother. Doesn't this look like his mother?

HUGH: You said the ape was called Caliph.

ALI: The ape was called Caliph.

HUGH: No it wasn't.

MR. MARLING: Can you show us the part where it says his name is Caliph?

ALI: Yeah!

HUGH: You're nuts. [pages through book]

ALI: OK, now I'll prove it. I'll prove it now. [turning pages] I'll prove that the ape's name was Caliph.

MR. MARLING: Can you guys find a place that proves that it's not [talking to the students who disagree with Ali]?

SCOTT: What page is it?

ALI: OK now, now, this girl [point to a picture in the text] was named Alice, right? And this guy, what's his name?

PAUL: Jonathon.

ALI: Yeah, John. That's not his mother and father. I'll prove to you that his mother was Caliph, because none of them are named Caliph and then look at the end.

HUGH: Tarzan.

ALI: [reading from the text] "I was born [inaudible]. My mother was an ape.

HUGH: His mother wasn't an ape. He just thinks that.

ALI: Caliph. Caliph. Here. There. [pointing to a place in the text] That little bit, part. "Her [inaudible] fallen to death Caliph had to take a chance. She jumped from one tree to another. The two trees were far apart. Caliph made it, but the baby did not. [some arguing which isn't audible]

ALI: The woman was called Alice, the man was called Jonathon Stokes, and the ape was called Caliph.

HUGH: But back here you said, their names are Alice and Jonathon, right?

ALI: Yeah.

HUGH: You said that they weren't the mother and father.

ALI: No, these were the mother and father but he grew up with Caliph.

This exchange, typical of other literature-sharing groups I listened to, has a give-and-take quality absent from whole-class literature discussions. Differences in interpretation aren't subjected to teacher evaluation (although I do ask if the tiger is really a saber-tooth), but worked out in a discussion in which students try to find support for their arguments and, perhaps, reconsider their reading of the text. There's also a certain authenticity to this discussion. Students are talking about their book, not just learning routines for talking about books as in our whole-class discussions. This discussion also gives Hugh an opportunity to draw on the reading he'd been doing at home about saber-tooth tigers. Similarly, in a literature-sharing group reading Arthurian legends, John compared what he had read to a movie on King Arthur he'd seen at home.

Overall, literature-sharing groups provided students with opportunities to engage in extended conversations in which they used language as a means of sharing, constructing meaning, debating, providing evidence, drawing on background knowledge and experience, and, at the same time, learning the give and take of ordinary conversation. As the Scary, Evil Book Club discussion on pages 16–19 demonstrates, students did not require my presence to engage in quality talk.

I should also note that, while literature-sharing groups worked fairly well, not all literature-sharing discussions were equally successful. Occasionally, students found the books they were reading uninteresting and sometimes I would ask questions that inhibited rather than stimulated discussion. Still, these small-group discussions demonstrated the potential for language learning that rarely appeared in the large-group discussions.

Siblings, Witches, and Killer Tomatoes

Writing conferences provided regular opportunities for students to use language as a means of collaborating on meanings and infusing the curriculum with their personal experiences (see Chapter 1). Perhaps because writing conferences were conducted either individually or in very small groups, writing conferences sometimes provided rare opportunities for students to take extended conversational turns within the structure of a classroom routine. The following excerpt is Nicholas's contribution to the sibling stories (see p. 46) that emerged when I talked to Roya about writing topics.

Me and my brother and sister and, me and my brother and sister, and my mom and dad, we went, we got my mom's friends and we went to the car because my mom's friends have this truck and they're getting some, um, furniture, right? From my grandma's house because she didn't want them anymore. And, um, me, my sister, and brother, three girls, me, my sister, and my brother and three girls were in this truck and, um, I was pretending like I was driving. And I pulled back the thing that makes it go back. And there was this hill. And behind it there was a house. And they brought a new car. It was a Porsche, a Jag, I don't know. And I crashed into that thing and I was rolling down the hill with the three girls and my sister jumped out. And we rolled over her and she got a cast.

Taken together the sibling stories provided a means by which Roya, Lila, Jeffrey, Catherine, and Nicholas were able to draw on their personal experience for writing while giving them the chance to tell a story. This kind of opportunity was particularly valuable for Nicholas, whose stories were often confusing although he did relatively well here.

Writing, like the literature-sharing groups, also provided students with opportunities to use language to construct meanings collaboratively. In the following excerpt Scott and Hugh worked together to construct a story about "killer tomatoes" all the while drawing on the knowledge of the Killer Tomatoes cartoon series.

Hugh: [commenting on what Scott had written] So "the tomato split up." How about "the killer tomato split up"?

Scott: Every day they would multiply.

Hugh: How about "every day they multiply."

Scott: What do you mean?

Hugh: Multiply. Don't you know what multiply means?

Scott: They transform . . . They don't transform. They're like this and they change into two. They come out from each other and there's two of them. And they keep going on more and more and more until there's a whole army of them. [This stimulates a discussion of recent movies they've seen.]

Hugh: How about every time the water comes on the, a tomato they'll turn into a killer tomato. Because that's what the lady did. She started washing a tomato and it turned into a killer tomato [referring to the cartoon show].

SCOTT: She takes a [inaudible] and pours it all over and it grows into a killer tomato.

HUGH: How the killer tomato grows up in one year and it comes up to be a grown up in one year. And after that year they had babies . . .

An excerpt from a writing conference demonstrates a different kind of collaboration in which Shyrose and I talk around a text as a means of helping her create a story that is more considerate of the needs of her audience.

Shyrose is reading her story about a witch to me.

SHYROSE: ". . . so she put them in bed and sold the house."

MR. MARLING: Sold the house? I don't get it.

SHYROSE: You'll find out . . . Then she said to the police . . .

MR. MARLING: Wait a minute. Now we've got a problem. You, all of a sudden you have the police here out of nowhere. Where did they come from?

SHYROSE: OK, OK, look. "Sold the house . . ."

MR. MARLING: She put the three girls to bed.

SHYROSE: Yea-uh.

MR. MARLING: I'm fine with you here. Then she starts selling the house and then the police come.

SHYROSE: No, no, no, no, no. And she sold the house to an old lady, OK?

MR. MARLING: While they were in bed? [an incredulous tone]

SHYROSE: Yeah, 'cause they were dead. Remember?

MR. MARLING: But you didn't tell us they were dead.

SHYROSE: Yeah, they were choked.

MR. MARLING: Choked? Could you put "to death" here then [indicating the place in the text she might add "to death"].

SHYROSE: Yah.

MR. MARLING: Choked to death.

SHYROSE: OK.

ROYA: [who's been listening] Who are the girls?

SHYROSE: [ignores the question] She sold the house to an old lady.

MR. MARLING: Why, what . . . I'm fine up to here [pointing to the text] Why would she put them to bed after they're dead?

SHYROSE: I don't know.

MR. MARLING: I'm having trouble with this part. She puts them to bed, they're dead.

SHYROSE: Yeah.

MR. MARLING: . . . and then she sells the house.

SHYROSE: No, no.

MR. MARLING: . . . and then the police come. Why do the police come?

SHYROSE: You don't get it. You don't get it.

MR. MARLING: As a writer you have to make sure that I [the reader] do get it. I'm a reader and I don't get it. Do you get it? [to a couple of children who have been listening].

CHILDREN: No.

MR. MARLING: I don't get it either. I think it gets a little confusing there.

SHYROSE: I'll take this part out [the part about selling the house].

In general, writing—like literature sharing and unlike the whole-class literature discussions—provided opportunities for my third graders to use language as a means of interacting, as a tool to support their learning, and, by participating in contexts that challenged their linguistic resources, to grow as language users, that is, learning to use language for more purposes in a wider range of settings. During writing and literature-sharing it appears that my knowledge about language may have made a difference. Science, however, is a more complicated story.

Isn't Science Supposed to Be Interesting?

In my classroom, science was a center-based program and three times a week my students worked at the science center in groups of three or four doing experiments and studying various phenomena. Sometimes the science center was organized around a theme of study (e.g., magnets, plants, mixtures) and sometimes we just did experiments I hoped would engage my students' interest. In either case, I imagined that a science center full of exciting experiments and interesting things to talk about would provoke a rich stream of hypothesis-testing and problem-solving talk. The science center would be the place, I thought, where my students would be able to use their language as a means of drawing on their background knowledge and experience to make sense of new learning. I also imagined that talk would make possible collaborative sense-making as children discussed and debated the processes they observed

A month-long study of plants in September using materials in a kit provided by the school board proved to be an immediate disappointment, however. Students conducted a series of observations and experiments on plant life without much enthusiasm or talk, leading

Roya to comment, "Isn't science supposed to be interesting?" So I embarked on a quest for exciting, provocative science experiments that would stimulate rich, lively talk. I bought no less than seven books filled with science experiments and challenges appropriate for elementary-age students and some of these experiments began to produce the kind of talk I'd hoped for. In early November, for example, I challenged students at the science center to explain the "layered water problem"[2] which led to the following teacher-moderated discussion.

SCOTT: [to the boy who put his finger in the water] Do you feel anything else?
MR. MARLING: Stick you finger in and feel all the way to the bottom [he does]. Do you agree that it's water?
HUGH: Maybe there's a little air in there.
PETER: Yeah.
SCOTT: Like maybe they put in the red and bubbles go all the way around the top and then the holes aren't big enough to let the water through.
HUGH: Yeah but the water, if you added a tray full of balls and you dumped the water on it, it would just, the bubbles would pop . . .
MR. MARLING: I did this this morning . . . I'd like to hear more about what you think about what's going on there.
ROYA: I think you put food coloring in.
MR. MARLING: You're right. I did put food coloring in there . . . [Teacher takes a new container, puts water with red food coloring in one container and water with blue food coloring in the other.] If I mix these together, if I pour this on top of this what's going to happen?
HUGH: It's going to go purple.
PETER: It's going to stay at the top.
MR. MARLING: You think it's going to mix together. You think it's going to stay at the top.
STUDENTS: [together] Yeah.
MR. MARLING: What do you think's going to happen Scott?
SCOTT: It's going to turn all purple.
MR. MARLING: How about you Razika?

---

2. I had prepared a cup in which there were two layers of water. The bottom layer was salt water to which I had added blue food coloring. The top layer was ordinary tap water to which I had added red food coloring.

RAZIKA: I think it's going to mix it all together.

[Mr. Marling mixes the solutions together.]

RAZIKA: See. I told you.

SCOTT: Maybe he put something inside it.

ROYA: He had to.

HUGH: Yeah.

PETER: It's all purple.

MR. MARLING: You put your finger in there and didn't feel anything.

CRYSTAL: Maybe you put something [inaudible] in there.

MR. MARLING: Where?

SEVERAL STUDENTS: In there!

HUGH: Maybe you put something in there to hold it.

STUDENTS: Yeah . . .

MR. MARLING: What do you think I could've put in there to hold it?

HUGH: Are you, you're not lying, are you?

MR. MARLING: About what?

HUGH: Like it's all, it's all [inaudible].

SCOTT: No, it can't be.

HUGH: I know.

MR. MARLING: I'm not lying that there's water and food coloring in there but there might be something else in there.

ROYA: So there is something in there.

MR. MARLING: What could it be? How could it work? [Teacher leaves.]

SCOTT: The water's cold. There has to be one way this happens.

PETER: I know how it happens.

HUGH: Maybe, maybe . . . he put ice . . . the top starts forming ice, then the bottom, then it goes from the top to the bottom . . . then he put a shape back in here . . .

RAZIKA: There's got to be something else in it [referring to the solution].

SCOTT: There is water and food coloring.

HUGH: I know.

PETER: Warm and hot water don't mix. He probably put food coloring in warm water and hot water in it.

SCOTT: And cold water.

PETER: The bottom should be cool and the top should be hot.

HUGH: Yeah, so it doesn't mix.

SCOTT: Why don't we try it . . .

HUGH: I'm going to try that ice idea and see if that works.

ROYA: What's the ice idea?

HUGH: I'm gonna put it in the freezer downstairs right now and then see if the top freezes, stay down there for a little while . . .

PETER: He just did this this morning don't forget. It's not like it froze overnight.

HUGH: If it froze overnight the whole thing would be ice.

SCOTT: It can't be ice [inaudible].

[Teacher returns and asks about their solutions.]

HUGH: . . . you took it down to the freezer and then you froze it . . . you just froze the top and then you poured in all the blue . . .

SCOTT: [interrupts] But by the time it got here that red would already be melted, the red would already be melted . . .

The layered water problem produced lively, animated discussion (although regrettably the boys do almost all the talking) full of hypothesis testing, problem-solving, and collaborative meaning making. After everyone had had the opportunity to talk about the layered-water phenomenon at the science center we even had an interesting, whole-class discussion in which my students compared and discussed various solutions to the problem.

MR. MARLING: What were your ideas about this experiment? Raise your hand if you have something to say.

PAUL: You put a little water in then a little plastic.

HUGH: No he didn't.

MR. MARLING: Why not Hugh?

HUGH: Our group put our fingers in and it went right through. There wasn't anything there.

MR. MARLING: Alright, Hugh. Other ideas? Wayne?

WAYNE: You had this kind of food coloring, and you put it in, and it kind of goes to the top.

MR. MARLING: Did you try it?

WAYNE: No.

ALI: I did.

MR. MARLING: What happened?

ALI: You had some special food coloring that went to the top.

MR. MARLING: I didn't have any special food coloring.

ALI: You must have had something special . . .

LILA: One of them is oil and one of them is water 'cause oil and water don't mix together.

MR. MARLING: Oh, that's interesting. Listen to Lila. What did you say Lila?

LILA: One of them is water and one of them is oil and oil and water don't mix.

MR. MARLING: That isn't what happened, but that's a very good thought since oil and water don't mix. Do you know what happens if you put oil in water and try to mix them up?

ALI: The oil will stay on top.

MR. MARLING: Any other ideas about what happened? Connie?

CONNIE: You put the red in the oil and the oil will stay at the top.

MR. MARLING: But I didn't use oil, OK. It's a good idea, but it's not what I did.

PAUL: Would it have worked?

MR. MARLING: I don't know. I don't have any oil to find out. [I then show how I did the experiment and ask them if they can explain why it works.]

MR. MARLING: Why do you suppose this water stays on top of this water? Troy?

TROY: Because the other one is salt water and salt water is holding up the tap water.

MR. MARLING: Why do you think it's holding up the tap water? Paul?

PAUL: Maybe if you put in enough salt the salt would float?

HUGH: That's what I think.

MR. MARLING: Why do you think that Hugh?

HUGH: Because salt evaporates.

MR. MARLING: Eventually it does . . . Any other ideas about why this stays on top?

CHARLES: 'Cause it rises up, when you put it in it doesn't go down to the bottom . . .

This is the kind of orderly, lively, and interested discussion that I rarely achieved in the large-group, literature-sharing discussions. Lila, who rarely participated in large- or small-group discussions, offers a particularly clever solution to the water-layered problem which is notable in itself. Charles's contribution is also unusual. It would seem that I was on to something and, at the time, that's how it seemed to me, too. The success of the layered-water problem encouraged my search for ever more exciting science problems. Over the course of the rest of the school year, however, I had only limited success using the science center as a means of encouraging rich, lively talk. Experimenting with *things that float, objects that displace water,* and *flying things* did stimulate quality talk. Other science lessons, on *static electricity* and *magnetic attraction,* for example, failed to engage my students' interest and did not generate much discussion.

Of course, not every science activity is going to be equally exciting, but listening to audiotaped discussions of science lessons and reading through my field notes has convinced me that the quality of talk at the science center depended on more than the mere presence of interesting activities. The science center worked best, at least in terms of encouraging rich, stimulating talk, if I actively supported what was happening there. Whole-class introductions of science activities seemed to help. Interesting discussions were also much more likely if I met with the students at the science center—even for just a few minutes—to introduce the activity, provide demonstrations, and pose a few questions as I did in the case of the layered water problem. This recalls the discussion of teacher support in Chapter 2. Quality discussions also depended on activities that were well planned, well organized, and well articulated. Many uninspiring discussions at the science center were traceable to inadequate planning. But most of all, I'm a bit uneasy about a science curriculum designed mainly to stimulate quality talk. A science curriculum built on the language of problem solving and hypothesis testing may be just right for third graders, but surely thoughtful, silent reflection also has a place in a science program. However, this isn't something I encouraged and I have no idea the degree to which it happened on its own.

I also worry about the coherence of a science curriculum that is tied so closely to exciting activities. Doing science should always be interesting, but it's doubtful that it always needs to be exciting. I expected that culminating scientific investigations with large-group discussions would give me a means of providing some coherence to our science curriculum, but, despite the success of the whole-class discussion of the layered water activity, these discussions rarely occurred. I always planned for them (i.e., they appear in my lesson plans), but I followed through on these plans only occasionally. There was just so much to do and I always worried about the inevitable behavior problems that accompanied large-group discussions. Part of the problem was that I always planned these discussions toward the end of the day when my students were tired and difficult to engage. Whole-class science discussions would have worked best first thing in the morning or right after lunch but these were times I reserved for reading and writing, which had a higher priority for me. Perhaps science failed to stimulate consistently the kind of quality talk I hoped for because I just didn't place a high enough priority on it. There was just too much to do—or maybe I just tried to do too much in one year of teaching.

I want to conclude this chapter by returning to the question: Did my knowledge of language make a difference in the kind of learning opportunities I provided for my third-grade students? Well, yes—and no. My knowledge of language learning environments did lead me to create opportunities for my students to use oral language throughout the day and across the curriculum. This worked best, however, when I had a clear sense of the kind of talk I was aiming for, as in the literature-sharing groups and writing conferences, and, occasionally, at the science center. I was also more likely to be successful encouraging particular kinds of talk—language for hypothesis testing or problem solving, for example—when I provided more explicit support for this kind of talk as in the literature-sharing groups where I posed specific questions and challenged students to provide evidence for their assertions.

But I was most likely to draw on my knowledge of language when I was able to listen to and respond flexibly to what was going on around me. My support of the science center and literature-sharing groups was based, in part, on my assessment of what was happening in these groups. But I never seemed to understand what was happening in the large-group literature discussions or, at least, I refused to try other means of addressing my goals for literature discussions; namely, learning to talk about books in literate ways.

It also seems that the degree to which I was and was not able to draw on my knowledge of language to create rich language-learning experiences for my students was often due to factors over which I had little control. The frequent behavior problems in my class meant that certain kinds of talk would always be difficult. Coping with twenty-four children and an overloaded curriculum also made it difficult to create space for relaxed talk. Again, the pressure to get things done—or, at least, my perception of the need to get things done—always restricted opportunities for talk.

I also believe that the degree to which I did succeed in creating space for talk was a function of the extraordinary freedom the teachers in my school enjoyed to construct and negotiate their own curricula. Unfortunately, this freedom is rapidly disappearing as Ontario school boards are yielding to the seductive attraction of learning outcomes and standardized tests. If I had to teach under these conditions I would find it much more difficult to create opportunities for meaningful talk.

This analysis reveals more examples of the inconsistencies and contradictions between my beliefs and my teaching practices. It's not just that I wasn't able to use my knowledge of language to the best advantage. Some of my teaching practices contradicted some of my basic beliefs about language. Here I'm thinking about the large-group literature discussions. I knew in advance large-group discussions would be problematic and day after day I had dramatic evidence that large-group literature discussions didn't do what I hoped they would do. Yet I continued this practice every day from September to June. I know there will always be a tension between "knowing and being, thought and action, theory and practice, knowledge and experience" (Britzman 1991, 2). The trick for teachers is learning to live with these tensions without beating themselves up for being human. This is something at which I was not always successful.

Finally, whatever success I had creating a rich language-learning environment for my students, I can't be certain about the relationship between the language curriculum I created with my students and what they actually learned. There is always an uneven relationship between instruction and learning, something I take up again in the final chapter of this book.

7

Multicultural Literature
Who Gets to Represent Whom, Why, and How?

Progressive educators, influenced by constructivist views of learning and liberal humanism, place a high priority on creating space in the classroom for students' personal identities. From a constructivist perspective learning is created through an interaction between new knowledge and old knowledge. Therefore, constructivists insist that the knowledge and experience students bring with them to the classroom play a central role in the process of making (i.e., constructing) meaning in school (Young 1971). John Holt (1982) observed that if students are not able to make connections between what they already know and what their teachers are teaching, they will soon forget what they have learned—if they learn at all. One of the reasons progressive educators place such a premium on talk in classrooms is that oral language is often the primary means by which students draw on their existing knowledge and experience to make sense of school lessons (e.g., Barnes 1976, Wells 1986). Liberal humanism, which celebrates the dignity and worth of the individual, leads progressive educators to value the individual personalities and unique experiences of each and every student. Rudolph Steiner's aphorism that children are God's gift to humanity is a defining moment in humanistic education.

As I indicated in earlier chapters, I've also been influenced by various currents in the progressive education movement to value student voice as a means by which students can negotiate space for their personal identities within the curriculum (see Chapters 1 and 2). I encouraged students to bring in personal treasures, for example, by setting aside a space to display them. Wayne, who brought in his hockey trophies, and John, who shared an old coin he'd found, were among several students who took advantage of this opportunity. I drew on Ali's expertise on tropical fish to help me care for the fish in our classroom aquarium. I regularly encouraged students to draw on personal experience for inspiration in their writing getting, for example, Shyrose to write about her family's trip to visit Elvis's house in Memphis, Roya to write about her family's escape from Iran, and Crystal to write about her "nosey sister." When students drew on these experiences to create books which became part of the classroom library their experiences became a part of the "official" curriculum—what Dyson (1993) calls "staking a claim."

Chart stories were another means by which I attempted to make space for students' personal lives in the classroom. When Troy published his first book, for example, I noted it on our daily chart story. When John's mother had a baby I acknowledged the event on a chart story. I also tried to connect with students' homes by inviting them to bring books from home to read at school and taking books from our classroom library to read with their parents. Knowing that Troy liked reading Hardy Boy books at home, I made sure we had several of these books in our classroom library. When Lila told me that she had read *The House that Jack Built* (Cutts 1979) to her mother, I suggested she read this story to our class. Powerful stories like *Sara Plain and Tall* (MacLachlan 1985) and *The People Could Fly* (Hamilton 1985) encouraged my students and me to bring our emotions into the classroom.

Arguably, all of these strategies provided at least the opportunity for my students to bring their personal lives into our classroom (Henry 1994), but, in general, the focus of these strategies was on students' individual identities. People do not, however, live their lives as autonomous individuals. Students' lived experience takes shape within various social, historical, and cultural contexts (Henry 1994). Looking back, I worry that the emphasis I placed on students' individual identities may have effaced the social and cultural contexts within which they lived their lives. In other words, without explicitly taking up the social, historical, and cultural contexts within which my students lived their lives I may have denied them any real opportunities to negotiate space for their voices within our classroom curriculum. There was one place within our curriculum, however, where I did explicitly take up the issue of students' cultural identities. I imagined that multicultural literature could be used as a means of connecting students' cultural, ethnic, and racial identities to our reading and writing curricula. My attempts to use literature as a means of representing my students' social and cultural backgrounds is the focus of this chapter. Four years after I finished my year teaching third grade it now seems to me that the ways I conceived of and used literature to acknowledge and represent my students' experiences were deeply problematic.

Since the story of my use of literature to represent my students' backgrounds began with an implicit belief about the potential of literature to connect to students' social and cultural lives, I begin by reviewing what other educators have said about the potential of diverse literary experiences in a multicultural curriculum.

THE CASE FOR MULTICULTURAL LITERATURE

The scope of multicultural literature includes "literature that represents *any* distinct cultural group through accurate portrayal and rich detail" (Yokota 1993, 157). In practice, however, the term "multicultural literature" tends to refer to "literature by and about people who are members of groups considered to be outside the socio-political mainstream of the United States" (Bishop 1992, 39), most often literature by and about people of color (Bishop 1992). Although multicultural literature comprises only about 1–2 percent of children's books published in the United States and Canada each year (Bishop 1992), it has been given a relatively high profile in journals, conferences, and publishers' catalogues. The attraction of multicultural literature is "based upon a fundamental belief that all people should be respected, regardless of age, race, gender, economic class, religion, or physical or mental ability" (Bieger 1995, 308) and the hope that literature can play an important role in multicultural and anti-racist curricula that seek to create space—both within and outside of schools—congenial to the range of human differences. Multicultural and anti-racist curricula may also use multicultural literature as a means of challenging social practices that limit the opportunities of some of our fellow citizens merely because of who they are. Some of the benefits that have been claimed for a diversity of literary experiences are included here.

An Opportunity for Students to See Themselves in the Curriculum

Commenting on what was missing from her school library, a fifth-grade African American girl observed: "Just look around this library. You don't ever see books about kids like us" (Reimer 1992, 14).

Educational researcher Annette Henry had a similar assessment of her school experience, "My school lessons never enabled me to make sense of my Blackness in positive, affirming ways ... [Teachers] selected lessons from an educational menu that rendered me emotionally and spiritually invisible" (1994, 298–299). Arguably, all children who are members of groups outside the socio-political mainstream have, at one time or another, felt slighted by school reading practices that do not include their experiences or their histories (Bishop 1992, Reimer 1992).

All children in our schools have a need—and a right—to see themselves reflected as part of humanity, a need which is denied to some students when the literature in the classroom reflects only the experiences, history, and values of the dominant culture. Since literature can play a strong role in valuing children's cultural heritage (Gillespie et al. 1994), each child also has a right to see their literary heritage acknowledged and celebrated as part of literature studies in school. A diversity of literary experiences increases the chances that our students will come to know, appreciate, and value their own literary heritage (Harwayne 1992; Norton 1990). The thoughtful use of multi-ethnic literature can also be used "as an important tool in helping all students develop a healthy self-concept, one that depends upon a knowledge of and a sense of pride in family and educational background" (Walker-Dalhouse 1992, 417). Research indicates that children prefer and engage more with books related to their personal experiences and cultural backgrounds (Allen 1995, Harris 1993). If a diversity of literary experiences encourages students to engage more in the act of reading, we would expect this to have a positive effect on students' reading ability and academic achievement.

If children do not see themselves reflected in school curricula, if their literary heritage isn't valued (i.e., it's ignored), or if they are exposed to negative or stereotypic representations of the groups to which they belong, they may come to feel that they, as members of marginalized groups, aren't worthy of positive regard (Bishop 1992, Taxel 1992). If children do not see themselves and their experiences reflected in school texts it is also less likely that they will read or value schooling (Harris 1993). As McCarthy and Crichlow put it: "The intolerable level of minority failure in schooling has to do with the fact that minority ... cultural heritage is suppressed in the curriculum ... [S]tudents fail *because* schools assault their identities and destabilize their sense of self and agency" (McCarthy and Crichlow 1993, xv, emphasis added). However, the wide range of racial, cultural, linguistic, and gender experiences represented in contemporary literature offers many students opportunities for identification with literary characters that have been denied to them throughout the history of American schooling (Dilg 1995).

An Opportunity to Promote Inter-Cultural Understanding

Readers my age may remember the song by the Youngbloods that pleaded with a generation to try to love one another and work together right now. There was a sense in the 1960s that understanding (i.e., "love") was the key to global, racial, and ethnic peace. This hopeful vision of human relations—if we just took the time to get to know each other better, we could learn to get along—is, for many educators, the primary attraction of multicultural literature.

Most of us readily accept the notion that literature has the power to transform attitudes and values (Eeds and Hudelson 1995). Arguably, multicultural literature, by increasing cultural awareness, can help students grow in their understanding of themselves and others (Norton 1990) and, by learning more about each other, promote tolerance[1] and an appreciation of other cultures and persons who are members of those cultures (Rasinski and Padak 1990). Certainly, the increased availability of books by and about girls and women and people of color are diversifying our experiences and "changing our ideas of time and life and birth and relationship and memory" (Greene 1993, 191). Multicultural literature can enable teachers and students to share in the diverse lives and feelings of literary characters rather than dealing only with "facts" which may or may not accurately portray the lives of others (Bieger 1995). As Norton puts it:

> Through carefully selected and shared literature, students learn to understand and to appreciate a literary heritage that comes from many diverse backgrounds. . . . From the past they discover folktales, fables, myths, and legends that clarify the values and beliefs of the people. They discover the great stories on which whole cultures have been founded. From the present, they discover the threads

---

1. The term *tolerance* itself is problematic since it implies a particular kind of relationship between one who *tolerates* and one who is *tolerated*.

that weave the past with the present and the themes and values that continue to be important to the people. (1990, 28)

Some books, by focusing on more than one culture at a time, may also promote cultural understanding by focusing on issues related to intercultural communication (Yokota 1994).

Still, mere understanding may not be adequate to challenge and transform existing relations of power in which certain groups of people possess a disproportionate share of society's social and economic goods. Literature may, however, provide a means for gaining insights into relations of power as well as an opportunity to critique and challenge the way social and economic power works in contemporary societies.

Basis for Critiquing Existing Relations of Power

Either implicitly or explicitly literature "provides statements about a host of critically important social and political questions: what it means to be human; the relative worth of boys and girls, men and women, and people from various racial, ethnic, and religious communities; the value of particular kinds of action; how we relate to one another, and about the nature of community, and so forth" (Taxel 1992, 11). Literature written by and for people from marginalized groups can provide students from dominant groups (e.g., White, middle-class, male, heterosexual, English speaking, and so on) some sense of the lived experience of people who have long suffered the effects of poverty and discrimination. Literature offers all students a chance to talk about the meaning of difference, to imagine how the world could be different, and to consider how to challenge practices that diminish the lives of our fellow citizens. In Walker-Dalhouse's (1992) class, for example, she used a discussion of skin color prompted by the illustrations from a children's book, to talk about melanin. Second-grade teacher Colleen Russell (1995) responded to her students' concern that the illustrations in the books they were reading didn't "look like them" to engage her class in a study of the way children's picture books portray females and people of color and to find ways to challenge racist and sexist practices in their classroom, the school, and the world beyond the school. Andrew Allen (1995), a second-grade teacher in a school populated largely by children of African, Asian, and Middle-Eastern descent, engaged his students in an extended discussion of the illustrations of people of color in children's books. Given the opportunity to discuss images of people of color in children's literature Allen's students rejected the illustrations of Black people in many picture books because, to them, they didn't look like "real" Black people (e.g., exaggerated features, shaded faces, White faces "colored" black, etc.). Karen Smith (1995) encouraged similar discussions among her students by sharing with them articles questioning the cultural accuracy of particular children's books. There are also numerous examples of literature providing a context for secondary students to examine issues of systemic racism or sexism (Britzman et al. 1992, Weiler 1988).

Diverse literary experiences may also have a more direct effect on the structures of schooling that have long disadvantaged students from non-dominant groups (Curtis, Livingstone, and Smaller 1992). School literacy practices that reflect the cultures, experiences, and perspectives of diverse ethnic groups may help to reduce racial and ethnic conflict and tension in schools and the social and economic prospects of students disadvantaged by the effects of poverty and discrimination by helping to improve the academic achievement of these students (Banks 1988). As long as groups of students are denied equal access to the economic and social rewards of schooling merely because of who they are (Black, Hispanic, Native American, etc.) we will never realize the dream of creating a truly just and democratic society.

Antidote to Monoculturalism

Underpinning traditional school curricula, including much available children's literature, is the assumption that there is a common culture in which we all share (or, perhaps, should share). In general, schooling is a reflection of the culture and experience of White, Protestant, middle- and upper-class students. The reality, however, is that America[2] is not a mono-cultural society and probably never has been. Diversity of culture, language, race, and ethnicity is the

---

2. Again, similar arguments can be made for Canada. I focus here on America because of my assumption that most of the readers of this book will be Americans and the fact that I myself am an American.

hallmark of the American experience. Multicultural education that includes diverse literary experiences may require a rethinking of what being an American means (Wong 1993), but it is an acknowledgment of what America is.

Arguably, a true, inclusive democracy makes room for the backgrounds and experiences of all its citizens (Greene 1993). Multicultural curricula reflect the multitude of backgrounds from which the children in our classrooms come (Yokota 1993) and help students entertain multiple ways of understanding and being in the world (K. Smith 1995). A mono-cultural curriculum, however, excludes the social and cultural identities of significant numbers of students in our classrooms and is, therefore, fundamentally undemocratic.

It is not only children from non-dominant groups who reap the benefits of multiculturalism. As Bishop observed: "Those who see only themselves or who are exposed to errors and misrepresentations are miseducated into a false sense of superiority, and the harm is doubly done" (Bishop 1992, 43). Multicultural education is based on the belief that the diverse mix of culture and language that is America has enriched and will continue to enrich the lives of us all.

Multicultural literature and multicultural education are not unproblematic as the discussion of my own experience will illustrate. Multicultural education has it share of critics from both the right and the left of the political spectrum. Conservative opponents, for example, "worry that a multicultural approach to education is too 'political' and simply panders to minorities, while also detracting from the 'basics' of education. Radical critics . . . think it is not political enough and see it merely as an attempt to placate minorities while leaving unchanged the wider social issues . . . that continue to disadvantage them, both in schools and society" (May 1993, 365). May, for example, is highly critical of what he calls a "spaghetti" or "basket weaving" approach to multicultural education (others refer to this as a "tourist" curriculum) that "emphasizes the *lifestyles* of minority children rather than their *life chances*" (1993, 365). This sort of tokenism only pretends to include the voices of minority students and, by so doing, actually participates in maintaining the status quo. As May puts it: "The valuing of cultural differences, although appearing to act solely for the best interests of ethnic groups, simply masks the unchanged nature of power relations" (1993, 365). Nor does token inclusion address basic pedagogical issues of working with students from a range of cultural and linguistic backgrounds. Educational practices that stress individualism and competition, for example, may conflict with the cultural backgrounds of students more used to collaborative, non-competitive approaches to learning. Superficial treatment of different cultural, racial, or linguistic groups can also reinforce stereotypes and misconceptions, including the notion that some groups are not an integral part of the dominant culture (Rasinski and Padak 1990).

There is also a problem with explicitly taking up the culture of others while leaving the Euro-centric culture underlying most children's literature unmarked (Wallace 1991, Wong 1993). Targeting the culture of non-dominant groups for explicit instruction, while failing to name the Euro-centric biases in curricular materials, tacitly signals the marginality of non-dominant groups and leaves unquestioned the status of Euro-centric culture as the norm (Norton 1990).

There is also the possibility that students may not always welcome having attention drawn to them and their backgrounds by teachers' selection of books. For some students, especially if they are the only students of a particular culture in the class, texts and discussion focusing on their cultural background may create discomfort and embarrassment (Dilg 1995). African American or Asian American students, for example, may resent being associated with literature which portrays African or Asian cultures as backward or primitive (Liu 1995). Similarly, the use of multicultural literature that regularly associates particular racial or ethnic groups with stereotypic images of urban poverty or school failure, no matter how accurately this describes some members of these groups, may negatively affect the self-esteem and academic achievement of students from these groups (James 1994).

The use of multicultural literature also raises questions of positionality—who teaches and writes about whom (Bishop [1992] notes that a substantial percentage of children's books about people of color are still being written by White authors)—and the dangers of homogenizing the experiences of any group of people (Dilg 1995, Paley 1989, Reimer 1992).

These are some of the pitfalls of multicultural education I will explore in the rest of this chapter as I discuss my own experience using so-called multicultural literature.

MULTICULTURAL LITERATURE AND THE WHOLE LANGUAGE TEACHER

As I indicated in the introductory chapter, there was considerable economic, ethnic, racial, religious, and linguistic diversity among my third graders. Four of my students were born outside of Canada.

Eight others had parents who had immigrated to Canada. Two of my third graders were African Canadians and one an Asian Canadian. Greek, Portuguese, Cantonese, Arabic, Farsi, and Urdu were spoken in my students' homes and several parents spoke little English. One fourth of my students were Moslems, the others Christian. Almost all my students came from working-class homes although several families received some form of public assistance. It was this incredible diversity that led me to use multicultural literature—which I understood to be books for and about people who fell outside the narrow conception of Canadians as White, middle-class, English- (or French-) speaking, Protestants of British descent (a profile which applies to less than half the people living in Toronto)—to create a curriculum that affirmed the range of social and cultural influences on my students' lives. To build up our classroom collection of multicultural books I used our school and public libraries, brought books from my own children's library, purchased books, and encouraged students to bring books from home. In the rest of this chapter I critically examine my efforts to use multicultural literature to create space in our curriculum for my students' social and cultural identities.

"I'm Not from Pakistan": a Folktale Study

> Today we read a Pakistani folktale, *The Talking Parrot* (Chia 1976)
> and I made a point of singling out Nader [I was led to believe
> he was from Pakistan]. When I made the connection between the
> Pakistani folktale and Nader he protested, "I'm not from Pakistan."
> (field notes, December 2, 1991)

At the end of September I began a folktale study and, over the next three months, I read and discussed more than fifty folktales with my students. They read many more on their own. I stocked our classroom library with dozens of folktale picture books and anthologies of folktales, many of which I displayed prominently on the chalkboard at the front of the classroom. I sent a letter home with students announcing our folktale study and invited parents to share their favorite folktale books with us. (None did, although Hugh convinced his mother, who was from Scotland, to come into our class and read us a Scottish folktale.) When I discovered that a home-school teacher who was working with a student in my class was an accomplished storyteller I invited her to perform for my students and, for the next few months, my class was treated to a captivating story every Thursday afternoon. I also encouraged my students to try their hand at writing their own folktales and, early in the year, many of their stories began "Once upon a time . . ."

When we discussed the folktales I read I asked students questions like: "Does this remind you of any other story we've read?" and "Why?"; "How is this different from other folktales (or other versions of the same folktale) we read?"; "How did you feel about the characters in this story?"; and so on (see Chapter 6). To facilitate these discussions I tried to read folktales featuring similar themes (e.g., trickster stories, rescue tales, etc.) on consecutive days. For instance, many multicultural books provided examples of folktales that functioned as "explanations" of natural phenomena. *Rainbow Crow* (Van Laan 1989), for example, is a story about the origin of light. An African folktale retold by Verna Aardema (1975) "explains" *Why Mosquitoes Buzz in People's Ears*. The Uncle Remus tales (Hamilton 1985) include a host of stories about how animals came to look or act in particular ways. Of course, these themes also appear in "mainstream" Western literature. *Paul Bunyan* (Kellogg 1984), for example, offers fanciful accounts of the clearing of the North American forests and the origins of the Great Lakes and the Grand Canyon.

Based on my assumption that children learn to read by reading, I expected that my folktale study would engage students' interests and invite (more) reading and writing. I also hoped that genre studies like our folktale and poetry units would help my students learn how to think and talk about literature in more interesting and enriching ways. At the time it seemed to me that a folktale study had the additional advantage of being a rich source of multicultural books which I could use to expose my students to a range of cultural stories, customs, and traditions. Our classroom collection of multicultural books, for example, included folktales from Asia, Africa, Europe, and North America (including Native American, Caribbean, Black, and Eurocentric folktales). It was as part of this broader effort to expose my students to diverse literary experiences that it occurred to me that I might make an effort to locate folktales that matched my students' cultural backgrounds. For the benefit of Ali, whose family had immigrated to Canada from Egypt, I read the Egyptian folktale the *Egyptian Cinderella* (Climo and Heller 1989). I also read Persian, West Indian, African, Portuguese, Greek, Chinese, Scottish, and Indian folktales in an attempt to acknowledge the cultural heritage of students like Charles, Denise, Lila, Nicholas, Connie, Hugh, and

Razika. In a couple of cases I was not able to locate representative literature. I couldn't, for example, locate any literature from Afghanistan (Fatima) or Kenya (Shyrose). I also drew on both literature and expository texts to acknowledge various religious observances important to my students. When I discovered that two students in my class were fasting for Ramadan, for example, I read several poems to my class about Ramadan. I also invited my Moslem students to talk with the class about how their families observed these traditions. A couple of weeks later, in order to acknowledge the religious heritage of my Christian students, we read about Christian practices surrounding Good Friday and Easter.

At the time I was teaching third grade I was generally pleased with my efforts to use literature as a means of acknowledging students' cultural and religious heritage. It wasn't until I rediscovered the episode where I grossly misrepresented Nader's background (see the excerpt from my field notes that opens this section) that I began to doubt the basic assumption underlying my use of multicultural literature to acknowledge explicitly and celebrate my students' cultural and religious backgrounds; that is, that I could have used literature to represent essential qualities of a student's ethnic, cultural, or religious background.

It's obvious that my selection of a Pakistani folktale to acknowledge Nader's cultural heritage missed the mark since he was from Afghanistan, not Pakistan (his family had spent a year in a Pakistani refugee camp to escape the war in Afghanistan.) But, as I reflected on my botched effort to represent Nader's background accurately, I began to doubt that I was any more effective using multicultural literature to represent the cultural background of Roya, Shyrose, Ali or any other student whose families had immigrated to Canada. First of all, it was unreasonable for me to have assumed that any piece of literature could speak to the culture and experience of all people from a particular continent, region, or country. Roya's family, for example, was from Iran and, therefore, shared a common history with other Iranians. However, her family's upper-middle class status—they were wealthy enough to buy their way out of Iran—set her family apart from most Iranians. Their status as secular Moslems also distinguished them from the fundamentalist Moslems who now run the country. I also suspect that Roya's family was much more open to Western influences than many Iranians. For these reasons alone it seems unlikely that Roya and her family shared a cultural experience common to *all* Iranians. It is even less likely that Connie, whose parents had emigrated from Vietnam, shared a common cultural heritage with the mainland Chinese—themselves a diverse mix of culture and languages—depicted in much Asian literature. And it is almost certain that Shyrose, whose family had migrated to East Africa several generations earlier from India, did not share a common cultural bond with many Black Africans. The reality is that Africa and Asia are culturally, ethnically, linguistically, and racially diverse places. African or Asian literature cannot represent the cultural backgrounds of students of African or Asian descent since there isn't *an* African or Asian culture as much as there are African and Asian culture*s*. The fact that libraries and bookstores tend to categorize multicultural literature by continent or region ignores this diversity, thereby contributing to stereotypic assumptions about particular groups of people. (Note that we do not talk about European literature referring instead to the literature of France, Germany, England, Scotland, Wales, etc. We know that Europe is culturally diverse and we do not pretend otherwise.) We cannot acknowledge differences between and among people if we pretend that they (Africans, Asians, etc.) are all the same.

If African literature cannot speak to the heritage of all Africans what can be said about the relationship of non-immigrant Black children to African literature? I would certainly want to distance myself from claims that the African folktales I read to my class somehow affirmed the cultural heritage of the African Canadian students in my class, but I did choose to read African folktales with these students in mind. Somehow I imagined that African literature would speak to my African Canadian students as if there existed a homogeneous African culture. The fact that the only student in my class who was actually *from* Africa was of East Indian descent gives an indication of how complicated questions of African identity and African culture really are. It's also doubtful that I any more accurately represented the cultural heritage of my Black students when I read Caribbean folktales (Charles and Denise's families emigrated to Canada from the Caribbean) since there is clearly not *a* Caribbean culture either. I wasn't so foolish, however, to assume that Black American folktales had any particular relation to African Canadian experience, although I did discover that Charles had a great attachment to Virginia Hamilton's (1985) anthology of Black American folktales, *The People Could Fly*, because his mother read these tales to him at home.

My efforts to acknowledge the religious heritage of my Moslem students by sharing literature and expository texts about Ramadan was also based on a tacit assumption that these students shared a common religious experience. Our whole-class discussions about Ramadan indicated, however, that there were significant differences in how my Moslem students lived Islam. I may have effaced these differences by reading texts to my students that presented a unitary description of Islam. My efforts to recognize Christian holidays probably fared no better since our readings and discussions did not acknowledge the range of ways Christians live their traditions either.

It is one thing to offer students diverse literary experiences as a means of exposing them to various cultural practices and literary traditions. It is quite another matter to use multicultural literature as part of an explicit effort to affirm, acknowledge, or celebrate the cultural heritage of individual children or groups of children as I attempted to do in my third-grade classroom. Using literature to represent students' cultural and religious heritages assumes an essential homogeneity in people's cultural heritage that clearly does not exist. People's cultural and religious identities are complicated by factors like race, class, language, socio-economic status, gender, and so on. As I suggested earlier, the ways Roya's family lived Iranian culture was complicated by their economic privilege and religious practices. It is also likely the males and females in Roya's family experienced Islamic and Iranian culture differently.

My efforts to match literature to students' ethnic backgrounds were based upon a homogeneous sense of culture that ignored the complicated ways people construct their cultural identities. Even my goal to improve cultural understanding was undermined by an approach to multicultural education that distorted the complexity of the people I tried to represent (McDermott and Verenne 1995). It is unlikely that the stereotypes produced by unitary constructions of culture could ever improve intercultural understanding or communication.

A multicultural curriculum that focuses on folktales and religious celebrations, as mine did, also misses the mark by assuming a stability in culture and cultural practices that ignores the complicated ways people go about making and remaking culture in their daily lives. Culture isn't a collection of practices or "the sum of 'mores and folkways' of societies" (Hall 1981, 22). The tourist approach to multiculturalism (Gillespie et al. 1994), implicit in the ways I used multicultural books in my third-grade classroom, reduced culture to folktales and religious celebrations. However, culture refers not so much to "food and festivals" (Henry 1994, 313) as to *relationships* between elements in a whole way of life (Williams 1981) or, as

McDermott and Varenne put it, culture is a "particular way of making sense and meaning" (1995, 325). Therefore, culture is not only *more* than the sum of its parts, it is *different* from the sum of its parts. Culture is a process by which people make—and remake—meaning in their lives and, as such, is not something people carry around with them, something they can transport from place to place. Connie's family, for example, didn't pack their culture into a suitcase and carry it to Canada. It may appear that immigrants to Canada or the United States are mainly in the business of preserving their cultures but, in fact, people actively remake, or reinvent, their cultures in order to make sense of their lives in new geographical (certainly geography influences the making of culture), social, and political environments. The reality is that all people—including those of us who do not have an immigrant experience—are constantly in the process of making culture. The problem with the sense of culture as a container of coherence is: "The container leaks" (McDermott and Varenne 1995, 325).

My tendency to use certain multicultural texts—folktales, for example—to represent the cultural heritage of some of my students failed to recognize this more dynamic sense of culture. Assuming a direct link between the culture of Connie's family and the culture of China assumed "some mystical pipeline of authenticity from Asian Americans to their 'heritage culture,' ignoring the fact that their [Canadian] experience has been a transforming one" (Wong 1993, 117) A particular Chinese folktale may have been part of the literary heritage of Connie's family but, as a representation of the culture of Connie's family, it ignored the vibrant and complex ways Connie and her family live culture in their daily lives. In Connie's case, certain folktales may have acknowledged a Chinese identity, but it's doubtful this identity had much of a relationship to the way Connie and her family actually lived their lives. Connie's family and other Chinese Canadians may work to preserve certain cultural forms or symbols, but the meaning of these forms or symbols in the lives of Chinese Canadians may be very different from their meaning for people living in China (Liu 1995). In some cases, the children of Chinese Canadians or other immigrant groups may resent, or even reject, efforts to link their identities to cultural forms associated with the place from which their families emigrated (e.g., Liu, 1995). (I'll say more about this later.) Perhaps worse, linking the experience of Asian or African Americans, for example, to folklore and traditions in faraway lands effaces the contributions these groups have made in shaping American and Canadian culture(s).

The need for students to see in texts reflections of their lives *as they live them* demands multicultural books that "stress *the Americanness of the group's cultural expressions*" (Wong 1993, 113, emphasis in original) reflecting their values and beliefs, rich in cultural details, including authentic dialogue and relationships and an in-depth treatment of cultural issues (Yokota 1993). Too often "teachers with good intentions select pieces of literature for classroom use and believe that because the story centers on a diverse group the book inherently represents a perceptive characterization and should be considered as a quality selection for children" (Pang, Colvin, Tran, and Barba 1992, 217). However, authentic multicultural texts do not merely include token minority representation or equate the culture of groups of Americans with "exotic" cultures in distant lands. Nor should difference be reduced to "details of skin color, clothes, houses, food, and holiday celebrations" (Fishman 1995, 76) as often happened in the multicultural curriculum I constructed in my classroom.

"I Didn't Ask You To . . ."

Since I imagined that multicultural literature would have a role in affirming and celebrating students' cultural background, I was surprised and disappointed when many of my students weren't particularly enthusiastic about my efforts to acknowledge their backgrounds. Ali, for example, behaved so badly when I began to read the *Egyptian Cinderella* (Climo and Heller 1989) (Ali's parents had immigrated to Canada from Egypt) that I asked him to leave the classroom. I was angry at the disruption, but also hurt that Ali didn't seem to appreciate my efforts to affirm his cultural identity (more accurately my sense of his cultural identity). I was even more upset a few weeks later when Ali disrupted a discussion of the religious meaning of Good Friday (in addition to being generally disruptive he shouted out "good" when someone offered that Good Friday was the day "Jesus was nailed to the cross"). When I confronted him with the observation that "the other students were considerate when I read about his religious traditions" he responded, "I didn't ask you to" (field notes, April 10, 1992). Looking back it seems clear that Ali may have been telling me something important about *his sense* of my efforts to use multicultural literature to represent his cultural identity. At the time, however, I merely dismissed Ali's comment as another example of rude behavior.

More often the children who I imagined the multicultural literature I read was *for* responded with silence. Roya, for example, had nothing to say about the Persian folktale I read to the class. Nor did Connie comment on any of the Chinese folktales we read. Razika, Roya, and Shyrose actually refused to help me with the pronunciation of certain words when I read about Ramadan. Roya claimed that she hadn't even heard of these words (which may have been true). Conversely, the Christian students in my class were not at all hesitant about discussing Christian traditions like Good Friday and Easter. In general, there were only a couple of times I recall students responding with any enthusiasm to "multicultural" books or stories that were meant for them. Charles, for example, loved it when I read West Indian folktales his mother read to him at home and Hugh was thrilled when his mother read a Scottish folktale to our class. However, I never observed a student spontaneously read one of the folktales that I imagined represented their ethnic or cultural background.

From my perspective, the use of multicultural literature was a way of explicitly acknowledging my students' ethnic, racial, and religious backgrounds. I imagined these efforts would lead to understanding and pride. This may not have been how the students who were singled out by these practices saw it, however. Associating Connie, Nader, Charles, Denise, Razika, Shyrose, Roya, and Fatima with exotic cultures and faraway lands marked them as different from ordinary Canadians at a time when most of them may have been trying to fit in. As much as Nader, the victim of frequent ethnic slurs and physical abuse, was trying to adopt behaviors that indicated he wasn't different from his peers, I was doing my best—through my use of multicultural literature—to say that he was different. Similarly, drawing attention to non-Christian students' religious backgrounds through stories about Ramadan, for example, may have been an unwelcome intrusion in students' personal lives which may also have had the effect of marking some students as *different*. Ali may have been a devout Moslem, but it isn't at all clear he wished me to draw attention to that fact. As he succinctly put it, "he didn't ask me to." To the degree that my use of multicultural literature marked some of my students as *different*, I may have undermined these students' own efforts to become mainstream Canadians (whatever that meant to them).

Ali's complaint that "I didn't ask you to" raises what is for me the crucial question in my use of multicultural literature in my third-grade classroom: *Who gets to represent whom and for what purpose?* What counts as an authentic representation of someone else's culture and who decides what's authentic is a problem all around. As McCarthy and Crichlow put it: "Issues of identity and representation directly raise questions about who has the power to define whom, and when, and how . . . [and] often minorities do not have central control over the production of images about themselves in this society" (1993, xvi).

What did I assume when I presumed to match representations of ethnic, cultural, and racial identities in books with my own reading of my students' bodies? Well, when I selected "Chinese folktales" to celebrate Connie's ethnic heritage, for example, I made assumptions about the relationship between Connie's physical appearance and language and a cultural identity which may have had little to do with the identities Connie and her family imagined for themselves. The African and West Indian folktales I chose to acknowledge the racial and cultural heritage of Denise and Charles assumed a Black or African identity that they did not choose for themselves either (and may not have chosen, for all I know). This isn't simply a matter of selecting more authentic books, that is, books that portray the lives of African Canadian or Asian Canadians (vs. Africans or Asians). A story about a poor African Canadian family living in public housing may be closer to Charles's lived experience than an African folktale, but it would still beg the question about who gets to represent whose experience. I may have considered Charles to be from a poor family, but he may not have had the same assessment of his family's economic circumstances. And what does it mean for me to decide that Connie is an Asian Canadian when she may only think of herself as a Canadian? I did not, for example, think of Lila as a Portuguese Canadian, Hugh as a Scottish Canadian or, more to the point, Catherine as a White Canadian. By what right did I assume racialized identities for Connie, Denise, or Charles? Like it or not, the practice of multiculturalism in my classroom often assumed that skin color and certain physical features were essential identity qualities.

The problem isn't that I made available to my students a range of cultural, ethnic, and racial images. A diversity of literary experiences permitted my students the opportunity to see themselves in curricular materials and exposed them to a range of cultural and ethnic images. The use of multicultural literature in my third-grade classroom did not, by its mere presence, impose racial or cultural identities on children. The problem is that I did, at least I tried to, match texts to the social and cultural identities I imagined for my students. I chose to use particular texts to represent the ethnic and religious identities of my students without regard to how they chose to represent those identities. However, it wasn't for me to represent my students' identities, but to create a space where my students could represent themselves or at least see themselves represented in the books in our classroom.

Many of my students did use the spaces for talk in our class and the opportunities to create their own books to infuse their social and cultural identities into our classroom. Roya, for example, often wrote about issues related to her identity as a Moslem and an Iranian. Other students, Razika and Shyrose, for example, resisted my invitations to talk about their religious and cultural backgrounds and preferred generic stories that didn't betray their ethnic or religious heritages. In either case, students retained the right to control how they would be represented in our classroom. Unfortunately, my approach to using multicultural literature gave my students little say in how they were represented. Speaking on behalf of my students' cultural and religious identities, instead of letting them speak for themselves, no matter how well intentioned, may have had the effect of reinforcing stereotypes that have been used to oppress those I imagined I was speaking for (Alcoff 1991). Ultimately, representing the experience of others as we expect it to be can never lead to either accurate and fair representations or to greater understanding.

A CRITICAL MULTICULTURALISM

At the heart of multicultural education is the assumption that getting to know each other better is the key ethnic and racial harmony. Of course, combatting racism requires more than just learning to get along. As May put it: "The valuing of cultural differences, although appearing to act solely for the best interests of ethnic groups, simply masks the unchanged nature of power relations" (1993, 365). Promoting understanding through exposure to a range of cultural practices doesn't challenge the structural barriers that deny many of our fellow citizens their fair share of our nation's social and economic riches. Anti-racist pedagogy, on the other hand, goes beyond multiculturalism by asking students to look not only at what makes us different (race, class, language, culture, and so on) but how difference is used as an excuse to exclude people from the mainstream of

American (or Canadian) life. In other words, anti-racist education stresses life chances instead of lifestyles (May 1993). It has been well documented, for example, how schools' preference for the values and experiences of middle-class students disadvantages students who are not from middle-class homes (e.g., Curtis et al. 1992, Gee 1990). Anti-racist education seeks to help students recognize and, ultimately challenge, social and institutional practices that limit people's social and economic opportunities merely because of who they are.

The use of multicultural literature in my classroom was largely in service of a food and festivals approach to multiculturalism. There were only a few times I used literature to get my third graders to think about sexism or racism. The following discussion, for example, followed my reading of two stories about slaves, *John and the Devil's Daughter* and *The People Could Fly*, both from Virginia Hamilton's (1985) collection of American Black folktales.

MR. MARLING: I read you two folktales. One about a Black slave who escaped the devil. I also read you one about slaves who flew away to freedom. I'd like to hear what you think about those two stories. What do you think?

STUDENT: I don't think they should work with babies on their backs.

MR. MARLING: Do you understand why they had to do that?

STUDENT: No.

MR. MARLING: They treated the slaves, not like people, but like animals. They didn't care about them. They beat them. They killed them . . . They took their children away from them to hurt them. The slaves lived in hell. It was worse than hell. So that's why they did that. They cared so little . . . There's a lesson in that, of course. The slave owners believed that some people were different because they were Black. But it's a lie. Because they believed they were different they hurt them. That's a sin. I'd like to know what you think about the stories. They're very sad stories [one of the reasons I'm talking is that I was overcome by emotion reading *The People Could Fly* which left me visibly choking back the tears]. Charles, how did those stories make you feel?

JOHN: Angry.

MR. MARLING: Roya, how did that make you feel?

ROYA: Did that really happen?

MR. MARLING: You mean the slaves flying like that?

ROYA: Yeah.

MR. MARLING: What do you think?

SEVERAL STUDENTS: No!

MR. MARLING: Why do you think they told the story like that then?

CATHERINE: To tell people what happened a long time ago.

MR. MARLING: OK. One reason was to tell people what it was like.

MR. MARLING: Hugh, why do you think they told the story like that?

HUGH: [shrugs his shoulders]

MARK: Not to think that Black people are different.

MR. MARLING: You think they told the story for that reason. OK.

CATHERINE: No Black people [inaudible]

MR. MARLING: Can anybody else tell how that story made them feel or why they told the story about slaves being able to fly away to freedom?

WAYNE: To help people stick up for themselves.

MR. MARLING: So you think they tell stories like that so people will stick up for themselves. That's a good thought.

MR. MARLING: Charles, how does the story make you feel?

CHARLES: Nothing.

MR. MARLING: Does it make you feel bad?

CHARLES: Nope . . .

MR. MARLING: Doesn't it make you feel sad?

CHARLES: From the beating and the carrying the baby.

MR. MARLING: That was very sad, wasn't it?

CHARLES: Yeah.

PAUL: That was really sad, but this movie was even sadder. He was going to get 40 lashes.

MR. MARLING: Who was?

PAUL: The guy [a movie about a slave who was shipwrecked with his masters and beaten].

MR. MARLING: These people were treated this way just because they were Black. Can you imagine that? Do you know why they tell stories like this? [pause] I think Wayne's idea that they tell stories like this to give people hope that they can stick up for themselves and fly away, get away, makes sense. These are sad stories. [discussion ends]

This discussion is one of the rare occasions when my students and I engaged in an explicit discussion of racism but, of course, I did most of the talking here and, for this reason it seems more like a lecture punctuated by a few questions than an interactive discussion. It was clear that my students were moved by these stories, however. During both the reading and the "discussion" you could have heard a pin drop—a very unusual circumstance in our classroom.

What is especially noteworthy about this discussion, however, is how limited it is in its scope. Racism is taken up in the historical context of slavery, something that "happened a long time ago" as Catherine noted. I made no effort to connect the racist practice of slavery with contemporary racism. The discussion of racism as something in the past may actually have done more harm than good since it provided space for arguments that racism is a thing of the past. (Neo-conservative writer Dinesh D'Sousa (1995) is a leading advocate of the remarkable position that racism is no longer an issue in American society.)

In contrast to the limited ways I used multicultural literature in my classroom, Colleen Russell (1995), a second-grade teacher in a Toronto-area school remarkable for its diversity, uses children's literature as a site where her students can take up issues of systemic racism and sexism. Colleen and her students look at who is represented in books and how they're represented. For example, her second graders discuss the various ways females are portrayed in children's books as well as the paucity of texts containing characters who "look like them." Importantly, Colleen invites her students to think about how to challenge racist and sexist practices in their classroom, their school, and their community. Colleen's literacy curriculum begins to realize the potential of multicultural literature to help students identify social problems and concerns and then make decisions and take action to resolve them (Banks 1988).

CONCLUSION

During my year as a third-grade teacher I managed to use multicultural literature to expand the range of students' literary experience, expose students to, and increase the probability that my students could see themselves in the books in our classroom. But, by trying to impose my own sense of students' cultural and religious identities I unknowingly engaged my students in a struggle over who controlled the shaping of their social and cultural identities. The "food and festivals" approach to multiculturalism that dominated my use of multicultural books effaced the complicated ways race, language, gender, and religion come together to shape students' culture as well as the active role people play in constructing culture for themselves. I also failed to exploit the power of multicultural literature to challenge social and institutional practices that deny many people access to the social and economic riches of Canada (and the U.S.) merely because of who they are.

Some readers may feel that I've been too hard on myself and I suppose I'd be resentful if someone else launched such a harsh critique of my literacy practices. After all, anti-racist education is as new to me as it may be to many of you reading this chapter. Therefore, this chapter shouldn't be taken as an implicit critique of teachers whose use of multicultural books resembles what happened in my classroom. We should all be pleased to have discovered the power of anti-racist pedagogy to challenge racist and sexist practices in our schools and the society at large and to help us imagine a more just and democratic society. I may never again teach small children, but this critique may help inspire other teachers and the students I work with at the university to fully explore the power of multicultural literature within an anti-racist curriculum.

8

"Spelling Is . . . a Worry for Me"

No Time for Spelling: An Unfinished Play in Three Acts

ACT I, SCENE 1 "THE TEACHER WORRIES"

TEACHER: Spelling is beginning to become a worry for me. Most of my students seem to be at the transitional stage of spelling development[1] and there are many students still using phonetic spellings including spellings which do not include all of the sounds. Peter is about the only student who seems to be using mostly conventional spellings. I am loathe to use spelling lists [Here the teacher's voice is pained.] but I think I need to do more than just mini-lessons. (field notes, September 19, 1991)

[*Onstage there is a prolonged silence while offstage the murmur of whole class and individual spelling mini-lessons, children reading, and students helping one another with their spellings can be heard.*]

TEACHER: I need to do more to support students' spelling development. One idea is five spelling words each week (to begin with) taken from students' writing. Every Monday they could make a list of these words in the back of their notebooks. (field notes, October 16, 1991)

TEACHER: Spelling is still a notable problem for Lila. Most of her spelling "errors" are phonetic spellings which include relatively few conventional features (e.g., "fiting" for "fighting"; "frand" for "friend"; "grlle" for "girl"; "asct" for "asked"; "navr" for "never"; and "ban" for "been.") (field notes, November 7, 1991)

---

1. Transitional spellings include features of conventional spelling but are still not "correct" (e.g., fite for fight, gerl for girl, etc.)

FIRST PARENT: When I was in school we sat in desks in rows. We had spelling books and memorized spelling words each week. I don't like these new teaching methods. I want Crystal to be a good speller.[2] [The teacher is heard mumbling something about the arrangement of desks in rows not serving the needs of kids like Crystal for whom school is often difficult.] (parent conference, November 11, 1991)

SECOND PARENT: I want John to bring home spelling words to study each week. (parent conference, November 11, 1991)

TEACHER: I'll see that John brings home spelling words from his writing each week. (parent conference, November 11, 1991)

NARRATOR: He never does.

ROYA: My mom thinks I'm a bad speller so she's giving me spelling words to learn at home. (field notes, February 19, 1992)

LILA: So is my mom (field notes, February 19, 1992)

[*Charles is among five students from Mr. Marling's third-grade class who have been sent to work with the art teacher on a special art project.*]

ART TEACHER: Mr. Marling, Did you know that Charles doesn't know how to spell his last name? I asked him to spell his name for me and Ali had to help him. (field notes, December 5, 1991)

ACT 1, SCENE 2 "GUILT AND FRUSTRATION"

[*As the curtain opens the teacher is sitting at his desk. The narrator tells the audience what's behind the pained look on this teacher's face as he sits motionless staring into space. He tells the audience of the guilt, the doubts, the feelings of incompetence this teacher is experiencing. The teacher sits quietly at his desk for several moments before a stagehand, sensing the audience's discomfort with this awkward moment, quickly closes the curtain.*]

ACT 1, SCENE 3 "LISTS, LISTS, LISTS. REALLY!"

NARRATOR: [Reading from the teacher's lesson plans] Introduce spelling lists today. (lesson plans, October 21, 1991)

---

2. For dramatic purposes I've transformed by field notes from the third to the first person. In some places I've used my memory to augment my field notes and produce a fuller dialogue.

TEACHER: I didn't remember to ask them to select some spelling words today, but I'll try to remember this for tomorrow. (field notes, October 21, 1991)

NARRATOR: [Reading from lesson plans] Today's goal: Start spelling lists as I had planned. Ask students to pick five words from their writing that they didn't spell correctly but would like to learn how to spell. Or maybe they could just pick words they'd like to learn how to spell from some other source like a book. Have them write these words in the back of their journal and then study each day.

NARRATOR: [Reading from lesson plans] Try again to begin spelling lists this week. (field notes, October 28, 1991)

TEACHER: Did a quick spelling mini-lesson on "gr." Did not do lesson on revising nor did I introduce spelling lists today. (field notes, October 28, 1991)

Finally started spelling lists earlier in the week, but didn't follow through. Need to keep with this ... (field notes, November 1, 1991)

NARRATOR: [Reading from lesson plans] Check their spelling lists. (lesson plans, November 4, 1991)

[*Onstage the actors are silent. Offstage this teacher and his students continue to talk about spelling in brief, whole-class lessons and within the context of students' writing.*]

NARRATOR: [Reading from lesson plans] Need to get serious about spelling lists this week. (lesson plans, November 11, 1991)

TEACHER: Didn't do the spelling lists again today. Need to make this a higher priority. (field notes, November 11, 1991)

NARRATOR: [Reading from lesson plans] This afternoon need to do writing mini-lesson and spelling list. (lesson plans, November 12, 1991)

TEACHER: Reminded everyone to do their spelling lists but only got to about thirteen students to see if they had. (field notes, November 12, 1991)

The problem with spelling lists is that it presents one more management problem. Perhaps need to monitor in large group instead of checking with each student individually. Also need to remind them of the purpose of the spelling lists and find a way for them to have little "tests." Perhaps working in pairs they could test each other. Also need to be consistent about doing this every Monday. (field notes, November 13, 1991)

[*The silence onstage signals the passing of several weeks, but continued discussions about spelling among the teacher and his students can be heard offstage.*]

TEACHER: I continue to be disappointed about spelling . . . I'm going to consider more seriously the use of spelling lists. I started to do this lately, but I didn't really have much enthusiasm for it and it fizzled out. Need to do. (field notes, December 6, 1991)

[*Several weeks have passed.*]

NARRATOR: [Reading from lesson plans] Resume (in earnest) personal spelling lists. (lesson plans, December 18, 1991)

[*More weeks pass and onstage the teacher says nothing about spelling lists.*]

NARRATOR: [Reading from lesson plans] Resume spelling lists. (lesson plans, January 6, 1991) This guy never gives up.

[*End of Act 1*]

ACT 2, SCENE 1 "CONSISTENCY— SORT OF"

TEACHER: Next I gave them ten minutes to write down five words they were going to learn to spell this week and gave them support to spell the words correctly. (field notes, January 6, 1992)

After French I gathered them on the carpet and told them that we were going to do a little spelling test. I began by giving them about fifteen minutes to retrieve their spelling words and study them. When they returned to the carpet I first asked them to tell the group how they went about studying their spelling words. Their strategies fell into three categories: 1) look at the word and look away or close eyes and practice; 2) write several times; 3) practice with someone else. Hugh added that he just looked at the words but didn't rehearse. Then I paired them up and had them give each other a "test." When they returned to the carpet . . . I asked who had gotten all five words right and then asked those who had missed a word to tell what word(s) they missed and attempt to spell them again. (field notes, January 10, 1992)

After lunch . . . I asked them to go and write their personal spelling words. I gave them about ten minutes to develop their lists. A couple of students used books to locate words for their lists. Many students brought their words to me and I provided them with the conventional spellings. (field notes, January 13, 1992)

NARRATOR: Finally!

TEACHER: Then I told them to make up personal spelling lists of six words which they could make up themselves or choose words from our list of "Olympics³" words or zoo words. (field notes January 20, 1992)

I let them study their spelling words for about ten minutes and then asked them to test each other. When I gathered them back onto the carpet I asked them again to describe how they went about studying their words and how many they got right. I let them know that we would now be studying seven words. I also asked them how many were still having trouble with spelling and only a few still admitted a problem (Crystal, Roya, and Lila were the only ones). (field notes, January 23, 1992)

NARRATOR: By George he's got it. By George I think he's got it! [With apologies to Lerner & Loewe]

TEACHER: I'm disappointed that we didn't do any spelling words this week. Crystal's spelling just isn't getting any better. The fact that she spelled balloon yesterday without any l's isn't encouraging. (field notes, February 28, 1992)

Again didn't do the spelling workshop. I need to find a time every day when we do something with our personal spelling lists. I'm not enthusiastic about spelling lists but so many of my students do poorly with spelling and this is such an issue for so many of the parents that I need to give lots more attention to spelling the rest of the year. (field notes, March 10, 1992)

NARRATOR: Uh, oh. Here we go again.

TEACHER: I've been much more consistent with the spelling drills this week. (field notes, March 27, 1992)

NARRATOR: Maybe he's back on track.

TEACHER: Didn't do a spelling lesson this A.M. The personal lists aren't ever going to be much help unless we do at least three times a week. (field notes, April 8, 1992)

NARRATOR: I don't think I can stand much more of this.

TEACHER: Then did a spelling lesson. Gave them about 10–15 minutes to study their spelling words. Also helped a few of them develop spelling lists using misspelled words from their own writing. Good idea but it's hard to imagine having enough time to do with twenty-three students . . . (field notes, April 9, 1992)

NARRATOR:: [Reading from lesson plans] Continue personal spelling lists (lesson plans, April 28, 1992). Ahhhhhhhhhhhhh!

---

3. We were doing an Olympics unit to go along with the 1992 Winter Olympics.

[*Silence onstage indicates the passage of several weeks while offstage there is lots of talk about spelling.*]

NARRATOR: On June 1st the teacher writes in his lesson plans "Personal spelling lists (may actually want to do this week)" and *never* speaks again of spelling lists. Praise the Lord.

[*End of Act 2*]

ACT 3, SCENE 1 "MORE 'BRIGHT' IDEAS"

TEACHER: A first grade teacher whose classroom I visited last year put the 100 most frequently spelled words on circles of construction paper and displayed them around the room. Each word had an associated number and when a student asked how to spell one of these words the teacher responded with the number of the word the child was trying to spell. I think I'll try this. (field notes, December 6, 1991)

NARRATOR: [Reading from lesson plans] Start getting frequently spelled words posted. (lesson plans, January 13, 1992)

Every morning before school for the next couple of weeks the teacher invited students to come in early to help him cut out circles from construction paper and copy words from a list of "most frequently spelled words" onto the circles. He taped each circle on wall space above the blackboards.

TEACHER: The frequently spelled words I've put around the room seem to be having no effect at all in my classroom. I've never seen anyone consult them (I should ask) and only once have I been able to refer to them when a student asked me how to spell a word. Maybe if I had put them up a few words a day in very dramatic fashion? I don't know. (field notes, February 28, 1992)

ACT 3, SCENE 2 "AN EVEN SHORTER-LIVED IDEA"

TEACHER: Last week I did a workshop on writing for a professional development day. There was a teacher at my session who told me about the spelling workshop she did in her class which sounded interesting. She does personal spelling lists (five words per student), but she has her students work in groups of four in which each student learns their words and the words of the other three students in their group. I might think about this or some variation on this idea. (field notes, February 27, 1992)

Today I did something like what the teacher at my PD presentation does in her class. I asked students to work in groups of four. I started by asking them to each come up with a personal spelling list of five words. Then I asked them to combine all the words of the people at their table to make a list of twenty words. I'll try to give them about ten minutes each day to practice their lists and give them a dictation on Friday. I'm not sure how I'll manage this, however.

NARRATOR: This idea was soon forgotten and the teacher never spoke of this again.

ACT 3, SCENE 3 "SEEKING HELP"

TEACHER: I should consult Temple, Nathan, and Burris's (1982) book on spelling and maybe ask some of my literacy colleagues at York University for advice. (field notes, October 16, 1991)

I've just ordered Sandra Wilde's (1992) new book on spelling. I need to read it as soon as I get it. (field notes, December 6, 1991)

Do lots more work on spelling; especially read Wilde's new book. (field notes, December 18, 1991)

Over the holidays I got a bunch of new books from Heinemann and began reading Sandra Wilde's new book on spelling. Spelling must be a very high priority for me the next few months. (field notes, January 6, 1991)

The spelling lessons may be getting a bit stale or at least the features we're talking about are getting more obscure. Need to consult Sandra Wilde's book on spelling or start thinking of other ideas. (field notes, February 27, 1992)

I started reading some more from Sandra Wilde's book yesterday and I was especially interested in the example of how one teacher dealt with spelling in a second- and third-grade class. I was impressed but frustrated by how difficult it seems for me to be as careful and systematic as she was. (field notes, March 23, 1992)

I MUST finish reading Sandra Wilde's book (field notes, March 10, 1992)

Try to finish Sandra Wilde's book to see if she has any other suggestions. (field notes, April 27, 1992)

[*As the curtain goes down, offstage the audience is still able to hear the sounds of individual and whole-class spelling mini-lessons, students helping each other with their spelling, students reading and writing regularly, and so on.*]

My daughter Anne isn't a very good speller. My wife and I find it painful to read Anne's work because we fear the probability that we will discover spelling errors. We worry that Anne's willingness to turn in work that hasn't been carefully edited for spelling will distract her teachers from the interesting things she has to say (clearly this happens to us) or, worse, lead her teachers to conclude that Anne isn't very smart (something that has happened with some of her teachers in the past).

Drawing attention to Anne's spelling isn't a great way to boost her self-confidence, but our concerns are not unwarranted. Americans and Canadians place a lot of stock in spelling as a measure of people's ability and their academic preparation, or, at a minimum, as a demonstration of the degree to which people take pride in their work. I've personally seen misspellings on letters of application for faculty positions at York University interpreted as a sign of carelessness that indicated a lack of real interest in the position. (It goes without saying that these people are not offered interviews.) And we've all heard of English teachers for whom some maximum number of errors in spelling, punctuation, or grammar resulted in an automatic reduction in grade. As a former teacher of students with learning disabilities, I also know how often teachers conclude that students have a writing problem when they merely have difficulty with spelling. I'll never forget a presentation I heard by a physician who used what I thought were perfectly regular (if incorrect) spellings as an indication of severe dyslexia.

Fair or not, children's spellings may also be taken as a reflection of the competence of their teachers. Teachers who send home samples of children's writing containing numerous misspellings risk the wrath of parents concerned that their children aren't being taught to spell words correctly. This explains, I think, the reluctance of some teachers (and principals) to share or display children's unedited written work. (I know of several schools where the principal has forbidden teachers from displaying children's work containing misspellings.) Newspaper and television reports on the literacy crisis[4] also impugn the competence of teachers who presumably can't teach children to read, write, or spell and may not be able to spell themselves.

---

4. See Berliner and Biddle (1995) and Barlow and Robertson (1994) for detailed critique of claims that our schools are failing to produce literate students.

During my year as a third-grade teacher I was reasonably concerned about the spelling development of my students. I also worried that my poor spellers might reflect on my competence as a
teacher and/or the holistic model of literacy and literacy instruction
that underpinned my work. The latter concern was particularly
salient for me since some of the parents and teachers with whom I
worked at Norwood School had made a point of sharing their skep-
ticism about progressive literacy practices that, in their view, paid
insufficient attention to the development of skills like spelling and
punctuation. As a university professor and researcher whose commit-
ment to whole language was well known, I worried that the principal, teachers, and parents at Norwood School would use my poor
spellers as evidence of the failure of whole language theory and
practice to address basic literacy skills. To be perfectly honest, I have
also been critical of teachers I knew who had rejected the use of traditional spelling programs (e.g., spellers) in the name of progressive
literacy practices without offering alternatives for providing explicit
support for students' developing orthographic knowledge. As a
teacher at my daughter's school told a group of parents: "We don't
teach spelling any more" and, as nearly as I could tell, she was right.

There was another way my concerns about the judgements of
other teachers affected my approach to spelling. At the time it
seemed to me that most of my students had difficulty with spelling,
but I had no frame of reference. All my previous teaching experience had been in special education. I didn't have much of a sense
for "normal" development so I was unsure of my ability to judge my
third graders' spelling development compared with students in
other classes. It didn't even occur to me to consult with other primary teachers at Norwood School and it's easy to imagine why I
didn't. To have done so would have risked a negative evaluation of
me and my spelling program.

The fact that I was concerned that my students' spelling development would reflect not only on me, but the entire community of
whole language teachers, may account for my nearly obsessive concerns with spelling instruction in my third-grade classroom. The
"onstage-offstage" metaphor in my little three act play is meant to
indicate the degree to which I focussed on what I wasn't doing
(onstage) to support my students' spelling development and how little I focussed on what I was doing (offstage). The sense that I wasn't
doing enough to support spelling development is, I think, a general
problem for all teachers who can never be too sure how their efforts

affect student learning (Lortie 1975). All of us can fairly wonder if our students learn because of our efforts or despite them.

I'm going to use the rest of this chapter to take a look at what I did do to provide regular support and direction to developing spellers in my third-grade classroom. I'm also going to take the opportunity to examine the spelling development of two students whose spelling development concerned me throughout the year even though I know that I can't be certain of the relationship between my spelling instruction and their spelling development.

MEANWHILE OFFSTAGE . . .

Since I believe that reading and writing are the principle means by which children learn to spell (Smith 1978, 1982; Temple, Nathan and Burris 1982; Wilde 1992) I think the most important way that I supported my students' spelling development was by providing frequent opportunities for them to read and write. Here, however, I'm going to focus on the explicit whole-group and individual support I offered my developing spellers.

Whole-class Minilessons

Early in the year I conducted whole-class spelling minilessons, focusing on specific features of English orthography, to increase students' knowledge of the rules and patterns underlying the English spelling system (for a detailed discussion of the English spelling system see Temple et al. 1982, Wilde 1992). The following transcription of a minilesson from January twenty-third is fairly typical of my whole-class spelling lessons.

[*Mr. Marling calls his class to the carpet for a spelling lesson.*]

MR. MARLING: Spelling words today [writes on chart paper "-ate"]
PAUL: Ate.
MR. MARLING: Words ending with a-t-e.
SCOTT: Cooperate.
MR. MARLING: Oh, that's a good one. Spell it.
SCOTT: Co- w [with questioning intonation] [Mr. Marling writes on the chart paper as Scott spells the word]
MR. MARLING: op (pronouncing the syllable)
SCOTT: o-p
MR. MARLING: er

Scott: e-r

Mr. Marling: ate

Scott: a-t-e

Mr. Marling: Peter? [Peter has raised his hand]

Peter: Wait.

Mr. Marling: Spell it.

Peter: W-a-t-e.

Mr. Marling: What does this word mean?

Peter: Something's heavy.

Mr. Marling: Okay. Something's heavy "wate" is w-e-I-g-h-t. There's another "wate," like I have to wait for Peter to come to the circle, w-a-I-t [a couple of students spell at the same time] So there is no word spelled w-a-t-e it turns out. Other words ending in a-t-e?

Ali: Gate.

Mr. Marling: Spell it.

Ali: G-a-t-e.

Mr. Marling: Scott? [who has raised his hand]

Scott: Mate.

Mr. Marling: Spell it.

Scott: M-a-t-e.

[*over the next few minutes children spell words like date, late, appreciate, etc.*]

Mr. Marling: Ali?

Ali: Hibernate.

Mr. M arling: Spell it.

Ali: H-i-b-b. No. H-i-b (pause) -e-r (pause) -n-a-t-e.

Mr. Marling: Good. Boys and girls, Ali started to spell hibernate "h-i-b-b." If it was spelled "h-i-b-b-e-r-n-a-t-e, how do you think it would be pronounced?

Catherine: Hib bernate.

Mr. Marling: Why?

Catherine: Because it has two b's.

Mr. Marling: That's right. Jennifer?

Jennifer: Eight, the number eight.

Mr. Marling: Spell it.

Jennifer: E-i-g-h-t.

Mr. Marling: This is another example of a word whose spelling isn't quite what we'd expect it to be. [*lesson goes on like this for a few more minutes*]

Unlike the personal spelling lists, which I followed through on only sporadically, spelling minilessons occurred almost every day. Over the course of the year these lessons focussed on initial and final sounds, short and long vowels, prefixes and suffixes, consonant doubling, silent letters (e.g., lam*b*, *wreathe*, fat*e*. . . .), consonant blends and digraphs, regular and irregular plurals, schwa, particular morphemes (e.g., -ous, -ious, -ate, -ite, -sion, -tion, -ing, -ance, etc.), compound words, and so on. My students seemed to enjoy these lessons and, like the lesson on "-ate" which included a brief discussion of consonant doubling and unconventional spellings (i.e., "weight," "eight"), these lessons usually drew students' attention to several features of the English spelling system at once.

My field notes indicate that these lessons sometimes connected to my assessment of individual children's spelling development. For example, a minilesson in early April reviewing short i and short e sounds responded to difficulties I observed in Lila's and Fatima's writing. When I observed that several students were confused over various ways to represent the "f" sound at the end of words we did a minilesson in which we generated a list of words ending in "f" which we then categorized.

-ff	*-ph*	*gh*	*-f*
off	photograph	laugh	deaf
puff	telegraph	rough	leaf
huff	graph	tough	reef
handcuff			beef
buff			wolf
stuff			barf
cuff			ref
			chief
			chef

A variation on these lessons was chosen in response to several students who were either reluctant to invent their own spellings or who still produced spellings which didn't represent all the sounds of words they attempted to spell (e.g., "prisable" for principal, "baouns" for balloons). These lessons, modeled on a lesson I'd seen conducted by Joy Shannon, a learning disabilities teacher in Denver, challenged students to spell words I imagined they wouldn't know how to spell. On March twenty-fourth, for example, I asked my students to try and spell *egregious* which resulted in the following spellings:

adrdgase	agrygus	agrajise	agreegus
agregess	agreguss	agryguss	
igreedguss	agrejus	agrejiss	

None of these spellings is correct, but each spelling makes sense phonetically. My field notes indicate that even Charles, who was always reluctant to invent spellings, sometimes participated in these lessons.

My sense is that these whole-class minilessons were usually fun and, I hope, useful (again, the uncertain relationship between instruction and student learning). They were not, however, the only way I responded to the individual needs of my students.

"How Do You Spell. . . ."

My field notes indicate that I was most likely to support my third graders' spelling in a context where they asked me how to spell a particular word. When Wayne and Ali were working on a sports column for our class newsletter, for example, they asked me how to spell "Redskins," "Broncos," and "Detroit Lions" and, in this case, I gave them the correct spellings. More often, however, I suggested a strategy for spelling unknown words instead of giving students correct spellings. Sometimes, I'd merely suggest students try to "do their best," advising them to "listen for the sounds" and reminding them that they could always edit for spelling later. This advice was based on the belief that learning to listen for sounds is an important development in learning to spell (Temple et al. 1982, Wilde 1992) and the assumption that a focus on transcription (spelling, punctuation, handwriting) often distracts writers from what they want to say (Smith 1982).

Encouraging students to "do their best" didn't always work, however. Charles, for example, was always reluctant to venture his own spellings and Ali sometimes worried that his unconventional spellings would make it difficult for him to read what he'd written the next day. To the degree that this was true (handwriting was also part of the problem) Ali and I sometimes reviewed what he'd written at the end of the writing period to deal with some of his less recognizable spellings.

Often I offered students more direct support when they asked, "How do you spell . . . ?" When Charles asked me how to spell "us," for example, I asked him "what sounds do you hear?" as I exaggerated the pronunciation "uhhhhh-ssss." He wrote "u-s" and then asked "U-s. Is that all there is?" (field notes, November 13, 1991).

Similarly, when Wayne asked how to spell "storm," I asked him to "listen for the sounds" he heard as I slowly pronounced "storm" and he wrote "s-t-o-r-m" (field notes, January 14, 1992). When this strategy didn't result in a conventional spelling pattern I usually did some sort of an individual minilesson. The following excerpt from my field notes describes an interaction I had with Troy in early October.

> During writing today I talked with Troy several times. Usually he wanted help with his spelling and when he asked how to spell climb I asked him what sounds he heard and he spelled, "c-l-i-m-e." I told him that was good, but then I gave a mini-lesson on climb and a couple of other words that ended in "mb" (e.g., lamb, dumb). Similarly, he spelled stairs "stars" and asked me how to spell it (he recognized that what he had written was stars). I asked him how to spell "air" to which he responded "a-i-r." (field notes, October 9, 1991)

Spelling by analogy was another strategy I suggested to students who were unsure of how to spell a word. For example:

> When Troy asked me how to spell "pound" and I asked him how to spell "found." he responded, "f-o-u-n-d." Then I asked him how to spell pound and he replied, "p-o-u-n-d." (field notes, January 10, 1992)

To the degree that whole-class minilessons and individual encouragement succeeded in getting students to rely on their own resources in trying to spell unknown words, helping students edit their writing prior to sharing it with a wider audience was the place I most often talked individually to students about spelling. Typically, I'd ask students to edit their work by reviewing the content and checking for grammatical usage, punctuation, and spelling, circling words they weren't sure how to spell. At some point I'd help them with their spelling by correcting many of their misspellings, but always taking advantage of at least one of the misspellings as an opportunity for a spelling minilesson.

One time Hugh disagreed with one of my spellings which led to a lesson on the use of the dictionary.

> I had asked Hugh to circle words he didn't know how to spell, which he had, so I wrote the conventional spellings for these words. [However] he didn't agree with my spelling of "koala" which he was sure was spelled with a "c." So I suggested he check with the dictionary. This also gave us an opportunity to talk about how

words in the dictionary are organized alphabetically. (field notes, February 14, 1992)

I also encouraged students to support each other's spelling development. When I was too busy to respond to students' requests for help with spelling I asked students to check with a friend although sometimes students would spontaneously offer their help. For example, when Connie asked me how to spell "Halloween" Denise "jumped up, picked up a copy of *Clifford's Halloween* (Bridwell 1973) and handed it to Connie" (field notes, January 16, 1992).

It wasn't always desirable, however, for students to ask their classmates for spellings. Charles became such a nuisance bugging other students for correct spellings that I had to insist that he stop asking other children for help with spelling, but I did enlist Razika's help to suggest other strategies he might use to write words he wasn't sure how to spell.

> Charles continued to pester other students for spellings during writing time. When I tried to encourage him to sound out himself he again complained that he didn't want to spell this way. So I asked him who he thought was a good writer in our class. He said, "Razika." I then asked him what he thought Razika did when she had to spell a word she didn't know. He said that Razika knew how to spell all of the words. So I called Razika over and asked her if she knew how to spell all of the words. Of course, she said that she didn't. When I asked her what she did when she didn't know how to spell a word she replied that she "sounded it out." (field notes, October 2, 1991)

Even with this sort of encouragement Charles continued to pester other students for spelling or he chose not to write at all.

Although I frequently worried that I wasn't doing enough to support the spelling development of some of my students the evidence indicates that I provided frequent, intense, and explicit support to my developing spellers. But did it help?

What Did They Learn?

Early in the school year Crystal and Roya were among the poorest spellers in my classroom. Both frequently misspelled words and neither used particularly sophisticated strategies to spell unknown words. They weren't the only poor spellers in my classroom but, by the end of the year, it seemed to me that Roya's spelling development had progressed more than any other student in my class. Conversely, it appeared that Crystal had made relatively little progress as a speller. Here I'm going to examine two samples of each girl's first-draft writing, one from early in the year and the other written toward the end of the school year, as a means of discussing these two students' spelling growth and to illustrate the uncertain relationship between spelling instruction and spelling development.

Figure 8-1 is a piece of writing Roya produced in early October. There are thirty-eight unique words in this sample (I counted only the first instance of words used more than once), twenty (53 percent) of which are spelled correctly. Fifteen of the correctly spelled words contain three letters or less. Even though many of the words in this writing sample are not spelled correctly, a closer reading of Roya's misspellings reveals that she is able to bring to bear a significant store of knowledge of the English spelling system to the spelling of unknown words. Each of her spellings at least attempts to represent phonetically all of the sounds in the word. Her spelling of "pinching," for example, uses "t-h" to represent the "ch" sound. When you recognize that the letter name for "H" includes the "ch" sound, this apparently unusual spelling is strategic and sensible. Her main problem appears to be representing short vowel sounds, but even here there is a bit more logic than at first meets the eye. The "a" in "caming" (for *coming*) and "wan" (for *one*) is a perfectly reasonable way to represent the schwa sound since in many words (e.g., *a* as in *a* dog) *a* represents the schwa. Her consistent habit of representing the short e sound with *a* also makes sense if you know that the letter name phonetically closest to the short e sound is *a* (see Temple et al. [1982] or Wilde [1992] for a discussion letter name spellers). Still, many of her vowel confusions (*lave* for *live*, *thas* for *this*, etc.) do not indicate any apparent logic.

Seven months later (see Figure 8-2) there was a noticeable improvement in Roya's spelling. In this sample 88 percent of the words are spelled correctly and many of the incorrect spellings are at least phonetically correct. The "-ght" in "light" (for *laughed*), for example, is phonetically correct as is the spelling of "wean" (for *when*) in which the "ea" for the short e sound resembles the pattern in words like bread, dead, and head. The logic behind her spellings of laughed, fall, and then (which she spells "light," "full," and "than") is not so clear but, still, her spelling, at least based on these

to day was My wrst
day My Bast frand
got Hrt and Some wun
Stirtd lifing and I Sode
Stop Bot He dadnt
Stop He Startd
panthing Me thets
way Iam navr caming
to thes school Iam
going to Lave wath
My gramar and now
I am Sary for not
caming

FIGURE 8–1   *Roya: October 10*

The first day of dance

The first day I went
to danc I was not good.
Edear my brother saw me he
light. And I told him "you
can not do Better." He
told me "I can do better
then you." So he asked me
my teacher if he code dance,
a My teacher said o.k.
he tried to do the running-
And
man. ∧ He full down. I
& light at him. All the
way home I light at him.

FIGURE 8–2   *Roya: May 20*

two writing samples, is much improved. In addition, the second sample shows her increased control of the use of capitals, periods, and quotation marks. My overall assessment is that Roya has done well learning the conventions of English orthography.

As I suspected, Crystal's progress as a speller was more modest than Roya's. In her first writing sample (see Figure 8-3) she has spelled only nine out of sixteen words (56 percent) correctly but, like Roya, there is a logic to many of her misspellings. For example, almost all her misspellings represent phonetically the sounds in the words she's trying to spell. Even her spelling of *wish* ("whs") makes perfectly good sense if we assume that she is using the letter name H to represent the *-sh* in wi*sh*. Her "wr-" in "wrint" (for *right*) indicates at least an awareness that the homonym *write* begins with wr-. But even phonetically

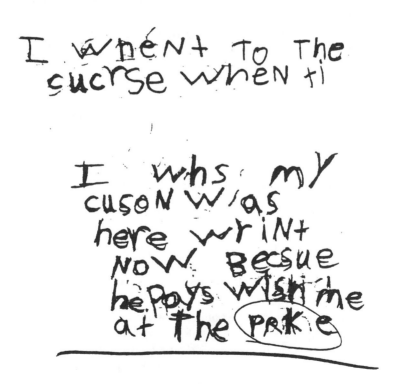

FIGURE 8–3 *Crystal: September 30*

there are problems here. She does not represent all of the sounds in her spelling of *plays* ("pays") and, in her spelling of *with*, she represents *th* wish "sh" which isn't particularly close to the "th" in *with*. Also, sometimes she adds more letters than are needed to some of the words she spells (e.g., "becsue" for *because*, "prke" for *park*). Arguably, Crystal added a letter or two to each of these spellings because she recognized that the correct spellings of these words included more letters than resulted from her phonetic spellings (Temple et al. 1982). It is difficult to see any particular strategy, however, behind the additional letter/sound in her spelling of *right* ("wrint").

Crystal's second writing sample—although marked by lots of misspellings—shows some evidence of growth (Figure 8–4). There is, for example, a modest increase in the number of words she spelled correctly (70 percent compared to 56 percent in the first sample). However, Crystal continues to rely on a phonetic/letter name strategy to spell unknown words (e.g., sisstr, lissns) and there continue to be sounds that are not represented in her spellings (e.g., "pust" for *pushed*, "thae" for *that*, "cvrsahn" for *conversation*[5]).

I can't be happy about the progress Crystal made with spelling and I know that her parents weren't either. It wouldn't be hard to imagine that her fourth-grade teacher saw Crystal's spelling development as a problem. Perhaps she even referred her to special education. I don't know.

This closer look at the spelling development of Roya and Crystal confirms my earlier impression that, over the course of the year, Roya developed into a much more sophisticated speller. It is also clear that Crystal did not grow much as a speller during her year in third grade although her spelling development is (somewhat) better than I recalled. The question I want to take up here is: what can I make of this? Should I take credit for Roya's progress and assume the blame for Crystal's slow development as a speller? It's difficult to take much credit for Roya's progress since I can't know exactly how the support I provided her affected her spelling development. I know that Roya's mom often drilled her on spelling words at home. Maybe that made the difference. Or, perhaps, Roya would have done just as well with spelling if I'd done nothing. I'd like to think I made a difference, but I can't know for sure. The relationship between my spelling instruction and her development is ambiguous and uncertain. Similarly,

---

5. I do not include "tink" for *think* as a missing sound because /t/ is a close approximation of "th" (Temple et al. 1982).

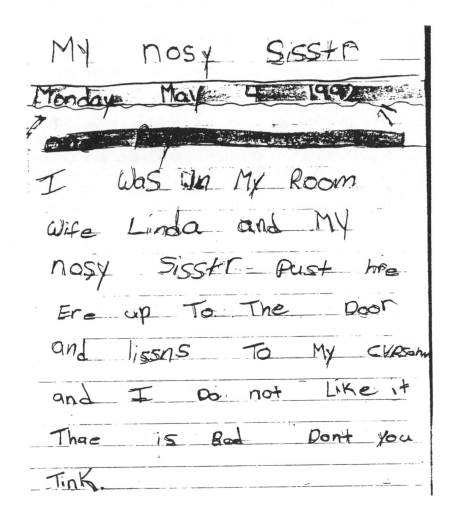

My nosy Sisster

Monday May 4 1992

I was in my Room Wife Linda and MY nosy Sisster Pust hre Ere up To The Door and lissns To My ckRsohn and I Do not Like it Thac is Bad Dont you Tink.

FIGURE 8–4. *Crystal: May 4*

I can't be sure of the degree to which I am responsible for the fact that, at the end of third grade, Crystal still wasn't a very good speller.

My tendency, however, is to take the stance that, while I'm not so sure about the effect of my support on Roya's spelling development, I should take the blame for Crystal's relatively slow progress as a speller. I wish I had done more for her. This is, I suspect, how most teachers react when their students fail to do as well as they hope they will. This attitude insures that teachers will always keep trying, which is laudable, but, by ignoring the uncertainties of human develop-ment, this tendency denies teachers much job satisfaction (Lortie, 1975). Since there will always be children who fail to learn as quickly as we expect, there is always cause for teachers to doubt their efforts and ability. I don't know how to resolve this dilemma since I cer-tainly do not want to suggest that teachers shouldn't worry when stu-dents aren't learning. They should. But whenever teachers respond to student failure by blaming themselves it will always be difficult to find much satisfaction in their work.

Unfortunately, there is now a tendency to blame teachers whenever children do below average work (the reality is that half of our students will necessarily perform below average on any standardized achieve-ment measure). Implicit in much of the criticism of schools by par-ents, politicians, and the business community is the assumption that every student should do better than every other student (Berliner and Biddle 1995) or, at least, that every student should be able to learn the same things at the same rate. This is, of course, an impossibility. But in this climate teachers will find it very difficult to feel good about themselves or the work that they do in their classrooms. Teachers must always strive to do their best, but unless teachers are able to work in a context that acknowledges the uncertainties, the ambiguities, the contradictions, and the variability of the human enterprise that teach-ing is, teaching will continue to be a very stressful occupation with limited opportunities for job satisfaction. The challenge for teachers and teacher educators is to find ways to confront idealized models of the good teacher who succeeds with every student—in which case we blame either the teacher or we blame the student and, if we blame the student he or she must bear the stigma of educational labels like learning disabled or mentally retarded. The current situation is a set-up that makes it difficult for large numbers of teachers and students to feel good about themselves and their work. For the sake of teachers and the students they serve we need an alternative that acknowledges the messy reality of life in classrooms.

References

Aardema, V. 1975. *Why Mosquitoes Buzz in People's Ears.* New York: Dial.

Alcoff, L. 1991. The Problem of Speaking for Others. *Cultural Critique* (Winter 1991–92), 5–32.

Allen, A. 1995. *Constructing Meaning: The Responses of Emergent Readers to Black Images in Children's Picture Books.* Unpublished master's thesis, York University, Toronto, Canada.

Allington, R.L. 1983. The Reading Instruction Provided Readers of Differing Reading Abilities. *The Elementary School Journal,* 83, 548–559.

Angeletti, S.R. 1993. Group Writing and Publishing: Building Community in a Second-Grade Classroom. *Language Arts,* 70, 494–549.

Atwell, N. 1987. *In the Middle.* Portsmouth, NH: Boynton/Cook.

Banks, J. 1988. *Multiethnic Education: Theory and Practice* (2nd ed.). Newton, MA: Allyn & Bacon.

Barlow, M. and Robertson, H.J. 1994. *Class Warfare: The Assault on Canada's Schools.* Toronto, Canada: Key Porter Books.

Barnes, D. 1976. *From Communication to Curriculum.* New York: Penguin.

Barrett, J. 1982. *Cloudy with a Chance of Meatballs.* New York: MacMillan Children's Books.

Berliner, D.C.B., B.J. 1995. *The Manufactured Crisis: Myths, Fraud, and the Attack on America's Public Schools.* New York: Addison-Wesley.

Bianco, M.W. 1991. *The Velveteen Rabbit.* Mankato, MN: Creative Education.

Bieger, E.M. 1995. Promoting Multicultural Education Through a Literature-Based Approach. *The Reading Teacher,* 49, 308–312.

Bishop, R.S. 1992. Multicultural Literature for Children: Making Informed Choices. In V.J. Harris (Ed.), *Teaching Multicultural Literature in Grades K–8,* (pp. 37–53). Norwood, MA: Christopher-Gordon Publishers.

Bloome, D. 1985. Writing as a Social Process. *Language Arts,* 62, 134–142.

Bloome, D. 1987. Reading as a Social Process in a Middle School Classroom. In D. Bloome (Ed.), *Literacy and Schooling,* (pp. 123–149). Norwood, NJ: Ablex.

Bloome, D. and Bailey, F. 1990. From Linguistics and Education, a Direction for the Study of Language and Literacy: Events, Particularity, Intertextuality, History, Material, and Dialectics. Paper presented at the National Conference on Research in English, Chicago.

Bogart, J.E. and Hendry, L. 1988. *Malcolm's Runaway Soap.* Richmond Hill, Ontario: North Winds Press.

Boomer, G. 1987. Addressing the Problem of Elsewhereness: A Case for Action Research in the Schools. In D. Goswami and P. Stillman (Eds.), *Reclaiming the Classroom: Teacher Research as an Agency for Change,* (pp. 4–13). Portsmouth, NH: Boynton/Cook, Heinemann.

Bridwell, N. 1973. *Clifford's Halloween.* New York: Four Winds Press.

Bridwell, N. 1985. *Clifford the Big Red Dog.* New York: Scholastic

Brilliant-Mills, H. 1993. Becoming a Mathematician: Building a Situated Definition of Mathematics. *Linguistics and Education,* 5, 301–334.

Britzman, D. (in press). Difference in a Minor Key: Some Modulations of History, Memory and Community. In M. Fine, L. Powell, L. Weis, and M. Wong (Eds.), *Off White: Readings on Society, Race and Culture.* New York: Routledge.

Britzman, D.P. 1991. *Practice Makes Practice: A Critical Study of Learning to Teach.* Albany, NY: SUNY Press.

Britzman, D.P., Santiago-Válles, K., Jiménez-Muñoz, G. and Lamash, L.M. 1993. Slips that Show and Tell: Fashioning Multiculture as a Problem of Representation. In C. McCarthy and W. Crichlow (Eds.) *Race, Identity, and Representation in Education,* (pp. 188–200). New York: Routledge.

Brown, M.W. 1956. *Big Red Barn.* New York: Scholastic.

Calkins, L.M. 1986. *The Art of Teaching Writing.* Portsmouth, NH: Heinemann.

Cameron, D. 1992. *Feminism and Linguistic Theory* (2nd ed.). London: MacMillan.

Carle, E. 1987. *The Very Hungry Caterpillar.* New York: Scholastic.

Carrick, C. 1978. *The Washout.* New York: Seabury Press.

Cazden, C.B. 1976. How Knowledge About Language Helps the Classroom Teacher–or Does It: A Personal Account. *Urban Review,* 9, 74–90.

Cazden, C.B. 1988. *Classroom Discourse.* Portsmouth, NH: Heinemann.

Chambliss, M. 1987. *I Know an Old Lady.* New York: Bantam Books.

Chia, H.C. 1976. *The Talking Parrot: A Pakistani Folktale.* Toronto: Dominie.

Christensen, L. 1994. Building Community from Chaos. *Rethinking Schools,* 9 (1), 1, 14–17.

Cleary, B. 1984. *Ramona Forever.* New York: Yearling.

Climo, S. and Heller, R. 1989. *The Egyptian Cinderella.* New York: Crowell.

Coles, G. 1987. *The Learning Mystique.* New York: Pantheon Books.

Crowley, S. 1989. *A Teacher's Introduction to Deconstruction.* Urbana, Illinois: National Council of Teachers of English.

Curtis, B., Livingstone, D.W., and Smaller, H. 1992. *Stacking the Deck: The Streaming of Working-Class Kids in Ontario Schools.* Toronto: Our Schools/Our Selves Education Foundation.

Cutts, D. 1979. *The House that Jack Built.* Mahwah, NJ: Troll Associates.

Delpit, L.D. 1988. *The Silenced Dialogue: Power and Pedagogy in Educating Other People's Children.* Harvard Educational Review, 58, 280–296.

Dewey, J. 1960. *The Quest for Certainty: A Study of the True Relation of Knowledge and Action.* New York: Capricorn Books.

Dilg, M.A. 1995. The Opening of the American Mind: Challenges in the Cross-Cultural Teaching of Literature. *English Journal,* 84, 73–79.

D'Sousa, D. 1995. *The End of Racism: Principles for a Multicultural Society.* New York: Free Press.

Dudley-Marling, C. 1990. *When School is a Struggle.* Richmond Hill, Ontario: Scholastic-TAB.

Dudley-Marling, C. and Oppenheimer, J. 1995. Student Ownership and Writing: A Critical Tale. *Qualitative Studies in Education,* 8, 281–295.

Dudley-Marling, C. and Searle, D. 1991. *When Students Have Time to Talk: Creating Contexts for Learning Language.* Portsmouth, NH: Heinemann.

Dudley-Marling, C. and Searle, D. (Eds.) 1995. *Who Owns Learning? Questions of Autonomy, Choice, and Control.* Portsmouth, NH: Heinemann.

Dyson, A.H. 1989. *Multiple Worlds of Child Writers: Friends Learning to Write.* New York: Teachers College Press.

Dyson, A.H. 1993. *Social Worlds of Children Learning to Write in an Urban Primary School.* New York: Teachers College Press.

Edelsky, C. 1991. *With Literacy and Justice for All.* London: The Falmer Press.

Edelsky, C. 1994. Education for Democracy. *Language Arts,* 71, 252–257.

Edelsky, C., Altwerger, B., and Flores, B. 1991. *Whole Language: What's the Difference?* Portsmouth, NH: Heinemann.

Eeds, M. and Hudelson, S. 1995. Literature as a Foundation for Personal and Classroom Life. *Primary Voices K–6,* 3, 2–7.

Everhart, B. 1983. *Reading, Writing, and Resistance: Adolescence and Labor in a Junior High School.* Boston, MA: Routledge, Kegan, and Paul.

Fishman, A. 1995. Finding Ways In: Redefining Multicultural Literature. *English Journal,* 84, 18–25.

Fitzgerald, J.D. 1973. *The Great Brain Reforms.* New York: Dial Press.

Five, C.L. 1995. Ownership for the Special Needs Child: Individual and Educational Dilemmas. In C. Dudley-Marling and D. Searle (Eds.), *Who Owns Learning?: Questions of Autonomy, Choice, and Control,* (pp. 113–127). Portsmouth, NH: Heinemann.

Floriani, A. 1994. Negotiating What Counts: Roles and Relationships, Texts and Contexts, Content and Meaning. *Linguistics and Education,* 5, 241–274.

Freeman, E.B. and Sanders, T. 1987. The Social Meaning of Literacy: Writing Instruction and the Community. *Language Arts,* 64, 641–645.

Freud, S. 1975. *Civilization and its Discontents.* Translated by Joan Riviere. London: Hogarth Press.

Gee, J.P. 1990. *Social Linguistics and Literacies.* Philadelphia, PA: Falmer.

Gillespie, C.S., Powell, J.L., Clements, N.E., and Swearington, R.A. 1994. A Look at the Newberry Medal Books From a Multicultural Perspective. *The Reading Teacher,* 48, 40–50.

Gillis, C. 1992. *The Community as Classroom: Integrating School and Community Through Language Arts.* Portsmouth, NH: Heinemann.

Gilman, P. 1985. *Jillian Jiggs.* New York: Scholastic.

Gilmore, P. 1983. Ethnographic Approaches to the Study of Child Language: Two Illustrative Cases. *Volta Review,* 85, 29–43.

Golding, W. 1974. *Lord of the Flies.* London: Faber and Faber.

Goodman, K. 1986. *What's Whole in Whole Language.* Richmond Hill, Ontario: Scholastic-TAB.

Goodman, Y.M. and Wilde, S. 1992. *Literacy Events in a Community of Young Writers.* New York: Teachers College Press.

Goodwin, M.H. 1991. *He-Said-She-Said: Talk as Social Organization Among Black Children.* Bloomington, IN: Indiana University Press.

Graddol, D. and Swann, J. 1989. *Gender Voices.* Oxford: Basil Blackwell.

Green, J.L. and Dixon, C.N. 1994. Talking Knowledge into Being: Discursive and Social Practices in Classrooms. *Linguistics and Education,* 5, 231–239.

Greene, M. 1993. The Passions of Pluralism: Multiculturalism and the Expanding Community. In T. Perry and J.W. Fraser (Eds.), *Freedom's Plow,* (p. 183). New York: Routledge.

Guarino, D. 1989. *Is Your Mama a Llama?* New York: Scholastic.

Hall, S. 1981. Cultural Studies: Two Paradigms. In T. Bennett, G. Martin, C. Mercer, and J. Woollacott (Eds.), *Culture, Ideology and Social Process,* (pp. 19–37). London: Open University Press.

Hallahan, D.P. and Kauffman, J.M. 1976. *Introduction to Learning Disabilities: A Psycho-behavioral Approach.* Englewood Cliffs, NJ: Prentice-Hall.

Hamilton, V. 1985. *The People Could Fly.* New York: Knopf.

Harris, M. 1993. Looking Back: 20 Years of a Teacher's Journal. In M. Cochran-Smith and S. Lytle (Eds.), *Inside/Outside: Teacher Research and Knowledge,* (pp. 130–140). New York: Teachers College Press.

Harris, V.J. 1993. *African American Children's Literature.* In T. Perry and J.W. Fraser (Eds.), *Freedom's Plow* (p. 183). New York: Routledge.

Hartup, W.W. 1983. Peer Relations. In P.H. Mussen and E.M. Heatherington (Eds.), *Handbook of Child Psychology, Vol. 4: Socialization, Personality, and Social Development,* (pp. 103–196). New York: Wiley.

Harwayne, S. 1992. *Lasting Impressions: Weaving Literature into the Writing Workshop.* Portsmouth, NH: Heinemann.

Heath, S.B. 1983. *Ways with Words: Language, Life, and Work in Communities and Classrooms.* Cambridge: Cambridge University Press.

Henry, A. 1994. The Empty Shelf and Other Curricular Challenges of Teaching for Children of African Descent: Implications for Teacher Practice. *Urban Education,* 29, 298–319.

Heras, A.I. 1994. The Construction of Understanding in a Sixth-Grade Bilingual Classroom. *Linguistics and Education,* 5, 275–299.

Herndon, T. 1970. *How to Survive in Your Native Land.* New York: Simon and Schuster.

Heshusius, L. 1982. At the Heart of the Advocacy Dilemma: A Mechanistic View of the World. *Exceptional Children,* 49, 6–11.

Holt, J. 1982. *How Children Fail* (2nd ed.). New York: Delacorte Press/Seymour Lawrence.

Irving, J. 1985. *The Cider House Rules.* New York: Bantam Books.

Jackson, P. 1968. *Life in Classrooms.* New York: Holt, Rinehart and Winston.

James, C.E. 1994. I Don't Want to Talk About It: Silencing Students in Today's Classrooms. *Orbit,* 25 (2), 26–29.

Jardine, D.W. and Field, J.C. 1996. Restoring [the] Life [of Language] to its Original Difficulty: On Hermeneutics, Whole Language, and "Authenticity." *Language Arts,* 255–259.

Kameenui, E.J. 1993. Diverse Learners and the Tyranny of Time: Don't Fix the Blame; Fix the Leaky Roof. *The Reading Teacher,* 46, 376–383.

Kavale, K.A. and Furness, S.R. 1985. *The Science of Learning Disabilities.* San Diego, CA: College-Hill Press.

Kellogg, S. 1984. *Paul Bunyan.* New York: Mulberry Books.

Kidder, T. 1989. *Among School Children.* Boston: Houghton-Mifflin.

Lakoff, G. and Johnson, M. 1980. *Metaphors We Live By.* Chicago: University of Chicago Press.

Larkin, J. 1994. *Sexual Harassment: High School Girls Speak Out.* Toronto: Second Story Press.

Lensmire, T. J. 1995. Liberating Student Intention and Association: Towards What Ends? In C. Dudley-Marling and D. Searle (Eds.), *Who Owns Learning?: Questions of Autonomy, Choice, and Control,* (pp. 167–184). Portsmouth, NH: Heinemann.

Lerner, J. 1993. *Learning Disabilities: Theories, Diagnosis, and Teaching Strategies* (6th ed.). Boston: Houghton Mifflin.

Lever, J. 1978. Sex Differences in the Complexity of Children's Play and Games. *American Sociological Review,* 43, 471–483.

Lin, L. 1994. Language of and in the Classroom: Constructing the Patterns of Social Life. *Linguistics and Education,* 5, 367–409.

Liu, Y. 1995. *Dragons and Chopsticks: When Will It End?* Unpublished manuscript, York University, Toronto, Canada.

Lobel, A. 1970. *Frog and Toad are Friends.* New York: Scholastic.

Lortie, D.C. 1975. *Schoolteacher: A Sociological Study.* Chicago, IL: University of Chicago Press.

Loughlin, C.E. and Martin, M.D. 1987. *Supporting Literacy: Developing Effective Learning Environments.* New York: Teachers College Press.

Maccarone, G. 1989. *The Return of the Third Grade Ghosthunters.* New York: Scholastic.

Maccoby, E.E. and Jacklin, C.N. 1974. *The Psychology of Sex Differences.* Palo Alto, CA: Stanford University Press.

MacLachlan, P. 1985. *Sarah, Plain and Tall.* New York: HarperCollins.

Macrorie, K. 1970. *Uptaught.* New York: Hayden.

Martin, A. 1990. *Karen's Ghost.* New York: Scholastic.

May, S.A. 1993. Redeeming Multicultural Education. *Language Arts,* 70, 364–372.

McCarthy, C. and Crichlow, W. 1993. Introduction: Theories or Identity, Theories of Representation, Theories of Race. In C. McCarthy and W. Crichlow (Eds.) *Race, Identity, and Representation in Education,* (pp. xiii–xxix). New York: Routledge.

McDermott, R. 1993, April. "An Anthropologist Reads from His Work." Paper presented at the American Educational Research Association, Atlanta, GA.

McDermott, R. and Verenne, H. 1995. Culture *as* Disability. *Anthropology and Education Quarterly,* 26, 324–348.

McDonald, J.P. 1992. *Teaching: Making Sense of an Uncertain Craft.* New York: Teachers College Press.

Moll, L.C. and Diaz, R. 1987. Teaching Writing as Communication: The Use of Ethnographic Findings in Classroom Practice. In D. Bloome (Ed.), *Literacy and Schooling,* (pp. 193–221). Norwood, NJ: Ablex.

Moss, J. F. 1984. *Focus Units in Literature: A Handbook for Elementary School Teachers*. Urbana, IL: National Council of Teachers of English.

Munsch, R.N. 1980. *The Paper Bag Princess*. Toronto: Annick Press.

Munsch, R.N. 1989. *Giant, or, Waiting for the Thursday Boat*. Toronto: Annick Press.

Murphy, S.M. 1995, July. *Celebrating Communities*. Paper presented at the annual conference of the Whole Language Umbrella, Windsor, Ontario.

Myers, J. 1992. The Social Contexts of School and Personal Literacy. *Reading Research Quarterly*, 27, 297–333.

Newkirk, T. 1992. Silences in Our Teaching Stories: What Do We Leave Out and Why? In T. Newkirk (Ed.), *Workshop 4: The Teacher as Researcher*, (pp. 21–30). Portsmouth, NH: Heinemann.

Norton, D.E. 1990. Teaching Multicultural Literature in the Reading Curriculum. *The Reading Teacher*, 44, 28–40.

Paley, V.G. 1984. *Boys and Girls: Superheroes in the Doll Corner*. Chicago: University of Chicago Press.

Paley, V.G. 1989. *White Teacher*. Cambridge, MA: Harvard University Press.

Palonsky, S. B. 1986. *900 Shows a Year: A Look at Teaching from a Teacher's Side of the Desk*. New York: Random House.

Pang, V.O., Colvin, C., Tran, M., and Barba, R.H. 1992. Beyond Chopsticks and Dragons: Selecting Asian-American Literature for Children. *The Reading Teacher*, 46, 216–224.

Pappas, C.C., Kiefer, B.Z., and Levstik, L.S. 1990. *An Integrated Language Perspective in the Elementary School: Theory into Action*. White Plains, N.Y.: Longman.

Parish, P. 1991. *Amelia Bedelia's Family Album*. New York: Avon Books.

Park, B. 1982. *Skinnybones*. New York: Bullseye Books.

Paterson, K. 1977. *Bridge to Terabithia*. New York: Harper and Row.

Peterson, R. and Eeds, M. 1990. *Grand Conversations: Literature Groups in Action*. Richmond Hill, Ontario: Scholastic.

Poplin, M. 1988. Holistic/Constructionist Principles of the Teaching/Learning Process. Implications for the Field of Learning Disabilities. *Journal of Learning Disabilities*, 21, 389–400.

Rasinski, T.V. and Padak, N.D. 1990. Multicultural Learning Through Children's Literature. *Language Arts*, 67, 576–580.

Reimer, K.M. 1992. Multiethnic Literature: Holding Fast to Dreams. *Language Arts*, 69, 14–21.

Rhodes, L.K. and Dudley-Marling, C. 1988, 1996. *Readers and Writers with a Difference: A Holistic Approach to Teaching Struggling Readers and Writers*. Portsmouth, NH: Heinemann.

Russell, C. 1995, November. *Using Children's Literature to Teach Anti-discriminatory Concepts*. Paper presented at the annual meeting of the National Council of Teachers of English, San Diego, CA.

Saul, J.R. 1992. *Voltaire's Bastards: The Dictatorship of Reason in the West*. New York: Penguin.

Schofield, J. 1982. *Black and White in School*. New York: Praeger.

Scieszka, J. and Smith, L. 1989. *The True Story of the 3 Little Pigs.* New York: Viking.

Sendak, M. 1963. *Where the Wild Things Are.* New York: Harper and Row.

Shannon, J. 1988. *The Big Enormous Turnip: A Russian Folktale.* Lakewood, CO: Link.

Shannon, P. 1994. Language as Property. In C. Dudley-Marling and D. Searle (Eds.), *Who Owns Learning? Questions of Autonomy, Choice, and Control,* (pp. 142–152). Portsmouth, NH: Heinemann.

Shepard, E.H. 1991. *Piglet is Entirely Surrounded by Water.* New York: Dutton.

Short, K.G. and Pierce, K.M. (Eds.). 1990. *Talking About Books: Creating Literate Communities.* Portsmouth, NH: Heinemann.

Silverstein, S. 1981. *A Light in the Attic.* New York: Harper and Row.

Smith, F. 1978. *Reading Without Nonsense.* New York: Teachers College Press.

Smith, F. 1982. *Writing and the Writer.* New York: Holt, Rinehart and Winston.

Smith, K. 1995. Bringing Children and Literature Together in the Elementary Classroom. *Primary Voices K–6,* 3, 22–32.

Swann, J. 1992. *Girls, Boys, and Language.* Oxford, UK: Blackwell.

Tannen, D. 1990. *You Just Don't Understand: Women and Men in Conversation.* New York: William Morrow.

Taxel, J. 1992. The Politics of Children's Literature: Reflections on Multiculturalism, Political Correctness, and Christopher Columbus. In V.J. Harris (Ed.), *Teaching Multicultural Literature in Grades K–8,* (pp. 1–36). Norwood, MA: Christopher-Gordon Publishers.

Temple, C.A., Nathan, R.G., and Burris, N.A. 1982. *The Beginnings of Spelling.* Boston, MA: Allyn and Bacon.

Thorne, B. 1993. *Gender Play: Girls and Boys in School.* New Brunswick, NJ: Rutgers University Press.

Van Laan, N. 1989. *Rainbow Crow: A Lenape Tale.* New York: Knopf.

Walker-Dalhouse, D. 1992. Using African-American Literature to Increase Ethnic Understanding. *The Reading Teacher,* 45, 416–422.

Wallace, M. 1991. Multiculturalism and Oppositionality. In C. McCarthy and W. Crichlow (Eds.), *Race, Identity, and Representation in Education,* (pp. 251–261). New York: Routledge.

Waller, W. 1932. *The Sociology of Teaching.* New York: Russell and Russell.

Weaver, C. 1990. *Understanding Whole Language: From Principles to Practice.* Portsmouth, NH: Heinemann.

Webster's New World Dictionary: The American Language (College Edition). 1960. Cleveland, OH: World Publishing.

Weiler, K. 1988. *Women Teaching for Change: Gender, Class and Power.* South Hadley, MA: Bergin and Garvey.

Wells, G. 1986. *The Meaning Makers: Children Learning Language and Using Language to Learn.* Portsmouth, NH: Heinemann.

Wigginton, E. 1985. *Sometimes a Shining Moment: The Foxfire Experience.* Garden City, NY: Anchor Books.

Wilde, S. 1992. *You Kan Red This!: Spelling and Punctuation for Whole Language Classrooms, K–6.* Portsmouth, NH: Heinemann.

Will, and Nicholas 1989. *Finders Keepers*. San Diego, CA: Voyager Books.

Williams, R. 1981. The Analysis of Culture. In T. Bennett, G. Martin, C. Mercer, and J. Woollacott (Eds.), *Culture, Ideology and Social Process*, (pp. 43–52). London: Open University Press.

Willis, P. 1977. *Learning to Labour: How Working Class Kids Get Working Class Jobs*. Farnborough, England: Saxon House.

Yokota, J. 1993. Issues in Selecting Multicultural Children's Literature. *Language Arts*, 70, 156–167.

Yokota, J. 1994. Books that Represent More than One Culture. *Language Arts*, 71, 212–219.

Young, M.F.D. 1971. *Knowledge and Control: New Directions for the Sociology of Education*. London: Collier-MacMillan.

Ysseldyke, J.E. and Algozzine, B. 1982. *Critical Issues in Special and Remedial Education*. Boston: Houghton Mifflin.

Wong, S.C. 1993. Promises, Pitfalls, and Principles of Text Selection in Curricular Diversification: The Asian-American Case. In T. Perry and J.W. Fraser (Eds.), *Freedom's Plow*, (pp. 109–120). New York: Routledge.

Author Index